To Marty,

Thank you !

May you find light and strength
on your journey.

Catherine Ida Campbell

true.

Moving Beyond Complex Trauma

Catherine Ada Campbell

Nautilus illustration and related chapter heading art
by Hellen Grig, used with permission.

Book cover design by Vila Designs • Nautilus cover art and related chapter heading art by Hellen Grig, used with permission.

ISBN: 979-8-9905092-0-7
Published by Perthshire Books

1 2 3 4 5 6 7 8 9 0

First edition 2024 Hardcover

For Jude and Autumn,
whose love and light guide my way.

Contents

Attention Reader

If you are a survivor, and at any point in reading this book
you feel triggered,
please honor that feeling.

Stop reading.
Put the book down.

Continue reading when (if) you are ready.
Know that I honor your journey.

Preface

This is not a self-help book. I am not a professional and even if I was, I know each person must find their own pathways to healing.

This is the unvarnished truth about a lifetime of one person dealing with systemic, complex trauma. I am a survivor who moved beyond what engulfed and shaped me as a child, and I share my experience, hope and strength with you.

I trust that whatever truths speak to you in these pages will illuminate and encourage your own journey.

*Note: Some names have been changed to respect their privacy. I share my story; not theirs. Those names are marked with an asterisk * the first time they appear.*

1

the phone call

Anything that is held in secret cannot be healed. The light cannot reach that which is locked away in the dark. - Donna Goddard

My apprehension rises as I dial the phone number. I'm in the bedroom because whether he answers or not – but especially if he answers – I don't want my husband to overhear the conversation.

The phone starts ringing on the other end. I take a deep breath. What kind of mood will he be in? Will he respond with the truth or shut me down as usual? I need to keep it light, like it's no big deal, just asking. The rules are firmly ingrained: We don't talk about the past. Period. Don't ask questions.

Here I am, breaking the rules.

My older brother Lee* and I had minimal contact, despite promising to stay in touch after Mom died almost a decade before. When we were kids, I trailed around after him like annoying little sisters tend to do. Lee seemed to hate me for whatever reasons he had. Like any abused animal or kid, I tried desperately to make him like me or at least stop calling me names or holding me down when Mom wasn't around and squeezing my thighs until I screamed in pain and fear. He also liked to call me names.

One night at the dinner table, I blurted out "Mom, what's a prick?" I was 10 years old.

Shocked silence. Then Mom asked quietly, "Where did you hear that word?"

"Lee called me that and I don't know what it means," I said.

Mom calmly turned her head toward Lee, who was flushed red and staring at his plate. Her tone was measured as she said, "Lee? Would you care to explain to your little sister exactly what that word means?"

Lee mumbled something about it being a bad word. The rest of the meal was eaten in silence.

Such was our relationship. After he got married and moved across the country, we didn't stay in touch. By then I was on my own and learned about his rare visits home from my mom or dad. Lee never told me he was coming and didn't ask to see me.

When his son was born, I sent him a copy of Kahlil Gibran's exquisite reflection on parenting, along with my congratulations.

Your children are not your children. They are the sons and

*daughters of life longing for itself. They come through you but not
from you. And though they are with you yet they belong not to you.*[1]

He didn't respond and by that time I no longer expected he
would.

The phone rang a third time. I wondered if he had caller ID and
knew it was me and deliberately didn't answer. The old shame was
pouring in, rushing to fill the familiar holes inside my heart. At
the age of 34, I still wanted him to like me. I wanted to understand
why he didn't.

I don't remember much about our childhood. The story I told
was almost rote, repeating the same details.

The First Story...

*I am born in San Francisco, California, but move to Portland,
Oregon when I'm four-years-old. My mom Riona* works as a
waitress most of the time at the fanciest places in Portland like the
Meier Franks Tea Room on the 10th floor of Meier's department
store. But in the summers, she works the West Coast Show's carnival
circuit with my father and me and my older brother in-tow. Most
of my days are spent going round and round on the Ferris wheel,
staring up at the bluest skies of midsummer and giggling each time
the wheel turned me groundward and the world spins from the dizzy
suspension of time and space.*

*I'm never spanked... except one time when my father Galen
thought I lied about who broke our venetian blinds. He takes me
to science museums, exhibits and the dog races. My father runs for*

state representative but loses. He graduates law school, though I don't think he works. He briefly has a job at a drive-in movie theatre when John Wayne's film The Longest Day comes out, about the Normandy beach landing. Because Mom works nights too, my father takes my brother and me with him and makes us wait in the car. I must have watched that film a dozen times.

In 4th grade I am a Junior Rose Princess bowing in my white taffeta dress embroidered with tiny red roses. I wave from a beflowered float in the Portland Rose Parade. I worship my big brother Lee, who is almost four years older than me. My mom misses most of my birthdays because she has to work the Puyallup Fair in Washington State. But she comes home with loads of leftover carnival prizes and stuffed animals and I have magnificent birthday parties.

Once, I am stung on my hand by a bumblebee. I thought if I held still, the bee would be charmed and follow me around like it did in the movie Snow White. But instead the bee betrays me with its stinger which is why I don't trust bees.

My mom and I share special times at Woolworth's five-and-dime store sipping a fountain coke.

I take ballet for four years and perform on stage. I love to roller-skate down the sidewalk. At Christmas we have a giant tree and tons of presents.

I am 10 when my father dies. Something about his heart. Mom marries a really good man named Jim. He is a Sergeant in the Marine Corps. My stepfather takes us on our first plane ride and first ride in a station wagon. He takes us shopping in real stores, instead of a thrift shop. I see live cows when we travel to his parent's dairy farm in Idaho.

That was the childhood I remembered. In my mind, each fact appears as a black and white photograph.

By the time the phone rang a fourth time, I was suffused with shame. Clearly, he didn't want to talk to me. A tiny whisper in my mind: just one more ring, then hang up.

"Hey." Lee's greeting told me he knew it was me. I took another deep breath.

"Hey, bro ..." I try to sound casual. "How are things with you?"

I had rehearsed this conversation in my mind before I dialed, mapping out the words I would say, then editing and rearranging them. So far so good.

"Not bad. What's up?" Lee asked.

"Oh, nothing much. I was uh, wondering about something. See, uh, you know I have this thing about bees?" I hoped he knew.

Bees terrified me. I avoided going outside for fear of spotting one. One time in high school I drove a bunch of friends in my VW Bug on a scorching hot day with the windows rolled down. One of my friends said "Shit, there's a bee in here." I don't remember what happened next except my friends told me I slammed the brakes on, throwing everyone forward, then opened the door and ran down the street about a block.

I remembered the incident with the bumblebee, but I reasoned my paralyzing fear couldn't have been caused by that, because I felt more betrayed than afraid.

Lee answers "Yeah ... kind of. You always freaked out. Why?"

That's what I wanted to know. I chose my next words carefully. "See, um, I got invited to a barbecue next week and I realized I don't want to go because it will be outside, and there's bees around. I know it sounds stupid. I kind of wondered, do you remember anything about me getting stung or something? I'm just trying to figure out why I'm so afraid of bees."

There. I qualified it for him, assuring him I wasn't asking about anything off limits, just a small harmless question.

"Mm...not that I remember," Lee said. "Of course, something might have happened in the places we got dumped every summer."

I frowned and said, "What are you talking about? We travelled with Mom and Galen in the carnival every summer." Lee and I had different fathers. Galen was mine.

Lee continued in a casual tone, "Nah, that's one of those stories you think is true, but it's not. Galen and Mom dumped us off every summer at different people's places. Don't you remember, when we were at Uncle Joe's and I tracked Mom down and told her to come get us out of there or I was going to take you and leave?"

I felt numb with disbelief and denial, while my stomach confirmed the truth in his words. Internal explosions gutted me. My voice shook.

"Wh..what? We were at people's houses? For how long?"

"Oh, usually they'd come back for us right before school started. But you remember, we had to start at other schools when they didn't get back in time."

I didn't remember. Why was my body so numb, my brain frozen?

He continued his train of thought. "Jeez, some of those places I probably blocked out because they were bad, really bad. That's why I got us away from Joe that time."

I grasped the phone so tight my hand hurt. I didn't want to hear anymore, I wanted him to stop talking.

"As bad as it got with Galen screaming and hitting Mom when he was drunk, it was worse at some of those places we stayed." he added.

Stop. I had to stop him from saying anything else.

"I need to go to the bathroom," I said and quickly hung up.

For more than 30 years I believed that first story I wrote above. I was confident that I had never been abused, and that every summer my brother and I travelled with our parents in a carnival. I remembered riding a float in the Portland Rose Parade, and that while my birthday parties were not always on time, they were special. I was certain I studied ballet.

Lee's phone call shattered everything I thought I knew about myself, my parents, and my brother. I would eventually find out that only one of above statements was true.

2

before my first breath

Trauma is a topographical map written on the child, and it takes a lifetime to read. – Natasha Lyonne

The human brain starts developing before we are born. In the book *What Happened to You?* Dr. Bruce Perry thoughtfully and clearly explains how it happens:

> Starting in the womb, the developing brain begins to store parts of our life experiences. Fetal brain development can be influenced by a host of factors including mother's stress; drug, alcohol, and nicotine intake; diet; and patterns of activity. During the first nine months development is explosive, at times

reaching a rate of twenty-thousand new neurons 'born' each second. (In comparison, an adult may, on a good day, create seven-hundred new neurons.)

My mother and father were married and living in San Francisco, California while pregnant with me. She already had a 3 ½ year-old son fathered by a boy she knew in high school, who disappeared upon learning that my mom was pregnant. My mom smoked cigarettes and worked on her feet all day as a waitress. My father was serving a brief stint in the Navy during this time. As an adult, I heard the story about him having rheumatic heart fever as a boy, during a time when penicillin wasn't available. He grew up knowing he probably wouldn't live very long. I wonder if that knowledge impacted the choices he made? I know that my parents had a volatile and at times violent relationship. I was born into strife, starting in the womb.

Consider that our brains slowly develop from the bottom up.

This explains why we have little-to-no impulse control as young children, and why we do impulsive and irrational things as teenagers and have no idea how to answer our parent's demand, "What were you thinking?!"

The truth is our brains are still underdeveloped at this time.

The first part of our brain to develop is often called our reptilian brain. More specifically the lower brain regions regulate our breathing, heart rate, movement, body temperature and so on. I consider this the primal brain gateway, that everything I see, hear, touch, taste and smell enters through for processing. According to Dr. Perry, humans have sensory systems inside their bodies that signal the brain when they are hungry or injured. This is called 'interoception.'

> The brain categorizes every bit of sensory input and then sends it up the triangle to other parts of the brain to integrate and process it further... This is the beginning of making sense of the world. As your brain starts to create the complex memories that store these connections, your personal catalog of experiences is being created...For one child, eye contact may mean, "I care for you; I'm interested in you." For another one, it may mean, "I'm about to yell at you." Moment by moment in early life, our developing brain sorts and stores our personal experiences, making our personal codebook that helps us interpret the world. Each of us creates a unique worldview shaped by our life's experiences.[2]

Before babies learn to walk, they have started to create a codebook to interpret their environments and experiences both positive and negative.

Here is a really important piece of information: Our primal brains are unaware of time or context. For example, say you're an infant, and you are startled by a loud sound. Perhaps someone has broken into the house in the middle of the night and a gun was fired. Maybe your parents are fighting. Or perhaps you are in the living room with the rest of your family watching the thriller action movie *Die Hard*. Whatever. Your initial response to the noise begins in your primal brain (i.e., "Am I Safe?"). If you are not comforted, embraced, or reassured, a neuropathway (or habit) is formed linking the sound to danger. As a result, a similar loud sound will likely trigger your flight/fight/freeze response in the future. Recent research reveals that *any type of trauma* can organically change a child's developing brain and as a result, the way he or she views the world.

Who Controls the Throne?

Imagine that you are the King or Queen of your own castle. Your brain is the castle, and you are its prefrontal cortex sitting on the throne. You, the prefrontal cortex *must* be obeyed. Everyone else living inside of the castle only exists to protect and serve you. Your amygdala consists of your armed guards who are constantly scanning inside and outside of the castle for threats. That is their main job, and they take this responsibility seriously.

If a potential threat is spotted, heard or even smelled, the amygdala – the guards – fire a shot to warn everyone to prepare to fight, run, or hide. Messages are sent to the motor functions, and the stress hormones of cortisol and adrenaline are released. Then everyone becomes hyper alert. Your breathing accelerates as your heart rate and blood pressure rise.

All of this happens in a microsecond.

Your hippocampus is the captain of your guards and is designed to help decide if the potential threat is real or not. Your hippocampus consults directly with you, so you can accurately put the situation into the right context. And based on your many years of experience, you either proclaim the threat to be real and order your legions to attack or defend the castle (your brain), or you decide the threat is not credible and order everyone to stand down and relax. Another microsecond passes.

But what would happen if there was a devastating attack, and your troops were overwhelmed? Your guards now become even more vigilant. Their captain is even more alert.

Now imagine if you are an infant or a child when the first attack happens. You have no years of experience or context. But from that moment on, your guards are scanning for possible danger and as a result fire the warning shots more often. Remember, each time this occurs your body produces more cortisol and adrenaline.

The guard captain has learned a lesson from previous attacks and thinks 'better safe than sorry.' As a result, you now doubt you can make the *right* decisions to protect the castle.

What if the attacks continue to occur over years? Soon your guards will start firing over and over. Because the captain constantly anticipates danger, your troops remain on high alert. You are living in a chaotic war zone. Your prefrontal cortex (you on the throne) develops strategies to cope with the dangers. Some of these strategies are referred to as adaptive, while others are maladaptive.

Adaptive coping strategies could include healthy eating practices, sound sleep, regular exercise, effective communication and/or strategic planning.

Maladaptive coping strategies might include drug and alcohol abuse, self-harm, avoidance, denial, dissociation, social withdrawal and/or suicide attempts. For some people, maladaptive strategies like anger and hurting others helps them *feel* like they have a sense of control.

What trauma experts have confirmed is that with repeated traumatic experiences, the amygdala begins to treat *every* threat as if it is happening for the first time and with the same intensity. Remember, the hippocampus is unable to tell the difference between the past and the present. The prefrontal cortex becomes less and less capable of controlling our fears and devises more strategies to help us cope. During this time, our memories may become suppressed, our impulse controls may be weakened, and hypervigilance may permeate our every waking moment.

That is what happened to me. My memories were locked away. And the things I could not suppress were somehow normalized.
Didn't everyone's mom and dad fight?
Didn't every big brother torment his little sister?
Don't all men like to drink too much?
I also blamed myself.
If I wasn't so weird...
If I wasn't so sensitive....
If I wasn't so stupid and trusting...

The consistent and systemic abuse I suffered as a child led my brain to be hypervigilant for attacks every minute of every day. At one point in my life, I thought I had a kind of superpower: I could enter a room and immediately scan for danger. Later, I found out that most children of trauma have an overdeveloped sense of what psychologist Stephen W. Porges calls neuroception. "Neuroception can be viewed as a sort of invisible sense or radar system that constantly scans the world for any and all external signs and signals that might help us determine how safe we are at any given moment."[3] We are all hardwired for neuroception. But mine was so hyperalert for danger that I didn't trust my interpretations of what might be safe and what might be real danger. As a result, I never felt safe.

An overarching message became ingrained in me – *anyone* can do *anything* at *any time* and I am helpless and powerless to stop them. Even after the first ten years of healing and recovery, my primal brain still responded to every experience with fear. But I didn't recognize any of that – at the time. Instead, I viewed myself as "brave" and "adventurous." I didn't see myself as someone who was always afraid.

This was my family tree:

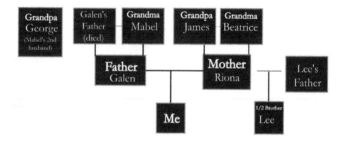

My father's dad died before I was born. Because Lee was older than me and had always been there, I didn't learn until much later that he was my half-brother. My family kept secrets, separated like the boxes on the family tree.

Keeping family, work, social relationships and most importantly, our interior lives compartmentalized felt natural. By the age of six I instinctively knew it was better to separate and hide all of the truths the adults around me insisted were lies. Keeping my feelings and memories boxed up in my mind was a necessary survival skill. Understand that for those of us who grew up in boxes, separation *feels* safer.

There were iron black boxes of childhood horrors labeled, "Don't think about" and "That didn't really happen." These boxes were locked up tight. I piled more boxes in the front to ensure that the black ones stayed hidden. I labeled the new locked boxes "Never be angry," "It's your fault," "No one loves you" and "You are shame." I tagged the other boxes by symptoms and stored them so far down that they became woven into the fabric of my cells. I kept all my boxes inside a deep underwater cavern in my mind and used every means necessary to keep my face above the ocean waves, never looking down.

I was so good at compartmentalizing my memories and feelings that for most of my life I didn't remember the first eight or nine years. Rather, I "remembered" that First Story, and every story afterwards explains part of it. Even today some of my memories appear as black and white photos in my mind, like the old-fashioned kinds with scalloped edges. No colors or emotions imbue the glossy stills, and I often see the years stamped on the bottom edge of the white frames.

I once thought that what you do not know – or did not remember – couldn't hurt you. But suppressed feelings and memories create immense pressure, seeping out in different ways.

In other words, there are always tell-tale signs.

Despite my "memories" of childhood, I knew there was something wrong with me because my parents, teachers, and other relatives confirmed it: *Cathy, stop rocking. Stop pulling your hair. Don't be like that. Stop laughing so loud, you are disrupting class.*

What's wrong with you? You're too sensitive. Stop being so naïve. Don't be so stupid. You have a serious problem, young lady. Stop...

I suspected whatever was wrong with me was my fault. So, I tried my best to fit in and kept most of my childhood hidden from everyone, especially from myself.

My healing journey began after a mental breakdown at the age of 21 incapacitated me for months. The only reason I wasn't institutionalized that time was because I assured the mental health counselor that I lived with my parents, and they knew about my symptoms and were taking care of me. That wasn't true. I did live with my parents, but I was an expert at masking what was really going on with me.

There are multiple disciplines that research and examine childhood and adult trauma, through different lenses. One such approach involves adverse childhood experiences (ACES). According to this approach, people with four or more ACES in their childhood are more likely to struggle with maladaptive coping strategies that affect their sense of self and their relationship with others. Similar maladaptive behaviors are identified and defined in the Diagnostic and Statistical Manual of Mental Disorders, 5th edition. Many survivors of child abuse turn to outside fixes and end up in 12-step programs, where they view their behavior through the lens of addiction treatment models. Meanwhile, neuroscientists have begun to break through old theories and conceptions about how our brains work and what happens to our brain when we experience abuse – as children and as adults. This book also addresses those theories.

But the linear thread of my 45+ years of healing is the heart of this book.

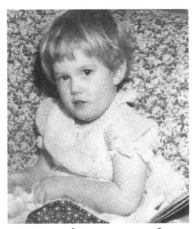

Me around age 3 in one of the frilly dresses my paternal grandmother Mabel* insisted I wear.

It's not true that we are what we remember. Rather we are more of what happened to us, whether we remember or not.

At a certain point in my healing journey, I experienced a moment of startling clarity – everything (everything!) about my life, worldview and sense of self was shaped by, informed by, responsive to and colored by my childhood trauma. The way I brushed my hair and teeth, how I stood, walked and carried myself, my problems with handling money, my interpersonal relationships and intimacy avoidance, how I dressed, spoke and behaved, what I believed and everything that I thought made me who I am, was simply a response to trauma. In that revelation I wondered, "Is there any part of me that is *true*?"

3

signs

Dissociation is the common response of children to repetitive, overwhelming trauma and hold the untenable knowledge out of awareness. The losses and the emotions engendered by the assaults on soul and body cannot, however be held indefinitely. In the absence of effective restorative experiences, the reactions to trauma will find expression. As the child gets older, he will turn the rage in upon himself or act it out on others, else it all will turn into madness.
— Judith Spencer

As an adult there were incidents from my childhood that I remembered but I didn't think of them as abuse or trauma. Example: hearing an adult decry spanking a child, I scoffed at the notion. I thought no, it's only abuse if they beat you to the point of bleeding or they break a bone. I believed that sexual abuse was only if you were penetrated or raped. I accepted the daily forms of abuse, like systematic bullying at school or constant punishment at home. Parental reprimands like yelling, slapping, neglect, withholding food as punishment, calling your child derogatory names, locking them in a closet or their bedroom and so on, were (and remain) deeply embedded in U.S. culture as acceptable child discipline and I didn't question that.

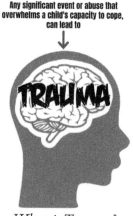

What is Trauma?

Mom used to chase my older brother Lee around the house with a wire coat hanger when he got in trouble. By the time she finally caught him she was so mad she just kept whipping him. I cried and begged her to hit me instead because somewhere deep in my mind I thought he would like me, and not call me names or tell me to stay away from him. He never seemed to want me around, but I later learned that he was a true hero, because his actions saved us – and possibly our lives - more than once.

We lived in a small, one-bedroom downstairs duplex in Portland. Lee and me slept in bunkbeds in a narrow, chilly glassed-in back porch with a row of small windows near the ceiling on the wall attached to the house. We often heard the sound of slaps against flesh, feet running, furniture crashing, my father screaming in rage and my mother angrily yelling. Lee tried to distract me from the drama with the clock game. He would hang one arm over the side of the top bunk and swing it back-and-forth like a clock pendulum. I was supposed to catch his hand, but he was always too fast for me.

From Lee's top bunk he could see into the kitchen. One night he saw Mom holding a butcher's knife, threatening Galen if he came any closer to her. We knew better than to try and intervene. We knew that interrupting them made them madder, but that night Lee didn't care. He jumped off the top bunk and ran into the kitchen. Both my parents froze when they saw him, then Mom said harshly, "Get back to bed right now! There's nothing going on." We were often told not to worry or wonder because nothing was going on, despite what our ears told us, our eyes showed us, and our nervous systems keyed into.

Lee never knew his biological father. Our mom said that his biological father was a boy she fell in love with while in high school who left her when she got pregnant. Lee was two years old when our mom married my father Galen.

I used to believe that I was only spanked once. My mom and brother were out of the house one day at work and school while my father was supposed to babysit me. He sat in front of the black and white television screen in his underwear drinking beer. Our dog General stayed with me on my lower bunk on the porch. A room in our home had a door that led to a dark dirt basement. When my father would get mad at General, he would drag him by the scruff of his neck to the basement door then kick him down the stairs. Seeing animals being abused always made me cry. My family's reaction was "You're just being too sensitive."

At some point in the afternoon, I heard loud crashing, and my father yelling and cursing. Then there was silence. I crept quietly into the kitchen and peeked into our combined dining room/living room. Galen was passed out on the couch. The venetian blinds covering the living room windows were broken and sagging. I returned to the back porch bedroom, worried that my father was either dead or sleeping and not sure which option was worse. After what seemed a long, long time I heard him call for me in that angry voice he had when he was mad.

"Get out here RIGHT NOW! Stand RIGHT THERE! NOW, WHO did this to the blinds?!" he demanded.

Somehow, I knew if I told him that he was the one who damaged the blinds I would be in more trouble, so I insisted that I didn't know. "Come here!" he yelled, standing up. Then his tone changed. He explained in almost a fatherly way, "I just want you to understand that if you had told me the truth, you would not be getting punished. But because you lied to me, you are getting a spanking."

When my father wasn't drinking, he would take me on adventures. He was fascinated by everything especially applied sciences, and he wanted me to have the same interests. Sometimes we went to a wonderful science museum in Portland called "OMSI" (Oregon Museum of Science and Industry). There was a giant manufactured display of the human heart inside the lobby that people could walk through. We visited a small auditorium at OMSI, where a life-size model of 'The Visible Woman' was on display. The model was encased in clear plastic that showcased her organs, veins and bones. During the presentation various parts of her body lit up as a female voice narrated, "These are my kidneys." "This is my heart." Afterward Galen bought me a small human anatomy model kit which came with dozens of parts to assemble. The model was see-through as well. It had removable internal organs and a realistically painted circulatory system. I remember my mom and my grandma Mabel being appalled. They said I was not old enough to be learning about how women are "put together!" I don't remember how old I was, but I think I was likely around 8 years old.

Another time, Galen took me to a biology exhibit at a nearby university. There were large rooms of displays. Two of the displays stood out – one was a beautiful large, white-feathered bird, dissected and pinned to a lab table. Tiny, numbered pins corresponded to the accompanying description. Galen pointed out the various pins and read them to me. I remember the white feathers and stains of dried blood among the internal parts. I knew my father was treating me like a grown-up so I swallowed hard and hid the urge to cry for the poor creature. Another display was a series of glass jars placed in order based on size. Inside each jar was a dead human fetus preserved with formaldehyde. Each fetus of a different month (in age) displayed the development of an unborn baby. Galen explained that sometimes nature knows when a baby shouldn't be born and that scientists studied the fetuses to help other babies be born healthy. He also suggested that my mom wouldn't understand and I shouldn't tell her about that particular display. I remember feeling proud that he trusted me to be smart enough to understand the science of it at the young age of just seven.

My father pursued any topic that caught his fancy, but he especially loved everything electrical. He collected old television and radio parts and tinkered with them in the basement building gadgets. For some reason I was terrified of electricity. I have a dim memory of looking at a dirt wall in the basement, a memory blurred by fear.

When we had a car that worked, Galen took me to bars with him. He forced me stay in the backseat while he went in but made sure the doors were locked. I knew he'd get mad if I got out of the car. He seemed to be gone for hours. It was hard to hold it in when I had to go to the bathroom, and I wasn't always successful.

I'm told my father was brilliant. He graduated law school in only two years with no undergraduate degree. My mom made herself a beautiful black velvet dress to wear to his graduation. I have a black-and-white memory of Galen in his graduation cap and gown.

It seemed like my mom could do anything. She was the primary breadwinner for many years and was proud of the tips she made at her waitress jobs. She taught herself to sew and made my ballet costumes. I didn't realize we were poor because she would scour the cupboards for cans of food to donate to neighborhood drives. My mom also gave us allowances of twenty-five cents and took us to the local Goodwill thrift store so we could buy things with our money. Lee and I always took a long time to pick out a toy or book.

Mom and I would ride the city bus to the Lloyd Center, one of the earliest shopping malls in the country. We couldn't afford much but we watched the skaters on the ice rink there, then went into the Newberry's store soda counter to sit on the round spinning stools as we sipped on Cokes. We held hands everywhere we went.

But there was another childhood, a hidden one. At a very young age I started exhibiting the tell-tale signs of trauma, and if any of those signs caught my parent's attention, I developed better ways to conceal those signs from them. My hidden childhood looked like this...

Being able to fall asleep was hard. I was scared to close my eyes because if I was asleep, I wasn't alert to danger. My startle response was so overdeveloped that I jumped in fear at unexpected sounds or sights. I dreamed of a safe place without other people. I was an avid fan of science fiction so after reading *Farnham's Freehold*,[4] a book about a family taking refuge in a bomb shelter under their house, I imagined such a place for myself. I also hoped to one day discover a deserted island where no one could find me.

I found comfort in designing the perfect underground shelter and deserted island. Both places would need to be hidden from detection. The shelter would have to be lead-lined, in the event of atomic bombs. The life support system would need a sustainable, renewable energy source and all waste would be recycled. I'd stock the shelter with enough food to last me approximately 20 years because I was confident that I'd die young.

The island idea seemed more practical because I could live outdoors and grow my own food. I worried about keeping stray boats away, so I devised underwater shields surrounding the shore about 50 yards out. Then I worried someone might spot me via the sky, so the island should have some kind of masking technology.

My brother Lee and me, hiding from the camera, circa 1961.

I don't remember when I started rocking. It feels like I have always moved, even when sitting still. Side-to-side or front-to-back were interchangeable. "Cathy, stop rocking!" was the refrain I often heard at home, in school, riding the bus, and in a car. In my sleep I would sit up cross-legged in bed and hold my pillow like a shield across my chest, bending over into a small huddle. The front and back rocking motion usually soothed me, but the side-to-side rocking felt even better. It was my way of coping with anxiety. I finally stopped the rocking when I learned healthier calming techniques. I was in my early forties by then.

My obsessive-compulsive behaviors also began at an early age. For years I counted my steps, challenging myself to reach a certain spot on the sidewalk within a certain number of steps. I felt real panic if I didn't make it and would have to start again. By the time I was twelve and starting 8th grade, I faced a series of counting numbers to certain beats before I could get out of bed each morning. Tap my left foot 10x against the sheet, then do the same with my right foot. Count to twenty using my fingers as fast as possible without missing a beat. Fail and start again. Put my right foot on the floor and tap 6x. Then do the same with my left foot. Repeat sequence 3x. Only then could I stand up.

Next came the rhyming. I had to pick a random word and go through the alphabet to find every word that rhymed with it. This was part of my morning ritual for years. After that came word association. Two unassociated words like blue and dirt. Now link them to make sense in as few steps as possible. Blue = color = different colors of rocks = rocks are in dirt = blue rocks in dirt. I tried hard to hide my counting and rhyming from everyone but wasn't always successful. Kids started calling me "weird" and "crazy."

I was terrified of electricity. One afternoon, during my junior year in high school, my mom asked me plug in her iron so she could iron some fabric. I froze and started backing back towards the door.

"Oh, for heaven's sakes, are you still afraid of plug-ins?!" my mom asked me in a slightly irritated tone.

"No, I just don't want to right now," I told her, hoping she would let it go. She didn't. In fact, her voice got stern, telling me to just plug in the damn iron. I started shaking and rocking my upper body back and forth. "It's time you got over this crap," she continued. She got up from her sewing desk and walked over to pick up the plug. "Now plug this in, and stop being silly!" she said in her no-nonsense-I've-had-enough voice. I started crying and pleaded, "Please don't make me," but she persisted. I finally did it. Then I bolted to my bedroom and hid under the covers. I stayed there until she called me for dinner. I felt deeply ashamed of my fear, but I didn't wonder why I was so afraid.

'Self-mutilation' wasn't a term anyone used in 1960s. I'm not sure it was called anything back then. My earliest memory of self-abuse occurred while living at our babysitter's house. I was probably 8 or 9 years old. There was an empty upstairs closet between mom's room and mine and sometimes when she was at work, I would sit inside the darkness and pinch myself 'down there' as forcibly as I could until the pain was too strong. Sometimes I took one of mom's stiff plastic rollers – the kind with the hard spikes – and wrapped my labia around it, squeezing. The sharp, piercing pain roiled through me. Another sign.

As time went by, I got more determined to hurt myself. At first the sensation of digging my nails into my inner arm was painful but also strangely comforting. I told myself if I became a spy I might get captured and tortured, so getting my pain tolerance built up was important. Over time, the self-mutilation included trying to hold in my urine when I went to the bathroom. I remember the intense waves of pain the longer I held back. It wasn't long before I could not pee without the ritual. I also had trouble with letting go of bowel movements, and constipation became part of my daily life.

I ripped the inside of my mouth, biting and chewing until I had a strip of skin long enough to tear off. Then another one and another. The inside of my cheeks were raw but I didn't stop there. My upper and lower insides of my lips were usually swollen and painful too. It was the taste and smell of my blood mingled with the prolonged pain that was oddly reassuring. My mouth was constantly sore, but I couldn't stop. It was a ritual I performed several times a day. Eating anything spicy meant more pain, and salty foods stung the wounds in my mouth.

During my teen years the self-mutilation increased. The harder I tried to repress my emotions – and going through puberty exacerbated everything – the more I felt out of control. I locked myself in the bathroom, sat on the toilet, grabbed a towel and stuffed it into my mouth so I could scream, as my body rocked violently back-and-forth. I went from digging my nails into my forearms to pulling out clumps of hair and sometimes leaving open wounds that scabbed over.

'Memory' was a word fraught with frustration. My mom and brother often dismissed the stories I told, insisting that they never happened. I didn't understand because the memories I shared with them were filled with funny and warm family events and experiences. How could they not remember?

At some point, I decided to remove any photographic evidence of myself in case I became a secret agent. I rationalized I might need to disappear for other reasons too and wanted to ensure no one could track me down from childhood photos. Surreptitiously I removed photos of myself from our family picture albums. Then I realized that other people had photos of me, so I did the same with my grandparents' albums. Today, there are very few photos of me as a child. Later in high school I stole the photos my friends had of me and to this day I prefer to be behind the camera – not in front of it.

It was around then that I started to wonder as many kids do, if I was adopted. Was that why I seemed so different than my brother and the other kids I met?

I asked my mom to show me my birth certificate and she said she didn't know where it was. I was sure she was lying to me. The next time the house was empty, I searched the drawers in my mom's bedroom looking for proof. There was a tall metal box on the floor of the closet and inside were file folders for various things such as her marriage certificate to our new dad Jim, her divorce decree from Galen, the official adoption papers from when Jim adopted us, Jim's birth certificate, my mom's birth certificate, Lee's birth certificate and... nothing for me.

Lee told me I was being stupid. He knew I wasn't adopted. So why did I feel so removed from other people – so different from my family? I gradually decided it wasn't because I was adopted; it was because I wasn't *human*.

I figured out I had been sent to inhabit this body and was on a mission to study human behavior. I was convinced a mothership would eventually arrive to take me to my real home. The 'beings' would expect a full report. So I started recording my observations of my family and the kids at school on small notecards that I kept in a file box with the label H.E.B.P.S.G. –Human Emotional Behavioral Patterns Study Group. I was 12 years old. For the first time I thought I knew why I was different. For the first time I had a purpose and value.

"Spacing out" was a phrase applied to me by high school friends. "Oh, Cathy's spacing out again."

Eventually this turned into the nickname, "Space cadet." I thought it was a sign of being accepted and was secretly delighted at the reference to outer space. My family had a habit of snapping their fingers in front of my face to get my attention and teasing me about my ability to block out my surroundings. It was normal for me to sit with my friends at a coffeehouse, feel myself grow numb and detached, then kind of drift away from the noise and sights around me. Sometimes I felt like my limbs were detaching from my body and floating off into a grey void. It's called dissociation, though I didn't know that at the time.

Most people recognize depression when they have it because it feels *different* than what they experience as normal. But I don't remember a time when I did not feel the thick, black undertow sucking me down under. When I first heard the word *depressed*, I wasn't sure what it meant. I wasn't aware enough to ask if what I felt was unusual. *Suicidal ideation* was another term I didn't know. But for the first 35 years or so of my life I thought about ways to kill myself, devising plans for it at least once a day. Those thoughts comforted me like a soft, warm blanket, so much so that I held on to the promise that I could always end my life if it got to the point that I couldn't stand it anymore.

I had regular nosebleeds in elementary school. Each time the school called my mother to come and get me. Since we usually didn't have a car, this meant she took off from her waitress job, waited for a bus, transferred to a second bus and then walked to my school to pick me up. Afterward

My mother and me at a beach.

we walked back to the bus stop and waited. My mom always seemed mad even though she tried to hide it. At some point in second or third grade as we walked out of the school doors, she said to me, "You know what's going to happen if you don't stop having nosebleeds? I'm going to take you to the doctor, and he'll put hot pokers up your nose to stop the bleeding. It's called cauterization. THAT's what is going to happen to you, young lady."

I didn't know why my nose kept bleeding. But clearly my mom was convinced there wasn't anything seriously wrong with me. Maybe she changed jobs so often because her bosses didn't appreciate her taking off mid-shift. Perhaps she thought I was trying to get attention. Whatever the reason, I continued to have nosebleeds after that day, but I learned to hide them from her and my teachers. Eventually the nosebleeds stopped completely. Except... when my mom slapped my face so hard it made my nose bleed. How old was I? Given I still don't remember anything before first grade, it would have been between first and fourth grade. It happened because I was supposed to take a bath in our big stand-alone tub, but I didn't want to take my clothes off. I started whining about keeping them on. Then I started crying, and my mother became angry and frustrated. She grabbed me and tried to force me into the bathroom. I resisted and... THWACK!! Her hand flew across my face. I felt and tasted the blood running down my lips. I had a hopeful thought that since I was bleeding, she would feel bad and turn back into the nice version of my mom. But she didn't.

"Get in that bathroom RIGHT NOW and wipe that ridiculous blood off your face. Then, get into that bathtub," she said sternly. I sat naked in cold bath water (it had cooled down by then) with my knees tucked under my chin, crying into my folded arms. I was certain my mother didn't love me.

When did I start wearing layers of clothes, particularly pajamas under my regular clothes? I got into trouble with Mom for doing that and at one point she started checking me before I left for school each morning. I thought if I wore lots of layers then an attacker might give up on me out of sheer frustration. I also remember sweltering in the Idaho summers but being determined to keep my leather jacket on. I hated being naked, so I avoided baths. Looking back, there were obvious signs of sexual abuse, but those memories were double-locked in an iron black box and then double-locked inside a second one.

My family rarely noticed the signs because I was a master at hiding, disguising and explaining them. I carefully studied other people to learn what was considered acceptable behavior and what would make me look more normal. Denial can be a survival tool, a mechanism to help us cope with emotionally distressing memories. The problem is it can also prevent us from healing, because the first step is always to acknowledge what's really going on.

I truly didn't believe there was abuse in my home. As a teenager and as an adult when the topic of physical or sexual child abuse came up, I would exclaim, *"Thank God that never happened to me!"*

Yet the signs were there.

4

what really happened, part i

It's all right if you can't remember. Our subconscious is spectacularly agile. Sometimes it knows when to take us away, as a kind of protection. – Kathleen Glasgow, Girl in Pieces

Researchers today understand much better that the crippling aftermath of many abused and traumatized children includes characteristics that impact and color their adult lives.

The first time I assessed my own behavior was in a 12-step support meeting for friends and family of alcoholics. Even though I wanted to deny what I was doing, I had to admit that I was using manipulation and control tactics to get my alcoholic husband to stop drinking. I also admitted and was ashamed of the many ways

I tried to manage the impressions other people had of me, from being a world-class people pleaser to outright lying to other people with made-up stories that I believed made me look like the person I thought they wanted me to be. Just because I was also lying to myself didn't make it okay.

The similarities between child abuse markers, and symptoms and outcomes from different assessment tools is indisputable. When I first read about how codependent people's lives can be affected when cohabitating with addicts, and then learned about signs associated with child abuse, I was taken aback again by the similarities. Years later I read about the adverse childhood experiences (ACEs) study and the associated outcomes for people who score 4 or higher. Psychiatrists and counselors often rely on the diagnostic and statistical manual of mental disorders (DSM-V) which list many of the same markers and symptoms.

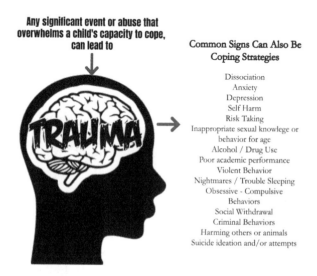

Any significant event or abuse that overwhelms a child's capacity to cope, can lead to

Common Signs Can Also Be Coping Strategies

Dissociation
Anxiety
Depression
Self Harm
Risk Taking
Inappropriate sexual knowlege or behavior for age
Alcohol / Drug Use
Poor academic performance
Violent Behavior
Nightmares / Trouble Sleeping
Obsessive - Compulsive Behaviors
Social Withdrawal
Criminal Behaviors
Harming others or animals
Suicide ideation and/or attempts

I realized that whether examined through the lens of ACEs, trauma assessments, the addiction/codependency model or the signs of child abuse, the more common maladjusted coping strategies are similar.

Not every trauma victim develops *all* of the maladaptive coping strategies listed above. There are a significant number of people who on the surface appear to be immune to traumatic experiences. But I agree with pioneering trauma researcher Dr. Bessel van der Kolk, that trauma *always* leaves a negative impact on the body and mind – an impact that can affect every area of one's life.

I wonder if our emotional and mental responses to trauma are universal?

It makes sense because we as humans share the same basic physical response to threats (i.e., fight, flight, or freeze). Our bodies are designed to react that way. If there is a universal response to trauma, I posit it is denial. I've met dozens of people who experienced trauma and *appeared* to be resilient to its negative effects. In other words, they just shrugged it off like it was nothing. These individuals turned their traumatic experiences into sheer motivation. They bury it. They deny it. These trauma survivors may think they are unaffected by the trauma, but I think there is always a struggle they think is unrelated.

People who have experienced trauma may struggle with depression. Or they may become thrill seekers. Moreover, these individuals may project a filtered persona to the world, not trusting anyone with their true selves. They may keep their feelings tightly in-check. Some of these individuals end up being manipulators or controllers who view life as a game to be won. I personally believe that any thoughts, emotions, or behaviors that hold us back from being our true authentic selves is detrimental. I also believe the source of this detriment is trauma.

In my life I have used many maladaptive strategies to cope with the things I had buried deep within. But my go-to maladaptive strategy was most often denial. Depression was my #2 coping strategy. Because this started at such a young age, the concept of hope was foreign to me – until years into my recovery. Most experts think of depression as a clinical term. While true, it's also a descriptive term. For instance, if you push something down (away from the surface) you create a depression.

At a very young age I learned the cardinal rule in dysfunctional families – "We don't discuss what goes on with other people." Early on I knew not to talk, trust or tell anyone *anything*. For over thirty years I *never* did – not even to myself.

The truth is I was abused as a child. Despite the Hallmark version of my First Story, my thoughts and behaviors told a very different narrative – a secret story kept hidden in those boxes, deep in my underwater cavern.

I was 9 years old when my mother and father declared bankruptcy and got divorced. In those days the creditors took *everything*, including furniture, dishes and linens and even children's toys. My mom explained to me and Lee that though two people may love each other it doesn't always work out, and that it had *nothing* to do with us.

"We will always love you both," she said. Despite her reassurances I still thought it was my fault. Lee was thrilled and warned me I better not be sad about the divorce. I had mixed feelings anyway, because part of me didn't want to be left alone with my father anymore and another part of me knew I was supposed feel sad but I didn't, and I felt guilty about that.

My mom, Lee and I moved into three vacant upstairs bedrooms at our elderly babysitter's house. I slept better there, though it was still hard to fall asleep.

One morning on my walk to school a car pulled up. My father was driving, and Lee was sitting in the back seat looking sullen. Galen told me to get in. I knew Mom would be mad if I did. His tone became stern and steely, "Get in the car NOW!" I did what I was told, and he took me and Lee to his mother and stepfather's home. I have vague memories of those weeks at my grandparent's house, but Lee filled in some of the details years later – when he was finally willing to talk about it. We had been kidnapped.

We were not allowed to use the telephone and we couldn't play outside in the front yard or across the street at the park. After a few days Grandma Mabel walked me to a nearby elementary school and enrolled me under a different name so my mom would not be able to find me by checking schools. Grandma Mabel kept stressing about how *wonderful* my life would be now that we were living with her. She bought me new school clothes – pretty, frilly little girl dresses and shiny black shoes. I didn't like dresses, but I didn't say anything because I knew it wasn't polite to shun a gift.

A few weeks later my mom showed up at my grandparent's home in a strange car with a man I didn't know. She and the man talked to Galen on the front lawn. I know this because Lee and I were watching from the upstairs bedroom window where we'd been ordered to stay until my mom and the man left. I remember Galen screaming at my mom, which caused Lee to ignore the order and run downstairs and out the door.

Grandma Mabel was busy ironing another one of my dresses at the time. She told me to get undressed and as she slipped the dress over my head, she told me that I didn't have to go with my mom if I didn't want to. "Grandma Mabel loves you and wants you to live here so all you have to do is tell your mother you want to stay," she said. I mumbled I wanted to go with my mom and that upset her. "It's just too bad you want to go with her. She's not as good for you as Grandma Mabel is. Grandma Mabel will miss you so much." She often spoke to me in third person.

When I walked outside Galen said sternly, "Get back in the house now!" I froze. Then my mom said, "Cathy, get in the car. Get in the car right now with your brother!" I started to cry as I moved towards the car. As I walked between them Galen grabbed a handful of my hair and yanked it, yelling "She's not going with you! You can have Lee but she's staying here!" Mom grabbed the other side of my hair and yanked me in the opposite direction toward the car, yelling back "You can't stop me anymore. She's coming with me!"

I was sobbing and begging them to stop fighting. That's all I remember, but I ended up leaving with my mom. Later, Lee told me that he had snuck out a few days before and called her from a payphone. Our mom then got a court order and with her attorney in tow came and got us. Once we were safely back at our babysitter's house Mom questioned Lee and me about why we got into Galen's car. Still crying, I told her it was because he told me to. My mom told me that in the future I should say, "NO" in a big voice when he asked me to do something I was not supposed to do. Then run away from him.

My father at a carnival.

I felt a crushing weight in that moment. I was powerless and helpless to stop Galen from doing anything but apparently it was my responsibility to do so. And say no in a loud voice? How often I heard, "Lower your voice, young lady!" if I showed I was angry.

Around that time a teenage girl named Marcy came to visit us for a few days at our babysitter's house. I think she was a cousin, the daughter of a great-aunt. My mom told her she could sleep in her double bed while Lee and I were supposed to stay in our own rooms. One night Marcy woke me up and dragged me into Mom's room, putting me in bed with her. Marcy started touching me under my pajamas, feeling my young nipples and sliding her hand down to poke a finger into my vagina. I laid still, frozen, pretending to be asleep, feeling frightened and confused. I wondered why she was doing that to me.

Another incident happened when I was in fifth grade. My

teacher's name was Miss Brat. One day as Miss Brat showed us how to work a math problem on the chalkboard, the boy next to me leaned over and slid his hand up my skirt and between my legs. I froze in shock as his fingers wormed under my panties. I slapped him hard against the cheek and he yelped. Miss Brat demanded to know what happened, but instead of admonishing the boy she ordered me to stop disrupting class. I was confused. The boy had done something wrong, and the teacher had blamed me so I must have been at fault. Shaking, I got up and headed to the principal's office where my mom was called.

When she arrived, she demanded that the principal handle the problem. That night our phone rang, and my mom spoke to someone for a long time. The next morning, she said I didn't have to go to school that day. She said I would be starting at a new school in a different district. Mom explained that teachers are not supposed to have favorites and should treat every student the same. But she acknowledged that teachers were human and made mistakes. Miss Brat admitted that for whatever reason, she simply didn't like me. Mom assured me that it had nothing to do with me and that sometimes, people just do not like other people. My mom's words didn't matter. I knew it was my fault.

My new fifth grade teacher was a man, but he seemed kind.

I saw my father sporadically after the divorce. Mom remarried and so did Galen.

When Lee learned about my mom's engagement he came into my room and grabbed my arm hard, saying, "Look here stupid.

Mom is going to ask you if it's okay if she marries this guy and if you know what's good for you then you'll say yes, got it? Besides, this guy is rich, and he treats Mom really nice."

The man's name was Jim, and we did think he was rich. Jim went to a job every day in a Marine Corps uniform. He drove a car that always worked. He ate like I imagined wealthy people did – meat with every meal, dessert after dinner and had a fridge stocked with Coca-Cola. After their courthouse wedding, we went from a diet of spaghetti and tuna on toast, to steak, ham, potatoes and corn on the cob. He and Galen had very little in common. Jim drank alcohol too but not to excess. He also refused to raise his voice, slap, argue with my mom, smack us around or do anything my brother and I expected. Instead, Jim held Mom's hand, opened doors for her and insisted that my brother and I 'hop to it' when we were told, no argument. Lee and I called him "Jim" at first, then "Dad" and later, I affectionately called him my "Pops."

Within months of their marriage, the few visits I had with Galen stopped because he got sick. Grandma Mabel took me to see him in the hospital. He was lying in a bed and said that he loved me and hoped to be up again soon. Days later my mom and Jim came into my bedroom and solemnly told me that Galen had died. He was 33 years old.

My mom said that he had been ill a long time and was now at peace. I sat on the side of the bed feeling like I was an actor playing a part. I knew I was expected to cry but I didn't know how to. Was I supposed to wail? Scream? Throw myself into my mom's arms? I desperately tried to figure out what they wanted me to do.

I covered up my face with my hands and tried to cry. Deep, deep down there was a sense of relief that was buried in guilt.

Harvard University researchers found that children need to maintain a connection with their deceased parents, such as believing the parents are looking down on them and/or guiding them. Many children believe that if they draw a picture or write a letter to the deceased parent, he or she will be able to see it.[5]

I didn't like it when people said, "He's still looking out for you." I pushed those thoughts as far away as possible and locked my grief into another interior box. I did love my father. Lee said that he was glad that our father was gone. At the funeral I had to sit with Grandma Mabel in the family area, even though I wanted to stay with my mom who sat in the general pews. Lee refused to attend the funeral.

Years later, I used the ACEs survey to aid in my healing and recovery, answering yes or no to the 10 listed experiences:

- *Child physical abuse*

- *Child sexual abuse*

- *Child emotional abuse*

- *Emotional neglect*

- *Physical neglect*

- *Mentally ill, depressed, or suicidal person in the home*

- *Drug addicted or alcoholic family member*

- *Witnessing domestic violence against the mother*

- *Loss of a parent to death or abandonment by parental divorce*

- *Incarceration of any family member for a crime[6]*

Incarceration of a family member was the only "no." By the age of 10 I had experienced the other nine.

Jim adopted us after Galen's death and so we had a new last name. Grandma Mabel was horrified and tried to convince me to tell my mom and Jim that I didn't want to be adopted. I did feel guilty, but Lee and I liked Jim. Plus, Mom wanted us all to have the same last name.

Later that year Lee and I were home alone. He called me into his bedroom – something he'd never done before. Then he started tickling me, which he knew I hated. When we were younger, Lee used to hold me down and squeeze my upper thighs. It felt like a jolt going through me and I would yelp and cry out which he found funny – until Mom heard my cries and told him to stop. This time he didn't touch my thighs. Instead, he put his hand underneath my shirt and cupped my breasts through my bra. I must have freaked out because the only other thing I remember was him coming into my room, apologizing and asking me to not tell Mom. I didn't. I didn't even tell myself because that incident was quickly boxed away until many years later when I was in a treatment hospital.

Mom changed after she married Jim. She seemed lighter somehow, laughing and hugging me every day. She didn't get as mad about things and her demeanor was calmer and more serene. It was clear she felt safe and loved. She and Jim held hands wherever they went and if I was with them, she held out her other hand for me.

We lived in a big house in Portland, the first real house I remember. I had my own bedroom on the second floor across the hall from Lee. I met my first friend, a girl my age named Teddie who lived next door with her parents and ten siblings. Mom said they were Christian Scientists which sounded very exotic to me. My mom explained that just because they believed differently than we did, I should be respectful and not ask too many questions.

She still worked as a waitress, but she must have cut back on the number of jobs because she was at home more than ever before. She even took on being the leader for my Camp Fire Girl troop. That summer, Mom didn't leave to travel with Aunt Holly in the carnival. After marrying Jim she left her carnie days behind.

After my father's death Grandma Mabel's attention towards me hinged obsessive. She decorated her guest room as a girl's bedroom and told me that it was mine – that it would *always* be there for me. Paintings of poodles adorned the walls and a lady's vanity set with a large mirror sat in the corner. Grandma Mabel brushed my hair with a special brush that she said was only mine and she bathed and dressed me when we were alone. I didn't like it. I was almost 13 years old before I gathered the courage to tell her that I didn't want her to bathe me anymore. She professed great hurt, insisting that "Grandma Mabel knows what's best for you."

Many years later I began to understand why I hated brushing my hair and why the sight of painted pictures of poodles made me recoil in disgust, despite loving dogs. Grandma Mabel used the hairbrush for nastier actions with me in that room than untangling my hair.

Another unfortunate message that connected back to Mabel was her refrain, "Jesus loves you, *just like Grandma Mabel*." I felt the presence of God but even hearing the word "Jesus" made me cringe well into adulthood.

Death and divorce in themselves can cause significant trauma for children, who naturally feel abandoned and who often blame themselves. In the span of 15 months, my parents divorced and remarried other people who had children of their own. Then my father died, and Jim adopted us.

But then he left us shortly afterward for a year to fight in the Vietnam War. As a result, we ended up leaving Portland for good. We moved to Hagerman, the small town in Idaho where Jim was raised, while he was deployed overseas. He wrote me a couple of letters while he was away. But though I was happy that he was thinking of me I still wasn't sure how to respond to him.

Jim was kind and affectionate, but I had scant experience with men like that. Grandpa Williams (my mother's father) died two months before my father passed, and I had no memory of visiting him, even though I'm sure that I did. My paternal grandfather died before I was born. Grandma Mabel's second husband (George) was the only grandpa I knew. I liked Grandpa George. When we visited the cabin he was building on the Oregon coast, he would give me a hammer, a couple nails and a piece of wood and encourage me to pound away. I have a vague memory of being very small and sitting on Grandpa George's huge foot while he bounced me up and down.

Jim was different, like Grandpa George.

I was certain he would eventually leave us or worse, die in Vietnam. Mom was also scared of that happening, though she tried to hide it from us. Sure enough, we found out Jim had been seriously wounded and had to be hospitalized for several months overseas. Mom freaked out of course, and Lee warned me not to aggravate her. He started acting like he was the man of the house, ordering me around and taking on chores that Mom usually did.

My response to the major changes in my life that had occurred over the previous 15 months was to add another maladaptive behavior to my toolbox. I had always been that child who continuously brought home stray dogs, tended to wounded birds, and knew every pet in the neighborhood by name.

I soon found stray dogs roaming the town and brought them home with me. At one point I had 13 stray dogs that I had adopted. I don't know how my mom was able to feed them all. Mom also took each new dog to a local veterinarian for shots and had them spayed or neutered. Six of the dogs walked with me to school each morning with three of them returning to meet me after school. These animals offered me unconditional love. I felt they needed and wanted me. I always believed that I took in so many strays because my heart ached for dogs who did not have a home or love. But as an adult, I realize that I was reacting to my many losses and upheavals.

When Pops came home, we moved to Camp Pendleton, California for his new assignment. That meant I had to find permanent homes for my dogs. I don't remember every placement, but I do remember that at one point Mom and Jim told me that they had a friend on a farm who wanted four of the remaining dogs. Writing this, I wonder what really happened to them.

I started 8th grade in Oceanside, California. On the first day of PE, the female gym teacher told us that we would be required to shower after every gym class. She kept our names on her clipboard and would stand by the open showers to make sure that we got completely wet and washed thoroughly before checking off our names. I wanted to run away and die. Not only did I have to get undressed in front of other people, but I also could see everyone else in various stages of undress. What if I didn't wash the way the teacher wanted me to? Would she make me do it over again? Would she take the soap and do it herself like Grandma Mabel did?

The next few days I faked being sick so I could stay home from school. But on the third day Mom insisted that I get on the bus. When it was time for PE, I remember holding one of my arms across my breasts and the other one over my vagina and hurrying through the shower as quickly as possible.

Shortly after, Pops was transferred from Camp Pendleton to Kaneohe Marine Corps Air Station on the island of Oahu, Hawaii. As a result, I finished 8th grade at Kailua Intermediate in Kailua, Hawaii. I spent my entire 9th grade there before my parents transferred me to St. Francis Convent High School in Honolulu for my sophomore year. I wasn't given a choice. I was getting in constant trouble. Then Pops was sent back to Vietnam, which meant a return to Hagerman to finish that school year. Somewhere along the way I briefly attended an experimental government program where I sat in an individual carrel and listened to taped instructions through a headset, filling out accompanying workbooks. Altogether I attended 18 schools before graduating high school.

It was when I was living in Hawaii that I told my mom I no longer wanted to go to Mass with her. She didn't get mad. Instead, she said, "Fine. But we live in a crossroads of the world here, with every religion represented. If you find another church that speaks to you more than the Catholic Church that's fine. You can attend your friend's churches or check out something else, but you *will* attend a church."

My friend Paula-Rene was a Jehovah's Witness and for many months I went to the Kingdom Hall with her family. I also spent an afternoon chanting with the Krishnas, a westernized sect of Hinduism. Mom and Pops took me to visit a Buddhist temple on the island. I went to church with friends who were Methodist, Lutheran, and Seventh Day Adventist. I found them all fascinating and developed a life-long love for recognizing the same gold threads in the world's tapestry of faith traditions. Some of the places I went – like chanting with the Krishnas – was to see if my parents really meant it when they said I could attend any church. I think they saw right through my ploy and didn't rise to the bait.

5

what really happened, part ii

The happening and telling are very different things. This doesn't mean that the story isn't true, only that I honestly don't know anymore if I really remember it or only remember how to tell it. – Karen Joy Fowler, We Are All Completely Beside Ourselves

I lived in Oahu when great changes were occurring in the U.S. The hippie culture was thriving, the Vietnam War was raging, and protests against the war and for civil rights dominated the nightly news. My contemporaries were experimenting with drugs beyond alcohol. On Oahu free weekly rock concerts took place all summer at Hanauma Bay beach. Kids hitchhiked everywhere. I desperately wanted to fit in. I was too terrified to try the kinds of drugs the other kids were taking – drugs like amphetamines, heroin, LSD, and marijuana. The idea of losing control of my mind and body paralyzed me with fear. But I talked a good story with my friends and a few times I stole one of my mom's valium pills, split it in half and took it. I liked the feeling of my muscles relaxing from their normal tense state, but I was also afraid of being caught.

My brother Lee graduated from high school and set off to see the world with no real plans. Before he left, he gave me a gift that would become my voice for many years. I was in my bedroom reading when the door flung open, and my brother walked in carrying his old six-string guitar, which had long been supplanted by his collection of electric guitars, a drum kit and other instruments.

Wherever we lived he started a band and if he couldn't find other musicians, he taught his friends how to play. Lee's first guitars (as a child) were made of cardboard. The old six-string guitar was his first *real* one, a used model our mom found in a thrift store.

The guitar was battered and only had two strings left. He tossed it on my bed and said, "Here, stupid little sister. I don't need this piece of crap anymore so you can have it." Then he left.

I was dumbfounded. It was the first time he had given me something that wasn't a mom-bought, obligated gift for Christmas or my birthday. I wrote my first few songs on that guitar. I had no idea how to play a guitar or even how to hold it, so I held it in a way that felt right. Since I couldn't read music, I pressed my fingers on the frets and memorized the sounds.

Years later I played in public for the first time and learned I was playing the guitar upside down – and backwards! Lee was impressed when he saw me play because he said that was how the rock and roll legend Jimi Hendrix played his guitar. I wish I played like Hendrix or Lee, who was a true musician with any instrument.

Writing and singing my own songs became another way for me to express my feelings. I wrote voluminously in journals, but the deep, deep-down pain and darkness only surfaced in my songs. My first song reflected my inner turmoil.

"Time is an eternity...
So ever changing, ever moving, never gone.
Spring and Summer pass, and Fall comes drifting down the lane,
it won't be long,
Before the winter's barren death comes creeping in, to the drain the
life from living souls,
And flowers then will never blossom anymore."

Cheery, huh?

When Pops returned to Vietnam for his second tour, I finished my sophomore year in Idaho. Being back in the rural desert of southern Idaho was a shock. Living in Hawaii had introduced me to a world of modern cultures, ethnicities and religions. I hadn't worn shoes in years, much less a dress or skirt. But here I was, once again living in a tiny, conservative farming town. The predominant religion was Mormon. At the high school the girls were required to take home economics classes as well as join the school drill team. The dress code was strictly enforced, with girls forbidden to wear pants or tennis shoes outside of gym or sports. I wore a floor-length pair of culottes one day and the principal sent me home to change.

I discussed the unfairness of the rules with my mom who suggested that I talk to the school board about it. I knew most of the other girls at school agreed with me. Not only was the dress code ludicrous, but it was highly impractical during the harsh Idaho winters when the ground was covered with more than a foot of snow. I knew the school board would never approve of girls wearing jeans like the boys did, so when I talked to the older, white men on the school board I emphasized that the girls wanted to wear the same kinds of new fashions that their wives were wearing at the time – pantsuits made of polyester. The men tentatively okayed a new dress code.

In my sophomore biology class, the teacher announced that we would be dissecting frogs. I was horrified at the thought of an animal being sacrificed just so I could see its internal organs. I believed that I could easily learn these things from a photo in a book. I told the teacher I would not be participating. He suggested that I see the principal instead. I first consulted with my mom and explained my reasoning. She said my argument was sound and she would back me up. I then talked to the principal and my biology teacher, and we reached a compromise – I would observe the dissections in class and be tested on them. A few months later the same teacher instructed the students to submit a project for the upcoming extracurricular science fair.

I raised my hand, "Is this science fair a requirement for this class?"

"No, it's not a requirement, but every biology student participates in the science fair."

"Are you assigning us the projects?" I asked.

"No, it's entirely up to you what kind of science project you would like to do," he replied.

Around this time, my mom decided it was time to give me 'the talk' about sex. Except, she was so uncomfortable about that she handed me a book instead, saying, "Ah...just in case you have any questions, this book should have all the answers you need."

The title was *Everything You Ever Wanted to Know About Sex But Were Afraid to Ask*, a national bestseller that came out in 1969. I was 15 years old when I read the wildly age-inappropriate book that detailed various sexual practices like sex orgies, sadism, exhibitionism, masochism and inserting objects into anuses and vaginas. The author's view on homosexuality was damning even for that time. As a young woman who had not dated, avoided boys and thought I was a virgin, the book was both foreign and frightening. One informative chapter was about sexually transmitted diseases (STDs).

I decided STDs would be a good project for the science fair mainly because I wanted to make my biology teacher regret that he forced me to participate. But after contacting the local health department for more information the project stopped being about revenge and became a serious mission to educate my peers on the topic. I discovered that any type of sex education and information was shockingly absent in the schools. Venereal diseases (VD) like syphilis and gonorrhea were still rampant, and yet few schools or parents talked about it to teens. I researched the history of VD and learned that during the 1930s, syphilis was epidemic across the U.S., and the government spent millions on a public campaign to 'stamp out VD.'

Between 1910 and the 1950s laws allowed local 'morals squads' of police to arrest women they suspected of having VD including thousands who were sitting alone in restaurants, walking with friends or even standing outside of churches. Without any due process these women were subjected to genital exams, and if found to have a sexually transmitted disease were incarcerated and sent to work farms. (I could find no record of similar action against men.) Learning about that practice horrified me and was one more affirmation that *anyone* could do *anything* at *any time* to me and I was powerless to stop them. Any mention of VD became socially-taboo again after World War II. As a result of my research, I was determined to change those views with my science fair project.

My biology teacher said flatly, "no." But I persisted, showing him the information that I'd gathered. He tossed the ball by saying I needed the principal's permission. Of course, the principal didn't want anything to do with the subject of VD so he told me that I had to get the school board's permission. I remember soft-pedaling my pitch to them and although there were some uncomfortable glances between the men, they okayed it.

By the time the science fair was over I had a reputation among my peers for being the person to ask about all things sexual. Armed with my knowledge of VD and that book my mom gave me, I was happy to dispense information in a calm, clinical way. I learned that knowledge is a way of helping people. It felt good to be wanted, even if only for what I knew.

Pops returned from Vietnam earlier than expected thanks to the Marine Corps' troop withdrawals. He'd been awarded the military's Purple Heart medal after he was wounded during his first tour. This time, he wasn't wounded physically but he had changed. No one called it "post-traumatic stress disorder" (PTSD) back then. I learned not to approach him when his back was turned, not to touch him to wake him up from a nap, and to stay in my room when he was in a bad mood.

I wondered why he didn't seem to like me anymore, despite my mom's attempts to explain something she didn't understand. For Pop's final assignment before retirement, he was stationed as a Marine Corps recruiter in Boise, Idaho. I was enrolled in the local high school for my junior and senior years. It was the first time I'd gone to the same school for two years in a row.

I was determined my senior year would be different. It was the last chance to join an extracurricular activity or be part of a group. Every time we moved, I met a few girls who were also considered misfits and we'd be friends until I moved again. I signed up for a drama class and soon realized that most of the kids were considered different like me. For the first time I felt like I fit in. I tried to dress like them, talk like them and act like them. So really, I wasn't fitting in, I was pretending. But it still felt wonderful to hang around other kids and *feel* like I was accepted.

I still dressed in layers, so when I found out boys and girls changed into costumes backstage together, I freaked. I already got teased about my large breasts and for being what a few kids said was the "last virgin in the senior high school class." I asked my mom to buy me a full slip that I could wear for performances under my costumes. She found a yellow satin one that covered me from my armpits to my knees.

I hated my body and neglected it. This included washing my hands and face, leaving my hair unbrushed and tying it back in a ponytail, not shaving my legs, and wearing minimal makeup if any at all. I was gaining weight and in the back of my mind, thought that would protect me from any boy's interest.

My new friends in drama class seemed like a tight-knit group of survivors who circled in and leaned on each other for emotional support. I was desperate to be liked and accepted by them. One of the popular theater boys was a sophomore named Jeremy*, and we became friends. Jeremy told me about the girls he dated and his dreams for the future. He also shared his poetry and journals with me. He was my first big crush, though I kept it a secret because the idea of any boyfriend-girlfriend relationship scared me.

Our relationship soon became what is described as excessive attachment or codependent which then turned toxic. I tried to change him, manipulate him and control him in overt and covert ways, while he was doing the same to me. I used all my learned coping skills to make sure he didn't leave me. Jeremy had a penchant for reframing conversations and events (whether I was there or not) into highly dramatic retellings that usually cast himself as the victim. And just as children of abuse often become abusers themselves, I felt driven to convince him that his memory was wrong. I started writing down our conversations so when he contradicted me, I would know I wasn't crazy. I was desperate for his approval while at the same time keeping him at a distance. I didn't recognize that I did exactly the same things he did – reframing conversations and events, including lying, to cast myself as the victim and him as the perpetrator.

That final year of high school was unlike any year before. For the first time, I hung out with a group of kids and after nightly rehearsals we would pile into my Volkswagen Bug and go to the local coffee shop to discuss the big topics that most teens focus on – life, relationships, sex, how mean our parents were and how we planned to change the world. Many of the kids talked about doing drugs and I told vividly false stories about living in Hawaii where "everyone" did drugs. My senior year was when I was given the nickname Space Cadet because apparently, I seemed 'spaced-out' to my friends.

One momentous thing happened that made me feel normal. There was a party at my house – an actual, high school party. My parents had left for the weekend, so Jeremy and I decided to have a party for our theatre friends. I had no clue about how to get alcohol, but Jeremy assured me that people would bring some to the party. What started as a group of about ten invited kids quickly mushroomed into ... I can't remember how many, but the house was trashed by the time everyone left. The next morning Jeremy and I decided to grab a fast-food breakfast before starting the clean-up process. My parents were expected back the next day so we thought we had plenty of time.

When we walked back in the house with our breakfast bags, we both froze in horror as my mom's you-are-in-so-much-trouble-young-lady voice boomed from the living room.

"Catherine? Jeremy? Would you both come in here, please?"

My legs turned to water, and I could barely stand. My stomach roiled and I wanted to throw up. We entered the living room to see my mom and Pops waiting for us.

"Sit down. Now" Mom said sternly, pointing to the couch. Her voice had a cold, low, steely tone. She didn't say anything about the fact I'd had a party without their knowledge or permission. Instead, she informed us that we would be cleaning the house "thoroughly" before I was grounded for two weeks.

She looked at Jeremy. "You are also grounded, young man! I trust I won't have to call your parents to make sure you stay grounded for the next two weeks, am I right?" Jeremy knew better than to do anything but nod.

My parents were at the end of the rope with my behavior. I talked back, blew off of my chores and slammed doors. They realized that their usual punishment of grounding was ineffective because I liked being grounded. It was a vacation from the emotional strain of dealing with them, school, and even my new friends. My room was a refuge with my guitar, books, typewriter, and record player. Other than emerging to forage for food or go to the bathroom, I was happy to stay put.

I don't remember the following incident. My Pops and my mom told me years later at different times that it happened. I had gotten into trouble for something, and they decided to ground me when I returned home from school that day. But first they stripped my bedroom bare except for the bed. When I came home and we had the inevitable "you're in trouble and you're grounded" talk, I left to go to my room. Pops said that I didn't come out for dinner, so at bedtime my mom opened my bedroom door.

My mom said, "You were sitting on the edge of your bed, staring at the wall, not saying anything. I told you to go to bed, and you didn't answer, but I thought you were just mad." Pops said that I was in that same position the next morning when they called me for breakfast, and this time my mom waved her hand in front of my face and raised her voice to get my attention. But still nothing. They decided to leave me alone and went to their respective jobs.

I remember feeling stunned hearing the story, wanting to disbelieve them but they were serious. "What happened next?" I demanded. Pops said, "Well, honey, you just stayed like that. Mom and I wondered if we should try to force you to move and I think she even wanted to call the doctor at one point, but we thought if we just left you alone you would come out of it when you were ready."

My mom said that on morning of the third day I joined them at breakfast and acted as if it was a normal day. She said they tried to question me, but I seemed confused. She told me what day it was, which I denied at first but then accepted. I would often get mixed-up on what day it was and couldn't remember entire blocks of my life.

They told me this story long after I left home. But even though I didn't remember anything, I was still shocked that they weren't more concerned at the time and didn't try to get me help. I believe that I had been in a dissociative or catatonic state. I didn't have a word for it at the time. I just kind of left my body. Years later I learned that this is called dissociation. Dissociation in both children and adults usually arises from trauma. Dissociation occurs along a spectrum, ranging from spacing-out - such as while driving and missing an exit - to being hyper-focused on a topic. Impaired memory (i.e., gaps in recall often associated with PTSD) is another sign of dissociation. Other signs include depersonalization and de-realization, which Dr. Milissa Kaufman describes as a "profound detachment from one's sense-of-self or sense-of-body, a sensation of being apart from one's self, perhaps viewing what is happening from a distance."[7]

By the time I graduated from high school and entered adulthood, my childhood coping skills and strategies had buried the *real* me. It's no surprise I failed as a young adult.

I graduated high school at 17 and shortly after Mom suggested I move out on my own. I wanted to leave home as much as they probably wanted me to leave. I clearly had problems and living with me must have been like riding an emotional roller coaster. I had a sharp tongue, and I could be mean even with my friends.

I was just hard to get along with. I gave off a signal that invited friends to get close to me, but this only went so far before I started conflicts, ran away, froze or self-isolated from them. Mom told me if I moved out, I would receive a monthly check from Galen's social security until I either turned 18 or turned 22 if I was enrolled in college.

Many of my friends were planning to go to Boise State University in town. I told them I was going too. I also told my Mom, who just nodded and said something about my grades better improve. Neither she nor Pops had been to college, so none of us had an inkling of how to go about it. A couple girlfriends asked me if I wanted to hang out during Orientation Day. I didn't know what that was and I hadn't actually applied yet. I knew there was paperwork involved but as usual I crossed my fingers and hoped it would magically work out.

On Orientation Day I stood in line with my friends for a student packet. When I got to the front of the line the student helper informed me that he didn't see my name. To save face I feigned confusion, hoping that he would give me a packet anyway. Instead, he directed me to another table where some adults were sitting.

I slid into the folding chair across from a woman who looked friendly. Her search for my name was futile too.

She asked me, "Do you remember applying? Maybe your parents did that for you?"

I nodded, happy to place the blame on my parents. The lady leafed through her papers again, smiled brightly and then said, "Don't worry, sweetie. I can help you take care of that." She asked me questions, filled out a form and sent me over to the main office. They had me complete another form so social security would pay my first semester's tuition. Then they sent me to another lady to get my schedule.

This was exciting! I was actually going to college! I imagined that people who attended college were adults with no more high school cliques or bullying. I also imagined college students sitting in a circle and having deep discussions and debates about whatever subject they were studying. I wanted to study science but my friends were majoring in theatre arts, so I told the lady to sign me up for those classes.

She asked me about my math, English and science grades and what foreign language I took in high school. I was confused. Why did that matter? I wanted to take theatre classes and help with stage productions. I told her I wasn't good at math, but I was pretty good in English and science. I also knew a little Spanish. She said, "Well, I'm going to sign you up for the basics this first semester, so you'll be taking English 101. It also sounds like you need Remedial Math 010." She wrote down the information. I still didn't know why I was being forced to take classes that had nothing to do with theatre, but I wasn't given a choice.

She handed me a copy of my schedule which included remedial math, English, Spanish and theatre arts. I left the office feeling crushed with disappointment. What was the point of college if you had the same classes you took in high school?

I found my friends sitting in the grass near the theatre arts building. They were going through a stack of books. Books? No one had given me books. Perhaps the books were handed out to people who had not pre-registered on the first day of class? I sat down and showed my friends my schedule. They nodded. Then one of them asked me which English class I was in. I didn't know how to read the schedule's details so I handed it to her. She frowned and said that it was "too bad" that we were in different English classes.

"Where are your books?" she asked. I looked down and finally confessed, "I don't know where to get them." Instead of laughing at me, she pointed to a building across the manicured lawns. "That's the bookstore," she said. "Go buy them there."

I nodded. Of course, I had no money and my social security check had already been spent. Besides I reasoned, it's not fair that I have to take math, English, and Spanish. My anger felt righteous. Turning my shame into righteousness was another coping tool I had mastered. I was beating the system! Other than my theatre class and signing up for stage productions, I did not attend any other classes at college. At the end of the first quarter, I received my grades. I had a 0.0 grade point average. There was one class I passed: Math 010. Because it was a remedial course, there were no grades, just a P for pass or an F for fail. Despite never attending class, the instructor gave me a pass, further cementing my distrust of public education.

Getting to school every day was a challenge. My beat-up VW Bug demanded gas to run. Thankfully my monthly $65 check from social security covered rent on my all-utilities-included studio apartment, plenty of ramen noodles, boxes of cheap macaroni and cheese, a carton of cigarettes and enough gas money for a week or two. It didn't take long for me to blow my monthly check on gas to drive friends around and buy more cigarettes and snacks. Within a couple months I was evicted.

Over the next year I was homeless. A friend's parents took me in for a few months and tried to help me get stabilized with a job. I would find a job only to lose it after a few days or a few weeks. The truth is I would give myself some reason – any reason – to not show up to the job because I was afraid of *everything* that appeared to be adult stuff, in the same way I had been so scared to turn 13. Without money there were times I stole food and other necessities from the store. That is...until I was arrested for shoplifting two packs of cigarettes and spent three days in the county jail. That ended my budding criminal career.

The year I turned 19 another momentous event occurred. I met a boy named Travis* and I lost my virginity to him (not realizing until years later that my virginity was gone years before).

I still hung out with Jeremy who was now a senior. He seemed upset when I told him the news, and said he thought my 'first time' would be with him. Those words sent my heart soaring and soon we had sex. For a few weeks I had sex with both of them – until Travis ghosted me. Jeremy and I decided that being sexual didn't add anything to our friendship. Deep down I knew that we weren't meant to be boyfriend-girlfriend, but I wished we could be.

By then I was sharing a studio apartment with Karen, my best friend from Hagerman. But we were polar opposites as roommates. I was a slob. The floors were covered with empty food wrappers, papers, books and other things. My dirty clothes were dumped in the bathtub, which meant that Karen had to move the piles to bathe. She was an immaculate housekeeper. Naturally we clashed.

Sometimes I would tell her to stay out of the apartment because I was going to cast a 'money spell' (which never worked). I wanted a quick fix to my problems and was willing to try anything – except hold down a job.

I often fantasized about having superpowers and debated which one to pick: invisibility or flight. Invisibility meant I could look behind the scenes of people's lives and find out the truth. Flight meant that I could escape traps or threats and be safe.

I quit college and spent a week at my parent's home in Hagerman. They were both retired by then. There was a travelling theatre company rehearsing at the local Grange Hall. I hung out with them for a few days before they left to go to Boise for performances at a local venue called Theatre in a Trunk. I was familiar with the stage because it's where I performed the role of the daughter in the play *I Never Sang for My Father*. (It was my one and only real speaking role on stage and I was terrible.)

The travelling theatre company's guest director offered me a ride back to Boise. His name was Lee Stetson, and he had worked professionally in Hollywood. Lee was curious about my life. "Do you have a boyfriend?" he asked on the drive. I said no and then he said the strangest thing, "Don't think I'm weird for saying this but I have a sense about these things – I think you're pregnant. That's why I asked you if you have a boyfriend." I cracked up laughing and assured him I was definitely not pregnant.

Back in Boise I couldn't pay my share of the rent and was homeless again. I spent a few nights on friends' couches. Then I found an outside storage room behind Karen's apartment building and snuck in every night. I had no changes of clothes. My daily attire was old denim coveralls, a tee-shirt and a long navy wool coat that my mom made me.

It was February by then and the fierce Idaho winter froze the landscape. I learned how to scan the streets and floors for loose change. I woke up each morning in an old chair in the storage room and then walked across the street to a gas station to use the bathroom and warm my hands with hot water. Warm water is the greatest gift when your hands are freezing and aching from the cold.

I walked seven blocks to Boise State University's student union building to relish the inside warmth. Hot water in the cafeteria was free and for 26 cents I could purchase a day-old loaf of bread and a small box of chicken bouillon cubes to stretch through a week. I used the hot water to make broth. My diet was supplemented by college friends who often left unwanted French fries or fruit on their trays. Because I still smoked cigarettes, I scouted ashtrays for smokeable butts (in those days, smoking was still popular and allowed inside of buildings.)

Looking back, I was on a ledge about to drop off. I am pretty sure I would have died had it not been for what happened next.

6

my first big break

Trauma is ... an experience we have that overwhelms our capacity to cope. – Dan Siegel[8]

A couple weeks later a friend asked me to go with her to get a free pregnancy test at Planned Parenthood. I was happy to support her but as we were chatting, I realized I couldn't remember the last time I had my period. I was certain that I wasn't pregnant despite not being on birth control and despite what the theatre director Lee had said on the way back to Boise. I thought a woman had to have sex dozens of times to get pregnant, and between Travis and Jeremy I'd only had sex a handful of times. I knew this because I kept track of my 'sexcapades' in my journal.

But I should have known better.

In high school I was the one who encouraged others to go to Planned Parenthood to get on birth control. How ironic would it be if I was pregnant? I decided to take a pregnancy test too while I was there with my friend. I peed in the cup they provided. Back then it often took a few days to get the results. I called the center after three days from a payphone. It was March 12.

The woman on the other end said, "Ah, yes, you are positive." I was confused. Positive? Was it positive that I wasn't pregnant or positive that I was? She clarified; I was pregnant! A rush of unexpected joy flooded through me, and I jumped up and down inside the phonebooth. Then I thought, "Oh no! Don't jump! It might hurt the baby!"

Abortion was not for me, but I also wasn't sure if I could keep the baby or if it would be better to give him or her up for adoption. My Planned Parenthood advisor invited me back to the office. She gave me a voucher to stay at the local YWCA for a week. Many cities had YMCAs and YWCAs, places where single men and women could find temporary shelter. That night I slept in a warm bed for the first time in over a month. I also took my first shower in weeks and ate a hot meal. By the end of the week Planned Parenthood arranged for me to move into Boise's Booth Memorial Home, a place for unwed mothers.

The Boise location was opened by the Salvation Army in 1921, and at the time I was there, offered free room and board and medical care.

Because I was 19 years old, I was given a room to myself. The other girls living there were between the ages of 12 and 17 with many of them arriving from other cities and states. These girls were sent there by their parents, insisting they give birth far away then give the child up for adoption before returning to their 'normal' life. Most of the girls wanted to keep their babies and fantasized that their boyfriends would come for them. They were so naïve but in retrospect so was I.

I knew that I had to inform the two prospective fathers. I have always believed that parenting should be a matter of choice not obligation. People *should not* have kids, just because it was 'expected.' Imagine how a kid would feel to learn their parents only had them because their grandmas and grandpas pushed them to do it? Or that their mom didn't even want kids but got pressured into it? Or their dad?

I wondered if I could keep and raise a child. Would I be patient enough? Was I willing to give up sleeping in for the next seven years or so? Seven-year-old children could fix their own breakfasts, right? Would I be able to afford a child?

I wasn't raised around babies and though I babysat kids in high school, none of them were under the age of two. I thought about the practical realities holding down a job, something I had not been able to do.

Travis said that he already knew. He had heard I was pregnant through the grapevine. I anxiously assured him that it was his choice whether or not to be involved in my pregnancy or the child's life. I didn't expect anything from him. I said I wasn't even sure that he was the baby's father. He nodded. I don't recall us speaking after that.

I still hung out with Jeremy but not as often once I left home and rarely when I was homeless. He was in his senior year of high school, busy with theatre and new friends. He immediately asked if he was the father. I told him the same thing I told Travis. I said I didn't think that he was, because we'd only had sex a few times. Yes, I was that uninformed. He gallantly offered to marry me. But we were both so immature and our lives were so messed up that the mere idea of getting married seemed both hopeless and terrifying. I reassured him that he probably wasn't even the father. He didn't look as if he believed me, so I lied. I insinuated that I had slept with more men than just he and Travis. I thought I was being noble, not wanting to keep him from his dreams but I wasn't being noble at all. I knew that I wasn't capable of having a healthy relationship with myself – let alone with him. It was easier for me not to know who the biological father of my baby was. And I still wasn't sure if I wanted to keep the baby or give him or her up for adoption.

Being pregnant changed me. It prompted me to turn my life around. I started exercising, walking and stretching. Deep in my bones I knew this would be my only pregnancy, so I wanted cherish this time.

I called my mom to tell her the news. "Mom, I'm pregnant."

"You're pregnant? Okay. What are your plans?" she asked. Her tone was distant.

Later I realized she was trying her best to support me – without being judgmental. She had also been an unwed mother when she gave birth to my older brother.

I found a part-time job as an office worker at a local live theatre company. I also applied for public assistance to access medical care and food assistance. I rented a small apartment within walking distance of my job. I was preparing for my child's birth. I talked to two people who had adopted children. I read books on parenting. Ultimately, I decided I could keep my baby. It was the first adult choice I made.

Many years later I asked Karen, "Why did you decide to be friends with me back then?"

She responded, "Well, we weren't *always* friends. There were times when you acted too crazy for me and I had to walk away. I got so mad at you when you became pregnant. That was so irresponsible. You were the last person on earth who should have gotten pregnant."

My beautiful daughter Andie* (short for Andromeda Sunshine) was born on a bright November morning and I was enchanted by everything about her. My mom came and stayed with me for about a week so she could help out with the baby. She prepared meals for me and snuggled with her new granddaughter. I asked Karen to be her godmother.

I was a practical new mother. I didn't have a crib or special room for my new baby, so the first several weeks she slept in an empty dresser drawer that I padded with blankets. The drawer was on the floor inside the small closet in the living room. I kept the door open. Eventually my friends at Theatre in a Trunk gave me a bassinet.

Breastfeeding was the most convenient and inexpensive option — no bottles or sterilizing to fuss with. When friends asked me what they could buy for a baby gift, I said disposable diapers. I found a backpack baby chair at a thrift store, and liked the papoose structure, so Andie could see the world.

If I developed postpartum depression, I don't remember it. But within months I started giving away my scant belongings. Decades later Karen reminded me why I did that.

"You were convinced that the mothership was coming for you to take you back to space and you didn't want to be encumbered by 'belongings' when they arrived." I asked her what happened after that and she responded, "Well, the mothership didn't come of course, and you just started collecting stuff again."

Every day I held my breath a little. I was scared that I might hurt my baby in some emotional way. I read that the first four years of a child's life are the most critical in terms of building a foundation. If a child feels loved, is expected to adhere to boundaries, has been encouraged to explore and learn, and trusts that his or her mom and/or dad are capable then the foundation is set. The child might veer off course or go 'window shopping' during their teenage years, but that foundation will remain strong. I told myself that if I could refrain from screwing things up during my baby's first four years then she would ultimately be okay.

But once again I found a way to sabotage my life. This time it triggered my first major mental breakdown.

It started when four of my friends moved into my small apartment. JoAnne and Tamara were friends from high school while Michael and Joseph were new friends. The five of us quickly became enmeshed with each other. Somehow, we acquired a beat-up van that Michael said we should drive to the country of Panama. I don't

Andie and me with our mini commune at my one bedroom apartment.

remember why. But the old van had a cracked engine block and would not run. Later it was decided to take a bus to California via Las Vegas, where Joseph's parents lived. I had no money and stayed behind.

After they left, I physically ached missing them, and looked for ways I could join them. With no credit to my name and no job, I purchased a brand-new Chevy Vega, telling myself it was meant to be because the car was named after the star Vega. I left everything behind except for some clothes, my guitar and of course Andie.

Even today I'm not quite sure if what happened to me on the trip was real or if I was showing the early signs of psychosis. I left one August evening. It took about 10 hours from Boise to Las Vegas. At my first gas station stop I met a trucker who suggested that I take a quicker, alternate route.

He warned me, "That road is pretty deserted, and pitch black at night. There are no towns around for miles. If you decide to take that route, make sure that you have a full tank of gas."

Andie was asleep in her backpack on the seat next to me. The trucker was right – within an hour my car headlights were the only lights for miles. No other lights could be found anywhere in the sprawling desert except for the extremely luminous and bright stars. The road stretched on without curves or inclines, so I was surprised by the pair of seemingly close lights in my rear-view mirror.

How did I miss those lights before?

The lights appeared to come closer. But once I looked into my rearview mirror again the lights had vanished. Where did they go? There was nothing except desert road and scrubby patches of sagebrush. The driver must have turned off the car's headlights but why? I travelled a few more miles when suddenly the lights were back – much closer to my car than before, and clearly descending from above the highway until they were level on the road again. My anxiety shot up. I pressed the gas pedal to speed up and watched in relief as the lights receded. Once again they vanished. But this time I knew that I what I was seeing was impossible.

Were those lights connected to a UFO? What it was an alien ship finally coming for me? I eased my foot off of the gas pedal.

Suddenly a ginormous jackrabbit jumped in front of my car, hitting it with a thud. I jerked, pressing hard on the brakes. Then another rabbit jumped in front of my headlights but this time, I was able to swerve and miss it. Then one rabbit after another popped into the scene. It seemed like dozens of rabbits came to the same place, all of them jumping frantically on the highway in front of my car. Each new thud startled me. My heart was racing. A few miles later I came across dead rabbits lying in the middle of the road and off to the side of it. Their little bodies were piled up into small clusters like pyramids and I knew someone – or something – had arranged them like that.

I felt primal fear – the kind that prompts you to fight, freeze, or flee. My response was to hit the gas pedal hard and drive as fast as possible even as I slammed through piles of dead rabbits. The blackness was overwhelming, and I had to slam on my brakes when the road ended abruptly.

My only choice was to turn left or right. Shaking with anxiety I chose left. It was the middle of the night when I first saw a scattering of lights. The road led into a tiny town, consisting of a few dark houses, a couple dark stores, and a tavern with lights on and three pickup trucks parked in front. I scooped Andie up in my arms and ran inside. There were a few men at the bar, and two more playing pool. The men got quiet and stared at me when I walked in with Andie. I went into the bathroom, touching the cold wall tiles, looking up at the bright lights, trying to calm down and reassuring myself that we were safe now.

There was a payphone inside the bar, and I used it to call my friends in Las Vegas. JoAnne answered. Just hearing her familiar voice calmed me and I told her everything that had happened. She assured me it would be okay and encouraged me to keep driving.

I left the tavern with Andie and drove back to the crossroads – this time going in the opposite direction. I remember my body was numb and feeling disconnected. I turned on the radio to help me focus but every signal was out of range. Eventually I found the main route and followed it until early morning when we reached Las Vegas.

Andie and I spent a few days there before my friends piled into the Vega and we all left for Santa Barbara, California. It wasn't long before we split up again.

I drove to Portland with the hazy notion to get a job and apartment. But because I had no money Andie and I were forced to sleep in the car for the first few nights before finding a local homeless shelter. Unfortunately, that shelter didn't allow children, but the manager said Andie and I could stay for one night.

The next day, another homeless woman told me that I should sell my blood for immediate cash. The blood collection site was in a dicey part of town and I was nervous walking in, especially since I had Andie in my arms. There was a line of men, most who looked homeless, tired and thin. I was paid after the blood draw, so I drove to the nearest grocery store and purchased high protein baby cereal for Andie. The weather had turned cold and I didn't want to keep her in the car another night so I reluctantly drove to my grandparents' house.

Grandma Mabel and George were thrilled to see me. Grandma Mabel hadn't changed. In fact, she had gotten worse. After her warm greeting, she informed me I should give Andie up for adoption and come live with her, while studying to be a dental hygienist or an x-ray technician. While in college I could meet a law student or med student and get married. According to Grandma Mabel, I would help put my husband through school before having more babies.

That was her plan.

She wanted me to stay in the room with the creepy poodle pictures on the wall. I felt a visceral reaction of fear and disgust and insisted on staying in the third bedroom. After two days I began to unravel and decided to stay with some friends I knew who had moved to Portland. Grandma Mabel was agitated by the news and pulled on my arm as I finished loading my bags into the Vega. As I picked up Andie's carrier, she tried to pull it from my hands, insisting that she would keep Andie for me. I must have flashed back to that scene with Galen and my mom because I froze with fear. Then anger set in.

"NO!" I yelled, pulling Andie away from her and quickly walking to the driver's side. I got in, leaned over and locked the passenger door. I placed Andie's carrier on the seat beside me. Grandma Mabel raised her shrill voice even louder as I drove away. I never saw her again.

I found a job as a receptionist at a photography studio in Beaverton, Oregon. One thing I had for sure, was a low, pleasant voice. Not only because I'd been told to lower it so often, but because of Grandma Mabel's voice. I did not want to sound like her.

I answered a *Roommate Wanted* ad from a young woman who also had a baby. Thanks to a Volunteers of America program I was set up with a babysitter. The brand-new Vega regularly broke down.

By then Michael, Joseph, JoAnne and Tamara had moved again to get seasonal jobs in northern Idaho. At the end of summer they visited me in Portland and asked me to drive them back to Santa Barbara, a fifteen-hour trip. I said yes without any concern for my job. We stopped at Golden Gate Park in San Francisco, but I don't remember anything else – until I was driving home on Interstate 5 a few days later, with Andie sleeping in the back seat.

I stopped at a truck stop in Red Bluffs as night fell and ordered a cup of coffee. Another young woman asked if she could join me. She was heading towards Klamath Falls, Oregon and suggested I follow her on the highway, which made sense to me. She asked me if I did drugs and if I had tried angel dust, a drug craze going around at that time. I knew it was a powerful hallucinogenic and the thought of losing control terrified me. I told her that I didn't do hallucinogenic drugs.

In the past when adults talked about teens being under peer pressure I didn't understand because in my experience, if I decided not to take a hit from a joint or drink alcohol (though I did both on occasion), it was no big deal to my friends. I was surprised when the young woman's response was outright belligerent. She challenged me to try it before judging. That's when I put my cup down, picked up Andie and told her I needed to get going. She agreed and followed me out. I decided to lose her on the highway, by taking a random exit that would throw her off.

I exited into the town of Redding, but she swerved off and followed me. I panicked. I bet she was wondering why I exited so abruptly. What could I tell her? I couldn't tell her that I needed gas because she saw me fueling up in Red Bluffs. It was my need to please people and avoid confrontation that led me into danger. I pulled into a busy gas station and parked behind the building. She parked next to me.

"Sorry, I have to go to the bathroom," I lied, heading past the gas pumps, and entering the convenience store. In the middle of the pumping stations there was a small, enclosed booth where an attendant sat. After using the restroom, I settled Andie into her car seat again, and then made one of the worst mistakes of my life.

The girl suggested, "Listen, why don't we park here for a few hours, and get some sleep? Then we can get going again."

I agreed. She invited me to sit with her in the cab of her truck and lit what I thought was a joint. She inhaled and offered it to me. I didn't want to take it but I also didn't want a confrontation. I took a small inhale and passed it back. We exchanged another hit then I returned to my car. My plan was to wait until she fell asleep then drive away.

The first wave hit me like a hammer. I was startled. Pot had relaxed me before but that felt nothing like this. Then another wave hit, and I saw my windshield glass distort, bend and melt. I said out loud, "Oh my God. That wasn't pot. Okay, stay calm. I'm hallucinating and it will pass. I didn't take much. Just be calm."

I looked to my left towards her truck. She was sitting on the passenger side watching me. *She knew.*

The third and fourth waves were even worse. I knew I had to get help for Andie. If that girl thought nothing of slipping me a hallucinogenic drug, what else was she capable of? What if she tried to do something to Andie? I opened the door and slid on all fours into the dirt. I remember reaching up and pushing the lock on the door so she couldn't get into my car. The next thing I remember I was clawing on the outside of the attendant's booth and trying to form words. I think I told the attendant to call the police because I had been drugged. But it's possible I was only making garbling sounds.

The next thing I remember is holding onto the open trunk of my car. There was a policeman with me and cars with flashing lights. I had moments of clarity, but they didn't last long. "Okay listen I only have maybe ten seconds so I have to talk really fast. Get Andie my daughter away from that girl. Here are Andie's diapers. She takes amoxicillin for an ear infection – one teaspoon every six hours. Don't forget. The last time she took it was ... okay, I'm leaving again..."

The policeman looked at me and said, "Okay...Do you want to press charges?" I returned to reality feeling confused. Don't the police automatically arrest people who have drugs on them? I said, "Listen, I have to talk really fast because I am BACK. Did you get

Andie? She takes amoxicillin for her ear infection and oh shit, I'm gone again..."

What felt like hours later I came back, and the policeman said, "Look, your license says you just turned 21 and she is 19 which means in California she is considered a minor and you are considered an adult. Let me ask you again, do you want to press charges?" Something in his tone told me that he was trying to convince me *not* to press charges, so I said, "no."

I don't remember anything after that – until I woke up the next morning alone in a jail cell. The door opened to a common area where a few women were eating breakfast. One of the women pointed to an untouched plate of food. It was like I'd wandered into an episode of the old television series *The Twilight Zone*. I was in an unfamiliar world, playing a role that I had no idea how to play.

The sheriff came in and motioned me to follow him to his office. I asked him where Andie was. He shoved a piece of paper across the desk. "This paper says you were never arrested, you were only held overnight for your own protection. Your daughter's safe with a foster family. I'll give you the address and let them know you're on your way." I stared at the paper, still fuzzy in my mind. The sheriff continued, "Listen, I believed what you said last night. As far as we can tell from the drugs she had on her, you were given angel dust. That's our best guess anyway without having your blood tested. But not everyone here agrees with me, and thinks you knowingly put your daughter in danger. I suggest you get your daughter and head out of town; do you understand?"

Gratitude filled me. I got up, went around his desk and tried to hug him. He held up his hand, and said, "That's okay. Just don't ... come back here, okay?" Then he gave me the tiniest smile.

After picking up Andie I drove home, hyperalert for any signs of danger. A couple weeks later I had a flashback after putting Andie to bed one evening. The flashback felt like my mind was fracturing. I also had an annoying cough and cold that wouldn't go away.   I found the free health clinic and was put on antibiotics, but they didn't help.

I don't remember how but later Andie and I moved to Santa Barbara and stayed in the one-bedroom apartment that my four friends were now renting. At some point my car got repossessed for lack of payment. I was getting physically sicker and weaker by the day. I couldn't stop coughing and mentally I felt like pieces of my mind were detaching and drifting away.

The next thing I remember is landing at the Twin Falls, Idaho airport with Andie. My Pops was waiting for me. He said my friends had contacted my mom, who then sent a plane ticket to bring me and Andie home.

There was a major piece of my story that was still missing but I wouldn't find out what until 5 years later.

7

cognitive change

If our thinking is bogged down by distorted symbolic meanings, illogical reasoning and erroneous interpretations, we become, in truth, blind and deaf. ~Aaron Beck, Father of Cognitive Behavioral Therapy

After I arrived back in Hagerman, I was sick for a long time. A doctor tried various antibiotics to knock out what he called a "massive body infection." But my physical condition was minor compared to what was happening in my mind. I was paranoid, and even a simple request to accompany my mom to the store sent my thoughts down a hollow tunnel of fear and suspicion. Why did she want me to leave the house with her? Would she drive me somewhere and then kill me?

I also heard things – sounds and conversations – that seemed real. The words weren't always clear and sometimes the sounds were amplified. Other times I felt like I had stumbled into a private room where people were talking about me. I was dissociating again. I was leaving my body and drifting away into a numb, echoing space of voices.

One day I borrowed my mom's car to drive to Twin Falls, the nearest big city about 36 miles away. I remember 'waking up' as I entered the city limits. Confused I looked around and realized that I had no memory of driving from Hagerman. I was afraid. What if Andie had been in the car? What if I had crashed?

Driving past the local hospital I saw a sign on an adjacent building – County Mental Health Department. Without thinking I pulled in, parked and went inside. I must have looked pretty scared or crazy because the lady at the front counter told me gently to sit down. She disappeared down a hall, then returned with a man. He asked me to come with him to his office. The man placed a blank form on his desk and asked, "Can you tell me your name?"

The only other thing I remember during my first session with Bob was him stepping behind me and asking my permission to rest his hands on my shoulders. Bob said something about sensing how stressed I was. He then made me promise to come back the next day to see him. He asked if I had someone who could come and pick me up. I assured him I was okay to drive myself.

Much later I learned my mental illness wasn't unusual

for someone like me. In one long-term study, as many as 80 percent of young adults who had been abused met the diagnostic criteria for at least one psychiatric disorder by age 21. These young adults exhibited many problems, including depression, anxiety, eating disorders, and suicide attempts.[9] Other psychological and emotional conditions associated with abuse and neglect include panic disorder, dissociative disorders, attention-deficit/hyperactivity disorder, depression, anger, posttraumatic stress disorder, and reactive attachment disorder.[10]

Over the next few months, I saw Bob three-to-four times a week. Eventually our visits went down to twice-a-week. He tried to get me to open up about my past, but I didn't understand why. I told him the 'First Story.' I said I knew something was wrong with me but it had nothing to do with my past. I didn't tell him about my blackouts, the voices or the paranoia. I didn't tell him because I was afraid that he would call the authorities and I would be taken away. On the flip side, I did admit to seeing things that were not always there.

I vaguely recall being on medication that seemed to dull my feelings and cast a haze over everything around me. The medication caused my brain to go quiet, causing me to feel ... nothing. It was called Thorazine, a medication used to treat schizophrenia and other psychotic disorders. I was only on it long enough to get stabilized.

After a few months Bob said he was transferring me to a female therapy group. He was concerned that I didn't have strong, healthy female relationships and didn't trust other women. He was right about that even though I couldn't see it at the time. The thing is ... I also didn't trust men.

I was afraid of being in a group of women that I didn't know and participating in whatever 'group therapy' was. Would they push me? Demand I talk?

My mind flashed to a night visiting my aunt's and uncle's bunkhouse when I was about 11 years old. They had five or six teenage foster daughters who slept there. The girls started teasing me about wearing a bra and then demanded I show it to them. I was scared that they would attack me if I didn't comply, so I lifted up my shirt far enough for them to see my bra. The girls laughed. One of them poked a finger into my breasts, joking about how large my boobs were. The other girls laughed louder.

Group therapy took place in a small attic room inside an older home that had been converted into offices. There were two counselors, but I only remember Sasha*. It took everything I had to walk through the door that first time. And when I was led upstairs to the attic office my uneasiness grew and I felt trapped.

Over time I learned to trust both counselors. The other women in the group also seemed safe but I was hypervigilant. I tried hard to manage their impressions of me so they would like me. I noticed none of the other women talked about hearing voices or feeling detached from reality, so I didn't say anything.

Cognitive Behavioral Therapy

The counselors used cognitive-behavioral therapy or CBT, which was developed in the 1960s by Dr. Aaron Beck. CBT is built partly on his observations and partly on the work done by earlier behaviorists like B.F. Skinner, Alfred Adler and Albert Ellis. Beck believed that what we do (behavior), what we think (mental), and what we feel (emotional) are interconnected. Put another way, our thoughts and beliefs have a direct impact on our feelings and behavior.

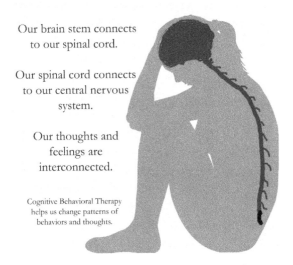

Our brain stem connects to our spinal cord.

Our spinal cord connects to our central nervous system.

Our thoughts and feelings are interconnected.

Cognitive Behavioral Therapy helps us change patterns of behaviors and thoughts.

I learned that the consequences of my disordered interpretations included symptoms of mental illness, but if I could learn to reframe information or events and also stop and interpret them differently, then I could respond differently.

One of Sasha's favorite questions to me was, "Where did that come from?" She challenged me to find the root of my emotional and mental reactions to any disturbing situation. For example, when Grandma Mabel called and pleaded with me to come back to Portland and live with her, my automatic response was fear and a desire to run. As a result, every time the phone rang at my parent's house I jumped, and my insides twisted in fearful anticipation that it was her calling again.

Examining the *why* of my feelings uncovered earlier memories of Grandma Mabel – the way she continuously criticized the way my mom dressed and raised me, all of the years she 'bathed' me, her shaming me for not wanting to stay with her after the kidnapping, and her attempt to take Andie away from me. I was afraid she would find a way to get me to do what she wanted. For the first time, I could identify how my present reactions were rooted in the past. In other words, they were based on my previous interactions with and perceptions of Grandma Mabel.

Another question my counselors asked was, "What can you do differently next time?" In Grandma Mabel's case I realized that I wasn't strong enough yet to interact with her. Sasha and I talked about my options, and I eventually decided to call Grandma Mabel. I wanted to tell her that I needed some space. Sasha role-played the conversation with me ahead of my conversation with Grandma Mabel. Sasha did a pretty good job of projecting Grandma Mabel's responses. Next, I wrote down what I wanted to say to my grandmother.

Then, I called her and said, "Grandma Mabel, I love you, but I need to ... *not* talk with you, or write to you for a while – at least until I get better. I will reach out to you when I'm ready. I appreciate your understanding." She said she didn't understand, "Grandma Mabel loves you, and only wants what's best for you!" She tried to shame me by saying, "Grandma Mabel knows what's best for you, just like she did when you were a little girl, and I took care of you. You know being with Grandma Mabel is good for you because I can help you get on your feet and get a good job!"

I'd learned in therapy that making choices for yourself didn't necessarily mean that your friends or family would understand – or support you. CBT taught me to stand behind my choices, and to recognize and deflect efforts to take them away. I didn't specifically respond to anything Grandma Mabel said. Instead, I kept repeating what I had written down. It took over 30 minutes for her to stop trying to convince me to do what she wanted me to do. I remember hanging up the phone and experiencing overwhelming relief, exhaustion, and guilt for standing up for myself.

CBT introduced startlingly new concepts to me about identity and choices. According to cognitive-behavioral therapists I am responsible for my own choices, which means it is my *choice* how to emotionally and physically respond to any given situation. I realized even though I detested the thought of being called a victim, I had a recurring inner message in my mind: that *anyone* can do *anything*, at *any time* to me and I am powerless and helpless to stop them. Sasha helped me recognize and own my choices. At first, I had trouble understanding that concept.

"Okay, let's say someone walks up to me, and slaps me across the face," I said. "How can I *choose* my response to it?"

Sasha explained, "In that second before you outwardly respond, you are making a *choice*. For instance, you could *choose* to respond with anger. Or you could *choose* to feel surprised. You could also *choose* to be concerned about the other person, perhaps asking them, why they did that? Or you might *choose* to respond with violence by slapping them back. Let's say you know the person and you have hurt them in some way. Then you might *choose* to understand why they slapped you. You could *choose* to feel guilt or remorse. The point is, in every situation there is a moment when you make a choice about your feelings and how you want to respond to the situation."

This realization can be both powerful and frightening. Frightening, in that the focus is no longer on *what* is being done to me or *who* is doing something but rather the focus lies on recognizing *my own* automatic reactions (for lack of a better term) that were programmed in me. I interpreted what Sasha was saying and what I had researched as meaning that it was all of my fault for feeling the way that I did. I was making a *choice* to feel that way. I wasn't understanding the point and blamed myself – again.

The therapists challenged us to think about how we could take charge of our health and well-being.

"What if you are fighting with your boyfriend, boss, or parents? What do you normally do when you start to experience overwhelming feelings?"

The answers varied – i.e., leave the room, tell the other person that you'll talk later, take deep breaths, and/or pause. Several women struggled with the idea of standing up for themselves.

"How do I tell my boss I don't want to keep discussing something?"

Group members told her to tell her boss that you have to use the restroom or that you just remembered another appointment and you need to go. Basically, do whatever you can to buy yourself a few minutes. Take some deep breaths, consider your feelings and *choose* how to respond.

There is another transition that happens when you experience change at the deepest levels. The type of people who are attracted to you and want to be around you also changes. You no longer seek out destructive people who treat you in unbecoming or unkind ways – ways you once learned to expect.

At that point and time, I was working at a small, quiet office at a trout farm. My job was to answer phones. As easy as that sounds there were moments when it took everything in me to stay focused and present in reality. I used stress-management techniques when I felt myself dissociating or filling with fear. I'd excuse myself and go into the bathroom. The office was in an old, renovated home and the bathroom had a grey tiled floor.

I lay on my back and felt the cold floor beneath me. Then I would take a breath, try to slow my breathing, stare at the acoustical ceiling tiles, and focus on counting each tiny hole in each panel. I was desperate to stay grounded in reality and not drift off and allow the echoing voices to distract me. I tried not to feel my numb body, as my arms detached and floated away. More deep breaths.

I kept repeating, "I can make *choices*. I can *choose* to stay in reality. I am in control." Often tears welled up, with the silent screams of my hidden past. I curled up, knees to my chest and rocked, sobbing into the sleeves of my blouse. Eventually I wiped melted mascara from my eyes and went back to my desk. Some days I needed to do these things multiple times. Slowly, slowly these times decreased to entire days, then a whole week went by, and I stayed present.

My biggest problem early on – at work and at home, was when the voices started speaking. In those moments it was impossible to know what was *real*. Were the voices and the detached floating sensations the reality? Or was reality the room I was physically in, even though the room and my body appeared to be a great distance away? It was sheer hell.

Every Thursday afternoon I left work early to attend group therapy. I told my boss that I had a weekly appointment, but I didn't go into detail, and he didn't ask questions. As the months went by, I was definitely changing. The changes were evident in my appearance too. It seemed like the more mentally healthy I felt, the more I lost weight without dieting. My overall health was improving too, and the self-mutilation eased except for the mouth tearing. At one point I realized I had more energy and I felt lighter and clearer.

It was like I had been buried underground in a cesspool of garbage and it took every bit of my strength to claw my way up to the surface. Once at the top I just lay there in the open air. It took a long time to gather the strength to actually sit up. After even more time had passed, I began clearing the ground around me and slowly picking my way through mounds of garbage until there was nothing left but plain dirt. No more lies and no more personas trying to be someone I wasn't. It was an incredible feeling. I was in charge of myself for the first time in my life. But I was still a long way from being cured. I fell into old responses at least once a day.

It was not enough to simply change the learned behavior. For example, I did learn to slow down old automatic responses – like negative reactions to something my mom said, or the immediate anxiety when I felt threatened – and take a moment to check myself and choose a different response.

With that act alone, I gave those around me grace. I no longer assumed the worst of them, but instead considered – for the first time – that maybe my first reaction wasn't even about what that person said or did. I discovered that Sasha's repeated question of 'where did that come from?' invited me to look back and identify the original triggers that created my gut response.

One relationship that benefited from the changes I was experiencing was with my mom. She had mellowed after she married Pops, and other than occasional biting remarks, her physical and mental abuse disappeared. My paranoia and anxiety arose from those early years, and as the cognitive behavioral therapy took hold, my paranoia slowly disappeared.

I recognized that perhaps there were circumstances I knew nothing about from her marriage to my father, and I leaned back into a survival tool many abused kids use: idealizing. I only remembered the good (or imagined?) mom I wanted to see.

In the tiny bedroom I shared with Andie, and quietly so my parents would not hear, I composed and sang this song I titled *Sandbox*:

I never had a swing set,
Or sandbox populaire,
I grew in berry bushes
And clouds up in the air.

Way down by forbidden railroad tracks,
That harbored bums who stunk,
Leaving behind their Olympia beer bottles
The drop or two we drunk.

Roaming dirty city streets,
Mud puddles galore.
No, my clothes were never very neat
And there weren't much food in store.

And Mister Rogers, he didn't live
In or near my neighborhood,
Multnomah Street, not Sesame,
Was where I spent my childhood.
So tell me Fisher Price,

Just where my dreams were bred?
When I didn't have a wind-up doll
To carry off to bed?

How did I come to be so tall,
Got a love for life flying everywhere.
When there weren't any nursery walls
And Mother Goose was never there?

I guess it was my mama's love and care,
'Cause she lift me up, she made me strong,
And she brought me up to where
I'm sitting here.

I slowly opened up and shared more of my therapy with her. She seemed to understand and was encouraging me.

I occasionally saw old friends and tried to share what I was learning about myself with them. Jeremy dismissed the whole notion of going to therapy, insisting that there was nothing wrong with me. I tried hard to convince him how beneficial therapy was for me but stopped short of telling him the truth about my symptoms. Instead, I told him I was "getting help with personal growth." I wanted Jeremy's sympathy and understanding but at the same time I didn't want him to think I was crazy.

"Trauma is much more than a story about something

*that happened long ago. The emotions and physical
sensations that were imprinted during the trauma are
experienced not as memories but as disruptive physical
reactions in the present."* - Dr. Bessell van der Kolk

After a year-and-a-half, I was ready to leave my parent's home
and move back to Boise. The paranoia and voices had faded, and I
had no more blackouts and few episodes of dissociation. My OCD
symptoms were diminishing though still present. I felt more *whole*
than ever before.

I moved into an apartment and found a job in the county
prosecutor's office. Ironically, I worked in the child support
department despite strongly believing that parenting should be
a matter of choice. Fortunately, the bulk of my cases involved
divorced people who had chosen to be parents.

About a month after moving, I contacted Sasha for advice.
Typical city noises somehow became louder after I moved into
my new apartment and time seemed to fluctuate, moving quickly
then slowing down and then picking back up again. I felt uneasy
and vulnerable in my new surroundings. I had a few memories of
living there before, but I no longer recognized people I once knew.
For instance, I had once worked with a man in theater and while
he was delighted to see me, I had no clue who he was or what
our relationship had been. The same thing happened with others.
If they looked thrilled, astonished, or surprised – whatever their

reaction was I mirrored it with my own.

But if the conversation went too far, I would stumble to explain. Sasha suggested that I say, "I'm sorry, but I'm having some memory issues." She assured me that my perceptions and feelings were normal and that my mind was simply adjusting to reentering life. "You are okay," she reassured me. "You have been living in a very quiet, supported environment for over a year, so it's normal to experience an alternate sense of time and place for a while." I hoped she was right.

John was the man I knew from theater. He invited me to join his writing group, who were working on a draft for a fantasy novel. Galahad* was one of the writers, who I eventually decided I was in love with. I didn't realize until much later that my crush stemmed from him being gay and not having any romantic interest in me. My protective pattern of seeking out romantically unavailable men was still entrenched.

Then I received a letter from my mom, asking me to call. I went to the nearest payphone and called collect. Mom struggled with back issues since her waitressing days and experienced an exacerbation in symptoms after a car accident. She had already had several back surgeries and after the last one was encased in a body cast for nearly a year. Afterwards she was able to move without pain. But she was also extremely tired and slowing down. Multiple medical tests had not discovered why my mom was feeling so bad. She told me that she and Pops had recently travelled out of state to meet with a specialist. The diagnosis was grim.

According to the doctor, my mom had a rare and untreatable condition called refractory anemia, a sub-type of myelodysplastic syndrome (MDS). But despite the name, my mom had plenty of iron. Her red blood cells were not maturing. At that time the only treatment was blood transfusions, which might possibly extend her life for a few years. I wasn't shocked or even particularly surprised. Instead, the news felt ... expected. Having my father die at 33 when I was 10 had prepared me for the possibility that my mom would also die young. She assured me she had a least a couple more years to live.

I felt hollow inside and didn't believe her. Her tone suggested she was trying to minimize the diagnosis.

Meanwhile, Galahad thought we should travel to the San Francisco area where his brother lived in the suburb of Fremont. Galahad said we could be singers and get a record contract. I was deeply and irrationally codependent with him and if he ever knew I had romantic feelings we never discussed it. Even though I knew the singing plan was not sensible, I leapt in and hoped for the best – my magical thinking again. We boarded a Greyhound bus with Andie, some clothes and my guitar and headed for California. I purchased bus tickets for all of us, using the $200 my mom gave me to use "only in case of an emergency."

When we arrived in Fremont, Galahad's brother Butch and his wife Dorothy let us stay in a vacant house they owned. After a couple days, my anxiety ramped up. How could I get a job with no car? How could I afford to buy a newspaper that contained

Help Wanted ads, the place (in those days) where job openings were advertised? Butch offered to hire Galahad for a construction project, but Galahad wasn't interested. I finally insisted we start rehearsing our music and then learned why he had always shown reluctance to sing with me.

Galahad could not sing.

He could barely hold a tune. After a week we were out of my money (Galahad had none). I had 3 pennies in my purse. This was the day before Thanksgiving. At Galahad's suggestion, we took Andie to a nearby park. Once there he announced to me that he was returning to Boise. I froze with shock and disbelief. What? Galahad's tone was apologetic while explaining how a friend had wired him a plane ticket. It felt like everything around me was spinning and my mind was turning bluish grey.

I asked, "When are you leaving?" and reeled again when he pointed to the transit bus stop across the park and replied, "Right now, so I can get to the airport in time." I couldn't move or breathe, and time slowed down as if I was dreaming. He gave me a hug and walked away.

What could I do? Andie and I walked slowly back to Butch and Dorothy's house. Dorothy casually asked, "Where's Galahad?" I whispered, "He's gone. He went back to Boise."

She stared at me in disbelief. "What? He left? He just left you here? Did you know he was going to leave?" I shook my head no and looked down trying not to cry. The tears spilled down my cheeks anyway.

When Butch got home, he threatened to go after Galahad and bring him back, but I knew it wouldn't make a difference. I had already moved from shock to survival. I said, "I'll call my folks for bus fare home and stay tonight at the empty house if that's okay. I'll be out of it by tomorrow." I was ashamed to ask my mom for money, but I didn't know what else to do.

Unexpectedly Mom said she was very sorry but couldn't help me. I had to accept that it was on me to get myself out of a mess ... again.

The next day was Thanksgiving.

I woke up cold and hungry. As had been my lifelong pattern I was unable to get to sleep until after midnight because any sound would startle me. That morning my three-year old daughter was already bouncing around the room. We danced to keep warm. Then we made and colored a 'turkey' from white paper plates. The only food we had was a wilted carrot and some canned green beans. I placed them on a slat of wood that was our makeshift table.

A knock at the door made me jump. Peeking through the curtains I saw Butch standing there with one of Galahad's cousins. The two men grinned, waved and yelled through the glass. "We're here to pick you up for Thanksgiving!" I was mortified. I cracked open the door to say, "No, thanks! We're fine." Butch wasn't having it. "If we don't take you home for Thanksgiving, Dorothy will kill me, so no arguments, just get Andie and come with us."

We were welcomed like long lost relatives. During the feast, a nephew who was serving overseas in the military called. The phone was passed around the table for everyone to say "hello"- including me. By the time dessert was served, the family had hatched a plan to lend me their spare car and take care of Andie while I looked for a job. I will never forget that Thanksgiving because of the love Andie and I were shown.

Within two days I was working as a temp at a grocery chain's corporate headquarters in accounting. Dorothy took me to a thrift store and lent me money to purchase suitable work clothes. I also went to California's local social services office and signed up for food assistance. By the end of the week, I had received a paycheck and food stamps. I refilled the gas tank of Dorothy's car and tried to give them the food stamps, but they refused.

Andie and I took a bus to Sacramento where my old friends from Santa Barbara now lived on a small plot of land with goats. Thanks again to social services, Andie and I moved into an unfurnished, rent-assisted apartment in nearby Rancho Cordova. I used an empty cardboard box as a table, and we slept on the carpet. Mentally I was still numb and heartbroken over Galahad's departure. It would take years before I learned about the effects of *abandonment*.

As is often the case in low-income housing, there were dangers around me. The young married woman living upstairs warned me not to leave my apartment at night because of criminal activity in the area. A single mom who seemed out of touch with reality, lived in the unit across from mine with her two young children.

One afternoon her kids knocked on my door. They said their mom was "acting crazy," yelling at them and waving a knife. I brought the kids inside and told them to stay put while I went over to check on their mom. The front door was open, and the mother was hiding behind her couch. She raised her head when she heard me say "Hello." As she stood up, I saw something glistening... she was carrying an open bladed knife. I tried to act natural by asking if I could use her phone. She seemed confused but nodded, then ducked down behind the couch again. I called the police. When they arrived, the woman became hysterical.

One officer interviewed the children and the other called the kids' father. When he arrived on the scene he was irritated that his ex-wife was having a breakdown, and that he was being asked to take care of his children. I felt outraged on the kids' behalf, wishing that I could keep them with me.

My mental stability was getting worse, and I knew something had to change. I purchased bus tickets and went home to my parents' house in Hagerman. This was the beginning of an extraordinary chapter in my life. It's also what propelled me back to therapy.

8

loss

Nothing that grieves us can be called little: by the eternal laws of proportion a child's loss of a doll and a king's loss of a crown are events of the same size. ~Mark Twain

When I returned to my parent's house in Idaho, my mom was receiving blood transfusions every week. I drove her to her appointments at the hospital when she was white, weak and barely talking. But after her transfusion her skin was pink and she was energetic, making plans to have lunch and shop.

I cherished those months before her death. We were finally coming together as women and embracing each other as friends and equals for the first time. We talked and talked.

My mom admitted to me that my father Galen had mental problems in addition to his drinking. She excused his behavior by saying, "It was always hard for him to relate to normal people, because he was a genius."

Mom and me.

One day mom and I were sitting on her bed when she said, "Honey, I feel guilty about something. I hope you have never felt like I didn't love you as much as Lee. I know I favored him." I knew that too, but I replied with, "Really? I had no idea. I thought I was your favorite!" She laughed in relief.

My parents asked me to feed their animals and plant the garden while they went out of state to help my Grandma Bea, who was dying of leukemia. Growing up, visits with Grandma Bea were infrequent but good. She got along well with everyone and acted like the grandmas I read about in books – the kind who could be stern but gave lots of hugs and enjoyed baking. Every year on our birthdays, Lee and I would receive cards with $1.00 bills inside. My heart ached when she died a few weeks later.

Shortly after, Mom told me she got word that Grandma Mabel had died of throat cancer. I was stricken with shame and ... anger. I borrowed my mom's car and drove mindlessly across the desert roads, screaming at the top of my lungs. I sobbed and howled through my grief and tears until I could no longer see the road. Then I pulled over and let my conflicted feelings consume me.

How could she die? I truly believed that the time would come when I would get a chance to confront her. Then maybe I could heal with her. But now that possibility was gone.

By Andie's 5th birthday I was working on-air at a local radio station. I had walked door to door in the business district asking if there were any job openings for a janitor or secretary. When I entered the lobby of a radio station, the woman at the desk said "No, but we are looking for a news reporter. Would you like to make a sample tape?"

I thought the experience would make a great story to share with my theatre friends, so I said yes. She put me in a sound booth, brought me some news wire copy, showed me how to work the recording equipment and left me alone. I honestly considered the whole thing as nothing more than an adventure and assumed my best imitation of a newscaster.

When I told the front desk woman I was done, she went to get the station's news director, who was a woman named Carol. Carol listened to my 'audition' tape and then said, "You're good. Where have you worked before?"

I was stunned, while a wave of shame rolled through me. Now I would have to admit the truth, that I was a fraud just wasting their time on a bit of fun. But Carol was undeterred and took me into the General Manager's office. His name was Dick, and he was an older man with twinkling eyes and a friendly smile. I told him the truth, and we started talking. After several minutes he said,

"Look, you have a great voice, and Carol says you're talented. I have a feeling you are radio people. So how about you work for us part-time for the summer, and if you still want to leave then you will at least have some money. But I think you will stay. I see something in you."

Dick was right. The broadcast world was full of people who frequently moved from one place to another, had quirky personalities, and who accepted me without question. I had found my home. Within a year I had been moved from news to on-air personality, working full-time on the overnight shift.

My paycheck was just enough to cover rent for an apartment, a private school for Andie, food and the laundromat. I couldn't afford a car or phone, so we walked everywhere.

Then a miracle happened. The grocery store across the street ran a promotion where customers could receive little squares of sealed pieces of paper with numbers inside. The right combination could lead to a $1,000 win. I won. It was the most money I had seen in my life, and I was determined to spend it wisely. My parents agreed to sell me their extra car for $400. I took the rest of the money to purchase car insurance and paid off Andie's school tuition.

The inevitable phone call came while I was at work. Pops said Mom was in the hospital 40 miles away and the doctor told him that she had maybe 48 hours left to live. Because it was late afternoon, we agreed that I would drive to Hagerman early the next day and we could go to the hospital together. I called a friend who agreed to keep Andie for me.

I woke that night, but not because the alarm had gone off. I felt relaxed and peaceful, yet disoriented. I felt my mom's presence in my bedroom. I looked at the clock. It was 3:47am. The hurt inside was gone, and a deep sense of stillness replaced it. I slept soundly until 6:00am. When I awakened, the curious sense of peace remained, coupled with a profound sadness. I knew that there was no longer a need to rush to Hagerman. I put on a pot of coffee and sat in my bathrobe, looking out the window at the lightening sky. I thought, "There's no need to hurry ... we won't be driving anywhere today."

It was raining as I pulled into my parent's driveway. Pops was standing in the kitchen, looking tired and worn. I went to him and we hugged tight. His voice broke as he whispered, "About three-thirty this morning, honey..." I whispered back, "Yes, I know..." and we stood there with only the sound of the rain outside.

I understood the five stages of grief. What I didn't know then, is that loving someone physically changes our brain, and as far as our brain is concerned, our loved one is gone yet still exists.[11]

A few days later, Lee told me that he was coming to see me in Twin Falls before returning home to where he lived in Tennessee with his family. This is my account of the events surrounding my mom's death. Like many kids and adults from abusive homes, I kept detailed journals to prove that an event really happened the way I remembered. The writing was a byproduct from the "don't talk, don't trust, don't feel" rule. This is my journal entry from that day:

We sat at my kitchen table, and Lee outlined the coming day. We would have lunch, fix my car, run an errand for Pops, and then I would go to the radio station for my shift. But it's not that simple. He knew it. I knew it. But Lee had obviously thought about that moment and needed to open at least one of the closed doors between us.

He said, "It's time that we started becoming friends, not enemies. Brother and sister instead of hateful strangers." His voice was shaky as he said, "I'm proud of you. I really do love you, and I hope we develop a strong relationship."

The words ... his words ... I had waited so long, so many years, to hear these things, but now I did not want to hear them. They had come on the heels of mom's death. There's just too much inside of me at the time that needed comfort and gentleness, with no intensity. I was too naked and hurt to want the situation between us torn open, no matter how sweetly it was done.

I had barely formed a thin shell – please don't crack it. Not yet. My mom had died, and now, this sensitive, strong man, who is my brother, was holding me, looking intently into my eyes. I could see a rush of feelings in him after a lifetime of cold stares... it was too much for right now. I wanted to stop this, wanted to only nod in agreement. I could not speak. I needed him. I loved him. I needed the closeness he had with mom. I wanted it to be simple with each other – no hint of regret or pain. There had been too much of that already.

We went outside to inspect my car. The oil needed changing. Then, Lee announced that he and Pops "discussed it, and I told him, I'd take care of it for you" ... This was the beginning. I turned away, blinking back new tears. This was the first time, the first moment, that I really had a brother. I had heard people say things like, "Oh, my brother looked at it for me" or "Yeah, my brother said he could fix it."

It is enough.

My mom's death released an unexpected feeling in me – freedom.

I felt guilty about that because I truly loved and missed her. I realized that the freedom came from a newfound lack of expectations. My decisions would no longer be judged or challenged. I would no longer have to worry about disappointing my mom. I remembered that Mom never encouraged me to date, bring a boy home or get married. I had always sensed her silent disapproval if I talked about boys. When I got pregnant, she accepted that there were two men who could be the father and seemed relieved when I assured her that I was no longer involved with either man.

Over the next twelve months both of my mom's sisters also died, which meant there were no women left before me in my generational train.

Eight months after my mom died, I met Walter*, a tall muscular man with tightly permed hair. I felt an immediate attraction. So did he because the next day he called me at the radio station and asked if I would accompany him to his company's annual picnic.

That was our first date and two weeks later he asked me to marry him. I knew I was pretending to be normal but told myself that it would be easy to be married.

The rules I had learned about how women *should* behave echoed in my head – 1. Take care of the house and 2. have sex when he wants (be agreeable). The fact that I didn't know how to cook worried me, but Walter fixed his own dinner most evenings. I worked the night shift six-days-a-week, and he worked days. On his days off he played golf or watched baseball on tv. I naively figured that I could still have a regular life, be Andie's mom, work in radio, read and play guitar and see my friends by myself.

Walter called his parents and announced our engagement, as I sat on the couch. After about a minute he hesitated and cupped his hand over the phone.

He whispered, "What's your last name?"

I whispered back, "It's Campbell, what's yours?"

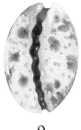

9

i do?

I've never heard a woman say, "My dad died of alcoholism, so I'm looking for a drunk with whom to settle down, have kids, and to save from self-destruction." Like most things with the disease of denial, it is much more subtle and subconscious. – Matthew Salis

Walter told me about his life. He loved baseball and was proud to have played in an AA minor league team in Minnesota. He was seven years older than me and had served in the Army in Vietnam. One night around Christmas I woke up to Walter crying. He showed me old scars on his knee and confessed that he had been captured and tortured in Vietnam, and they had rammed sticks into his knee. He said when he was released the army transferred him stateside where he had a lengthy stay at a rehab center while physically healing. He still had nightmares about what happened to him. Walter said the capture and torture happened around the holidays and that's why he hated Christmas.

I was determined to prove to him that he was safe with me, and that I understood his feelings. I assured him that I didn't need any gifts. At least that would relieve his shopping stress, I told myself. The truth was I hated the idea of getting a gift from anyone because of shame. I felt like I didn't deserve gifts.

The first time Walter lost his temper I felt scared and guilty. I obviously had set him off by disagreeing with something he said, so I tried to talk him down with calm, measured tones and apologies. The night before our wedding he went off again, this time punching a hole in our bedroom wall. I remember going outside, sitting on the back porch and staring at the bright stars in the quiet Idaho sky with the sound of his yells echoing in my ears.

I whispered, *"I know, God. I know this is wrong, but I just want to be 'normal' and married. I swear I can do it. I can make it work."*

The next day we were married by a justice of the peace at our home. That afternoon we held a housewarming party for our friends and announced the news. Walter kept drinking and getting more boisterous. Then he called for everyone's attention. He said, "I married the *perfect* woman, so I want to play her the *perfect* song on our wedding day!" I cringed when I realized that the artist was Jimmy Buffet singing his hit, " *Why Don't We Get Drunk and Screw.*" Walter grabbed me, cupping my breasts in his hands while we danced, causing most of our friends to politely turn away. I was embarrassed. But I also chided myself for not being freer and easier like Walter. I had always mentally distanced myself during sex. If that didn't work, I sent my thoughts somewhere outside my body until it was over. I did the same thing with Walter.

A week or so after we married, I scheduled a uterine hysterectomy due to early cancer indications. The surgeon told us not to have sex for at least six weeks after the surgery. But a week later I said "Okay" to Walter's persistent urging. The result? I started to bleed heavily and felt extremely weak. Walter felt terrible. He helped me change the sheets and offered to take me to the emergency room. I said "no." I didn't want my doctor to know I had gone against his orders. I told myself it was my own fault for not saying no to Walter.

Walter and I fell into a typical codependent pattern. I tried to control him by steering any problem away from emotional responses towards logical and rational thoughts. I was sure I could find the right words, the right argument, to convince him. I told him that it was okay for him to be angry but not to take it out on me. He railed back, blaming me for trying to tell him how to express himself and that if I really loved him, I would accept the way he exhibited anger.

I eventually believed him.

Neither of us had a clue about what an honest, intimate relationship looked like. Tellingly, in the six years that we were together I never unpacked my belongings except for clothes and toiletries. My journals, books, knickknacks and mementoes were sealed in cardboard boxes in the spare bedroom. Walter had a vision of what his wife should be, and I had a vision of what he should be, so neither of us saw the other person for who they really were. I didn't want him to know me because I knew if he saw who I really was, he would leave.

As the months went on, more typical patterns of an alcoholic-codependent relationship emerged. I stopped playing guitar because it felt too personal and risky to play in front of him and he complained if I wanted to play alone. I acted like the martyr to his perpetrator, even though I believed our problems were my fault.

My mental health was deteriorating again, and I started experiencing moments of dissociation. This time I didn't hesitate before reaching out for help, though I didn't tell Walter. I sat down with a counselor and launched into why I had problems – I was probably grieving the loss of my mom and not handling it well. I wasn't truly giving myself in marriage and I held back. I was afraid to let my husband know me. George, my counselor asked me about my marriage. I told him that Walter was wonderful and loved golfing and watching sports. I said Walter was sweet to my daughter. We only had problems when I did something to set Walter off, like begging him to talk about his day or when I stayed too long at work.

George asked, "Does your husband drink? Do drugs?" I shook my head emphatically and said, "Oh no, not at all. He has a beer once in a while but that's about it." In reality, Walter routinely drank at least one six-pack of beer a day and smoked pot. The counselor asked about domestic violence and I quashed that notion too. Walter had not beaten me with a belt or his hand, however he did grip and squeeze my arms or legs too hard while holding me down or against the wall. I regularly had bruises on my body.

One day while having lunch with my Pops, I pushed a sleeve up to grab the ketchup. He frowned and said in a still and measured tone, "Where did you get those bruises?" I knew immediately what he meant and made up an excuse about being clumsy and bumping into walls. I don't think he believed me.

George thought it would be valuable to have Walter join the next counseling session. Right then I knew I would never return. Over the next few months, I was hypervigilant every time I left the house, worried that I would run into George and he would insist I return to his office. I still felt powerless over my own life.

Unlike typical codependents, I didn't try to control Walter's drinking for one simple reason – I didn't believe he had a problem. The idea that he might be an alcoholic scared me. I pushed those feelings down and rationalized that he couldn't have a drinking problem, since he only drank beer.

There was a sick dynamic in our relationship. I was the 'superior one,' the calm and rational one, and he was the one with all of the problems – the one who couldn't control his anger. I told myself that because I was supportive and understanding, it meant he couldn't find fault with me. Instead, the focus would always be on Walter, and I would be considered a good wife for being so 'nice.' But the truth was I tried to control him so I could deflect attention away from my own behavior.

Though I told myself Walter wasn't an alcoholic I decided to try Alanon, a support group for friends and family members of someone with a drug or drinking problem. Maybe I would learn how to *fix* Walter's drinking problem (that I didn't think he had), while maybe fixing what I thought was wrong with me – I was too afraid to challenge or confront people and I was too willing to say "yes," to whatever Walter wanted just to keep the peace. I needed to learn how to handle stress better. At this point, I was oblivious to the obvious – I needed to be honest with myself and work on my own issues.

At my first Alanon meeting, I walked into a basement room at a Presbyterian Church and saw several people sitting around a table. There was a coffee pot and disposable cups on a smaller table. I looked around the dingy room and saw a display of pamphlets with the name *Alanon* on them. One title was, *"So You Love an Alcoholic."*

I had devised a story – I had an uncle with a drinking problem and wanted to know how to help him. The group leader read this off of a laminated card:

"We welcome you to the Monday night Alanon meeting and hope that you will find in this fellowship the help and friendship we have been privileged to enjoy. We, who live or have lived with the problem of alcoholism understand, as perhaps few others can. We, too, were lonely and frustrated, but in Alanon/Alateen we discover that no situation is really hopeless, and that it is possible for us to

find contentment, and even happiness, whether the alcoholic is still drinking or not. We urge you to try our program. It has helped many of us find solutions that lead to serenity. So much depends on our own attitudes, and as we learn to place our problem in its true perspective, we will find it loses its power to dominate our thoughts and our lives.

The family situation is bound to improve as we apply the Alanon ideas. Without such spiritual help, living with an alcoholic is too much for most of us. Our thinking becomes distorted by trying to force solutions, and we become irritable and unreasonable without knowing it. The Alanon program is based on the 12 Steps (adapted from Alcoholics Anonymous), which we try, little by little, one day at a time, to apply to our lives, along with our slogans and the Serenity Prayer. The loving interchange of help among members and the daily reading of Alanon literature thus makes us ready to receive the priceless gift of serenity.

Anonymity is an important principle of the Alanon/Alateen program. Everything that is said here, in the group meeting and member-to-member, must be held in confidence. Only in this way can we feel free to say what is in our minds and hearts, for this is how we help one another in Alanon.

I listened carefully. But when she read the part about spiritual help, I paused. Was Alanon a religious organization?

She continued:

The Alanon family groups are a fellowship of relatives and friends of alcoholics who share their experience, strength, and hope in order to solve their common problems. We believe alcoholism is a family illness and that changed attitudes can aid recovery. Alanon is not allied with any sect, denomination, political entity, organization, or institution; does not engage in any controversy; neither endorses nor opposes any cause. There are no dues for membership. Alanon is self-supporting through its own voluntary contributions.

Alanon has but one purpose: to help families of alcoholics. We do this by practicing the "Twelve Steps", by welcoming and giving comfort to families of alcoholics, and by giving understanding and encouragement to the alcoholic.

I appreciated the part about not being connected to any sect, denomination, etc. But the mention of voluntary donations raised a red flag. How much? Money was tight already. Also, this whole approach sounded like I was supposed to change myself instead of Walter, and I was already understanding and supportive of him.

Next, she invited everyone to recite the Twelve Steps. At last! I thought to myself, I can hear what the actual program is about. Everyone around the table picked up their small blue book or recited from memory.

1. We admitted we were powerless over alcohol – that our lives had become unmanageable.

Well, I wasn't actually powerless over alcohol – but maybe Walter was or perhaps he was not. And my life wasn't unmanageable. I mean compared to where I had been mentally and emotionally, I was doing pretty well.

2. Came to believe that a Power greater than ourselves could restore us to sanity.

I felt uneasy. First of all, what's the "power greater than ourselves" and second, I certainly was not insane. I mean, I knew what crazy was.

3. *Made a decision to turn our will and our lives over to the care of God as we understand Him.*

Okay, I liked the part about "as we understand" because that opens it up for everyone no matter their religion or disbelief. And "turning my will and my life over to the care of God" was a concept I was familiar with as a lapsed Catholic who had once considered a vocation in religious life.

4. *Made a searching and fearless moral inventory of ourselves.* That sounded kind of like Catholic confession.

5. *Admitted to God, to ourselves, and to another human being the exact nature of our wrongs.* Definitely confession.

6. *Were entirely ready to have God remove all of these defects of character.*

Say what? That sounded suspiciously like the 'born again' revivalists, who preach sudden and miraculous transformation by "letting Jesus Christ into your heart!" The idea of giving up my autonomy and control to God scared me. I'd been wary of letting anyone try to change me.

7. *Humbly asked Him to remove our shortcomings.*

I was still reeling from that 6th step.

8. *Made a list of all persons we had harmed and became willing to make amends to them all.*

That one was okay. I didn't believe I had harmed anyone though.

9. *Made direct amends to such people wherever possible, except when to do so would injure them or others.*

I immediately focused on the escape clause.

10. *Continued to take personal inventory, and when we were wrong, promptly admitted it.*

Admit it to who? To myself? In that case, I can do that.

11. *Sought through prayer and meditation to improve our conscious contact with God, as we understand Him, praying only for knowledge of His will for us, and the power to carry that will out.*

Again, a reasonable approach to any spiritual practice.

12. *Having had a spiritual awakening as a result of these steps, we tried to carry this message to others, and to practice these principles in all our affairs.*

I felt dismay. I didn't believe in proselytizing.

"Would anyone like to share?" the woman asked. Another woman spoke up. "I will. Hi, my name is Susan. This last week has been hard. My son got arrested again, and this time when he called, I said, 'no' to bailing him out. Then as soon as I hung up, I called my sponsor because I knew if I didn't, I'd go to the jail and bring him home. I've always been there for him, but Alanon has taught me to stop rescuing him. I can't change him."

There was a moment of silence, then a blond-haired woman said "My name is Sheila and I'm a grateful member of Alanon. I keep on keeping on, one day at a time because that's all I can do at this point. My husband stopped drinking two years ago but he refuses to go to AA, so all of the issues that he had when he was drinking are still there. I do detach, but sometimes I'm so angry I just want to scream at him. Then I remember, I'm trying to change my responses to him and not keep thinking that if I say the right thing, convince him with the right words, or show him how miserable he's making me and the kids, he'll magically change because I know he won't. We're supposed to go to my parents' house for Christmas dinner and they drink. Every time my family gets together my dad gets drunk and mean, and my sister does her usual thing and tries to calm him down. I just want to yell. I'm thinking maybe we shouldn't go this year. But then my mom will be pissed at us – mainly me – for not making her fantasy about the perfect family get-together happen. So, I don't know what to do..." she trailed off, looking around the circle.

I wanted to tell her not to go. All she needed was some encouragement and reassurance from the group to make her decision.

But before I could work up the courage to speak someone said, "My name is Darla. I understand what you're saying, totally. My mom is an alcoholic-drug addict and she's a master manipulator when it comes to getting the rest of us in my family to enable her. Plus, my dad and siblings are just ... I don't know ... like toxic to be around. I stopped going to family events for about a year because I was struggling with letting go of trying to fix them. I kept coming to these meetings instead. After a while, I realized that the best thing I can do for myself and my relationships, is to practice detachment from their problems and focus on my own behavior."

I was confused. Sheila clearly wanted advice, but the rest of the group wasn't telling her what to do. In future meetings I slowly learned no one was telling anyone what they should or shouldn't do. Alanon members share their own experiences, strengths, and hopes. Most groups had a no cross-talk rule to remind everyone of that. It took me a long time to learn how to be supportive of other people's journeys and not tell them what they should or should not be doing or feeling.

After the meeting I made a beeline for the literature table and picked up several pamphlets. One of the women came up to me, and said, "Welcome!" She added, "I hope to see you again."

I did attend more meetings. I also bought my own copy of the little blue book titled *One Day at a Time in Alanon*. The book contained 365 short one-page readings, one for each day of the year, and the Twelve Steps were at the back of the book. Also in the book were the Twelve Traditions, which are used as a guide for each Alanon group. I don't remember the excuse I gave Walter for being gone once a week. But over time I found my way to other Alanon meetings, encountering a few women who became my soul sisters and who are still in my heart and life today. I became aware that the more I moved forward toward sanity, the closer my marriage came to smashing apart.

10

intervention

When we adjust to dysfunction, including dysfunctional relationships, the cost is high. We end up paying with our very beings, the essence of who we are. – Thema Bryant[12]

We tried marriage counseling. Walter said that he didn't understand why we needed to go but agreed to give it a try. I explained to the counselor how we met and married so quickly. He told the counselor that I was perfect in every way and didn't think we had any problems, except for me taking "everything so seriously, and looking for clouds in silver linings." The counselor informed us that we hadn't taken the time to really court or get to know each other. He suggested that we have a date night once a week. Neither of us mentioned Walter's (by now) heavy drinking and pot-smoking problem. We went on two date nights before we both dropped it.

I only saw Walter get out-of-control drunk twice, both times
when he drank hard liquor instead of beer. The worst time was at
his company's holiday party. By the time we left, Walter was livid
with rage – furious with his supervisor. The more I tried to calm
him down, the angrier he got. Once home and after the babysitter
left, he berated me, grabbed me and pushed me against the wall,
while screaming in my face. I remember shaking and crying, which
only set him off more. He kicked over the coffee table, smashed his
hand through the drywall in the living room, and started throwing
knickknacks at me. I begged him to stop and be quiet because
Andie was sleeping. Instead, he banged his fist on her bedroom
door. Next, Walter stomped back into the living room, opened the
front door and started throwing my belongings outside into the
snow.

I knew I had to leave. Andie came into the living room crying. I
hugged her and we headed to the car. Walter followed us onto the
porch, still yelling. I was numb. I drove away, found a payphone
and called a co-worker to ask if we could stay the night.

When we arrived at her home, she had a cushion laid on the floor
with a blanket for Andie, who went to sleep almost immediately.
My co-worker asked if I wanted to talk and when I whispered,
"no," she nodded and left me alone. I felt numb and couldn't
sleep.

The next morning we were having coffee when her phone rang.

Walter had tracked me down. He was crying and whispered, "Catherine? What happened? I woke up this morning and our house is a wreck. I called everyone looking for you. What happened? I don't remember anything."

The hollow vacant feeling inside me expanded because I knew that he was lying. I told him he got mad the night before and I left with Andie. He said that he was sorry and understood that he couldn't just take it all back. He also swore that he would never do that again. I had nowhere to go and no money for a motel room. Andie and I returned to the house that night. Walter had brought my stuff back inside and straightened up the living room. There were still holes in the wall and Andie's bedroom door was still splintered where he'd kicked it. Over the next several days I moved slowly as if I was underwater. I contacted a low-income rent-assisted apartment complex in town and applied but had to wait a week for an apartment to open up.

I told Walter that Andie and I were leaving. He was silent with anger but since it had only been a week since the incident, he didn't protest too much. I left the furniture since I had no way of moving it myself. And as usual I was determined to do everything on my own. I was ashamed. I knew deep down that our problems were my fault. I knew I wasn't being honest with myself, much less with him. In Alanon I was starting to understand that addiction is a disease process, and I needed to learn to detach from the disease and stop trying to control and blame him and make myself out to be the victim in his story. I hated that last idea – I was no one's victim. Anything that happened to me was my own fault. Walter had his share of demons but so did I.

Slowly I realized that the reason why we had an instant attraction was because I was a codependent, and he was an addict. The two go together like coffee and cream. Some part of me recognized my father's drinking in Walter, although the idea that Galen had been an alcoholic wasn't something I could acknowledge yet. Much later I admitted there were deeper reasons.

Over the next few months Walter visited me at the apartment. I told him about going to Alanon meetings but stopped short of suggesting he had a drinking problem. On one particular visit he announced that he had started going to AA meetings and had been sober for a few weeks. I was thrilled to hear that. Maybe this would be the solution for us, and he would grow and change along with me. We moved back in together, this time in a new place with a big backyard. Andie quickly became friends with four sisters who lived down the street, and I became friends with their parents. Erv was a minister for the local Church of the Brethren and Joan was a nurse. They were so good and solid together, working as a team. There was a genuine friendship between them – something I lacked with Walter.

Even though Walter swore he was attending AA meetings and had a sponsor, not much changed with our relationship dynamic. My efforts were designed to convince him how bad he was acting and to cement my role as the long suffering and superior spouse. My attempts to control Walter were subtler than many co-dependents but just as damaging to the both of us.

I suspected Walter was still drinking because he came up with excuses to go out to the carport multiple times a night. I checked and found his stash of bottles. I didn't confront him. Instead, I talked to my Alanon sponsor and she helped me understand my choices – 1. leave him, 2. stay with him and keep practicing detachment, or 3. try an intervention to get him into rehab.

I didn't know what an intervention was, so I contacted the Walker Center, a local treatment facility. I met with a counselor named JC who, along with his wife Dagmar would later become like family.

JC explained how an intervention works. He then asked me who in Walter's life had "leverage" – in other words who could *make* him go to treatment. I knew it wasn't me. I learned it's usually not the codependent significant other because he or she has a history of continuing to excuse, deny, and forgive the alcoholic's behavior.
Walter had no incentive to think that I might actually leave him if he refused treatment. But I knew he valued his career, and his boss was willing to help.

On the day of the intervention my whole body shook with anxiety and fear. I was so proud of Andie as she read her letter to Walter, telling him she felt scared when he got mad and she didn't like the way he drank so much. When I read my words, I couldn't even raise my eyes from the page. I didn't want to look at Walter, because I could feel his rage from across the circle we sat in. It was his boss who convinced him to seek treatment. My fear skyrocketed once Walter angrily agreed to seek help. My years of denial were shouting, "But Walter is not an alcoholic, and he is going to kill me for doing this." I had a bag with some of Walter's clothes and toiletries in the car, and he left with JC to go into rehab.

That night I couldn't sleep. I was convinced that the Walker Center would quickly discover the truth – that Walter just had an overreactive, crazy wife.

The center's policy for new admissions consisted of 3 days of detox, then another 4 days of therapy before the patient could talk to anyone outside. I dreaded the 7th day but when the phone rang, Walter appeared to be in a good mood. He told me that he was fine and asked me to bring some stuff to him during visiting hours the following day. Walter acted happy and excited to see me, which surprised me.

Then he said, "Okay, so there's this thing called 'Family Program,' where you and Andie can attend for three days. You're supposed to tell me how you feel about my drinking. Oh, and one more thing..."

What he said next left me speechless. "You know how I told you that I was in the military and got captured? Uh, well ... that didn't happen. I was never in the Army. The scars on my knee are from a sports surgery. Also, I was never in AA ... until now. And I didn't play minor league baseball in Minnesota. One more thing, I never lived in California. So don't say anything about any of it during the Family Program, okay?"

I was shocked and stunned. I didn't know what to say. Who did I marry? Was anything he'd told me about himself true?

As Walter had instructed, I didn't say anything about all the lies he told me. But he must have admitted to some or maybe he got caught in one of his webs of lies, because the first time I heard him introduce himself in the family group circle, he said, "My name is Walter. I'm an alcoholic and a pathological liar."

During the Family Program the patient and their families spent a good deal of time learning about alcoholism and the disease of codependency. Much of what I heard in Alanon rang true – my focus on the "identified patient" in the family (Walter) meant that I didn't have to focus on my own illness. Thus, I was invested in keeping the family communication dynamic the same because the idea that it was me who needed to change scared me. As long as I could keep the water around me churning in chaos, my nose would stay above water, and no one would be able to see what lay underneath, especially me.

It was extremely important for me to hide those buried boxes from myself. That's when it dawned on me. I understood why I had married someone who wasn't capable of honesty or self-knowledge. It was so I would always be the smarter one, the more self-aware one, and I wouldn't have to risk self-honesty much less being vulnerable to someone else.

I knew I was an addict too. I was a workaholic.

In the U.S. *workaholism* is highly valued in the marketplace when in reality, true workaholics are masters at making people think that they are indispensable, hard workers. Most of these individuals have a hard time getting things done. For instance, I could take an 8-hour day of tasks and stretch it into a 12-hour day. If I came close to finishing my workload my anxiety rose, and I looked for ways to make my work perfect, which meant not finishing my tasks on time. My perfectionism (another character flaw touted as a value) was my shield against moving forward. I truly believed that my value lies in what I could do – not who I was. At an Alanon meeting I once heard, "I'm a human *doing* and not a human *being*."

It's true that I found my worth in what I could do for others rather than who I was. When I worked in broadcasting, twelve-to-fourteen-hour days seven days a week were not uncommon. On the overnight shift I brought Andie with me and she slept on the carpet of the conference room. Once my show moved to evenings it was the same thing. I would wake her up at 11:00pm when my shift was over.

After my hysterectomy, I was told not to lift anything more than 10 pounds for three months and to avoid stairs for at least three weeks. The radio station was up a long flight of stairs in a business office and after the first week off I couldn't stand it. My mind was racing. I felt anxious and scared not being able to work. I called my boss and insisted I could come back the next week. About six weeks after the surgery my boss asked me to handle a remote broadcast at one of the advertiser's business promotions.

"Of course!" I said, completely ignoring my doctor's orders of no lifting.   The remote equipment included a large amplifier, a remote signal box, microphone, headset and at least 50 feet of extension cords. Altogether it weighed around 100 pounds. I was determined to haul it all downstairs, lift it into the radio station's van and get it set up by myself. I should have asked for help but workaholics are terrified that if they cede any responsibility, they will be perceived as 'less than.' I'd always perceived myself that way and felt my only value was in working twice as hard as everyone else.

The next day I couldn't move. The pain in my lower and mid-back was crushing. Walter took me to the emergency room. According to the doctor, my 'steering wheel' was now in the 'back seat.' As a result, I would need physical therapy, which meant taking time off from work.

That wasn't what I wanted to hear.   I made an appointment with a chiropractor instead who took x-rays and told me the same thing. He gave me physical therapy exercises and said if I followed his orders, I could probably avoid surgery. I faithfully did the exercises and when the treatment ended, the chiropractor took another x-ray and told me that I was now restricted from lifting more than 25 pounds for the rest of my life. He gave me a letter to give to my boss.

At the time, I still didn't recognize that my workaholism was an addiction. Between my fixes of going to work, I obsessed about how I could be better at my job, how much more I could take on to prove my value and counted the hours until my next shift started. I permanently injured myself as a result. My addiction intensified until I was rarely home with Walter. I was the station's public service coordinator, continuity director, on-air talent and advertising writer and producer. When the traffic director left, I assured my boss that I could handle that job too until someone new was hired.

After about a year my new boss intervened. Dick had left the station for another job, and the new manager was a woman named Kris. She called me into her office and told me that she wanted to "loan me out" to a friend who was opening a business. The friend needed help creating forms, setting up supplies and establishing policies and procedures for her new staffing agency. I would be gone from the station for six weeks. I panicked but of course said, "Okay."

Tears spilled down my cheek and I felt unwanted. Why would she do this to me? She gently said, "Catherine, I know how much you love your job but it's important to have boundaries too. I see you here hours before and after your shift nearly every day. You're working too much. You need a break. This is a good opportunity for you to step away for a little while and have a life outside of work." Shame flooded through me because she seemed to see deep into my heart. She saw what I didn't want to admit to myself.

The first week I barely slept, my whole body craved the radio station. I went through the grief stages of denial, bargaining, and anger. Anger at my boss because she did this to me. Anger that my new boss strictly enforced how many hours I could work at her office. Gradually I accepted my fate because I knew it was only for six weeks.

I felt overjoyed and relieved when I got back on-air.

After Walter left the Walker Center, he found a sponsor and started to regularly attend AA meetings. Every Tuesday night for the next two years, we attended the rehab's aftercare group. During the weekly sessions, the identified patient and their family member(s) shared how the week had gone, problems that came up, and solutions that worked, if they did. We learned that all our relationship problems were echoed by the other couples present. We were all rooted in shame and as a result avoided true intimacy.

I had been in Alanon for more than two years by then but still wasn't capable of *real* honesty. I shared what I thought would make me look good, including nodding and agreeing with whatever the old timers in the group said. I wanted to get better and help my marriage but every time I reached an intersection of awareness and self-growth I hesitated, for one simple reason.

Shadows and dark places were my comfort zone. It was all I'd ever known. Stepping forward was like abruptly stopping in the middle of the ocean and letting those deep caves of boxes and the black undertow of depression suck me under. I had no reference point that would keep me from drowning. I skipped a few weeks of meetings and slid back into my familiar codependent behaviors and negative coping strategies. My whole life was spent churning up the ocean surface and now the waves had calmed. I was afraid of letting go. The darkness was painful and confusing but at least it was familiar. My anxiety and depression were still intense, and I coped with them with workaholism, obsessive exercising, and sneak eating, in addition to my lifelong behaviors like self-mutilation and rocking.

Walter and I joined a private couple's group that some of our friends in recovery belonged to, including JC and his wife Dagmar. Addicts and codependents don't learn how to socialize and communicate without alcohol or impression management. We met once a week at one of our homes. Sometimes we just talked about our week but more often, we used this time to learn and grow together. We watched the 1986 PBS series "*Bradshaw on the Family*," which featured renowned family dynamic expert and speaker John Bradshaw. We talked about what we'd learned, and how those same dynamics played out in our own families of origin, and current relationships.

Bradshaw popularized the terms *dysfunctional family* and *inner child*. The latter made me squirm. I didn't think I had an inner child, though my physical and emotional response to the term was definitely reactional. Bradshaw portrayed a typical family as a hanging mobile with each piece acting out a particular role in the system. The balance of the mobile was reliant on the other moving pieces. If one piece moved in a different direction or detached from the mobile, it threw all of the other pieces off balance.

I thought it was a brilliant way to illustrate what happens when alcoholics stop drinking and start recovering, or when the codependent spouse/significant other starts detaching. In our couple's group and in the two years of aftercare, it was easy to see codependency more consciously while unconsciously trying to make the addict return to old, familiar relationship dynamics. I recognized that I needed and wanted to change my behavior, but I still portrayed and expected Walter to be the sick one. While I appeared to work on my recovery, I was subtly manipulating the impression others had of Walter, so the focus stayed on him.

Here's what I wasn't owning up to – I had never been in a true, honest, intimate relationship, not even with myself. I had no idea what that was. I didn't allow Walter to know the real me because I was just beginning to know myself. We were both enmeshed in our dysfunctional relationship and while I told myself I wanted to change that, deep down I knew our marriage was more role-play than real. When we met, neither of us were emotionally capable of being truly present. In recovery I was slowly becoming more self-aware and vulnerable. By then it was clear that I had very little in common with Walter.

I had to admit to myself that I didn't love him for who he was. In shorthand, he was an alcoholic, and I was a codependent, and we were drawn to each other like flies-to-honey. That isn't love.

Melody Beattie's 1986 book, *Codependent No More,* became a bestseller and the term *codependent* entered the lexicon of alcohol and drug counselors and 12-Step meetings. In Beattie's introduction, she writes, "This book is about your most important and probably most neglected responsibility, to take care of yourself."[13] I almost set the book aside while reading the first chapter because I didn't think the personal stories fit me. I flipped through the pages, looking for a list of concrete ways to help myself. Beattie quoted Earnie Larsen's definition of codependency which rang true: "Those self-defeating, learned behaviors or character defects that result in a diminished capacity to initiate or to participate in loving relationships."[14]

I knew from cognitive behavioral therapy that many responses and behaviors were learned from an initiating event or series of events. But then I learned about the word *react*.

> "Codependents are reactionaries. They overreact. They underreact. But rarely do they act. They react to the problems, pains, lives, and behaviors of others."[15]

Beattie identified many codependent behaviors such as feeling responsible for other people's feelings and actions, feeling almost compelled to 'help' by giving unwanted or unasked for advice, or telling other people what to do, trying to please everyone, and being afraid to let others be who they really are.

I felt as if I had been stripped naked on the pages of a book.

During Alanon meetings I'd learned about detachment and resolved to apply those techniques. I reached another crossroads of growth but this time I didn't feel the fear as much as shame and a determination to change. I told myself that since my father Galen wasn't an alcoholic and I was never abused, maybe I wasn't very codependent so it wouldn't take long for me to get better. (Isn't denial sneaky?)

Beattie laid out symptoms that can occur as a codependent progresses in the disease, including depression, suicide ideation, hopelessness and mental illness. This made me reflect and wonder, was there something in my childhood that first impacted me and caused my symptoms or was it because Galen had mental problems and so did Grandma Mabel? But I still clung to my denial.

The early 1980s into the 90s were exciting times in the field of addiction. Drug and alcohol treatment centers were trying new therapies, in addition to the standard individual and group therapy sessions supported by 12-Step meetings. Also, a new 12-Step group called Adult Children of Alcoholics (ACOA) was formed locally. Researchers were discovering that an addict's family members often have mental health and addiction issues of their own. Studies explored if there was a quantifiable impact on those who lived with an alcoholic or drug addict. My Alanon sponsor suggested that I attend an ACOA meeting but I preferred to read a book about it first, since reading meant I could more easily control my response.

Besides, I still believed my First Story.

In Claudia Black's book, *It Will Never Happen to Me*, she explains that *at least* half of the alcoholics she has treated come from alcoholic families. Black was an early pioneer who addressed the effects of living with an alcoholic (or drug addict) on their spouses and children. She was the first to coin the phrase, "Don't Talk, Don't Trust, Don't Feel" as a shorthand to describe what children from alcoholic homes learn.

We don't talk about what's going on.

We can't trust our senses and feelings.

It's better that we don't feel at all, in fact.

I learned those lessons too well. I remember a particularly bad fight between my mom and Galen. Lee was peeking through the curtained window from his top bunk, watching them in the kitchen. I was upset because the screaming frightened me. Then we heard my mom say in a steely tone, "I'll kill you if you come closer!" Lee said she had a big knife in her hand to ward off Galen. Then there were crashing sounds. Next the front door opened and slammed shut.

Mom was crying. I got out of bed and ran to find her. I asked, "What's wrong, Mommy? Why were you and Daddy fighting? Where's Daddy? I'm scared!" My mom stopped crying, smiled and said, "Nothing's wrong, don't be silly. We weren't fighting, we were just having a discussion, so don't be scared. Daddy went outside for a little bit, and he'll be back soon. You get yourself back to bed and go to sleep." I felt deeply confused. I knew what I had heard. I knew what Lee said was going on. And I *thought* I knew what I was feeling but my mom said, "No, that's not what happened," so that means I'm wrong. Over time I learned to doubt my perceptions and mistrust what I heard, saw and felt.

The Don't Talk rule isn't just germane to families dealing with alcoholism or other addictions. "We don't tell other people what happens in our family" is a near universal law unto itself. Your mom's drinking. Your dad's drinking. Your parents smoking pot or using other drugs. Your parent's fights. Physical and sexual abuse by a parent or other family member. Your mom's fragile health condition. Grandma's cancer. Dad's jail record. Bankruptcy, poverty, homelessness, a parent losing his or her job, being unemployed, having a mental illness, not having a car, your mom's explosive temper, being hungry, etc. etc. etc. Instead, kids are subtly encouraged to *manage* the impression outsiders have by striving to look good and appear as a "normal family."

Claudia Black also introduced the concept of different roles in family systems. In her work with adolescents and adults from alcoholic families, she discerned how children adapt by assuming specific roles.

The Responsible One (or Hero Child) is often the oldest child who takes on the responsibility for everyone in the home, and particularly the alcoholic. This child believes that if he or she behaves *perfectly*, gets good grades and other achievements, things will magically get better in the family. This child believes that they must be responsible themself and others, because mom and dad can't do it. In fact, often the internal message becomes, adults and other authority figures are not to be trusted.

Another role a child assumes in the family is what Black calls the Adjuster.

"*adjusting children* find it wiser to follow, and simply not draw attention to themselves. This behavior is less painful for these children and makes life easier for the rest of the family as well. The role of the adjuster is permeated with denial, without the focus on others."[16]

The third role Black identified is the Placater. "In every home, there is usually at least one child, who is particularly more sensitive—one who laughs harder, cries harder, and seems to be more emotionally involved in everyday events."[17]

I related to this child. My mom, Lee, and Pops told me for years to "Stop being so sensitive!" or "Oh, you're just too fragile. You need to harden up."

Black writes, "This child's feelings are hurt more easily than the other childrens'. Yet, he likes to make others feel better. The Placater finds the best way to cope in this inconsistent and tension-filled home, is by acting in a way which will lessen his own tension and pain, as well as that of other family members."[18]

Placaters are often well-behaved children, 'people pleasers,' and the ones that a parent points to and says, "At least we don't have to worry about him or her." I tried my best to make my mom and

Lee love me by being silly at times, and during my teen years by attempting to understand them intellectually. I even tried to help Mom and Pops by using my budding knowledge of psychology to point out their parenting errors. They laughed at me.

Black's fourth family role is the Acting Out Child. Rather than assume a role that tries to protect against the chaos in the home, the Acting Out Child becomes the focus. These children often get into trouble at school and at home, fight with siblings, and fit the stereotype of delinquent kids. These kids also tend to hang out with other troubled kids, have low self-esteem, and are often called "too emotional." My brother took on the Acting Out role during his last year of high school. He constantly fought and argued with my mom and Pops, experimented with drugs, broke curfew, and lied. After he graduated, he hitchhiked around the country, homeless until he was down to his last dime. Then he would collect call my mom and ask her to wire him some money.

But a strange thing happened after he left home; a vacuum was created in our family system. And so I stepped into Lee's role. I started challenging the rules and talking back. I later learned that kids can often take on more than one role in the family.

The *Children of Alcoholics Screening Test* is located in the appendix of Black's book. The test contains 30 questions. A score of 6 or more indicates that the person may have grown up in an alcoholic household. In my denial I scored 0 and felt vindicated. I wanted to say to my Alanon sponsor, "See? I don't need to go to any ACOA meetings."

I also read the national bestseller *Adult Children of Alcoholics* by Janet Geringer Woititz, Ed.D. According to Woititz, "Your judgment of others is not nearly as harsh as your judgment of yourself, although it is hard for you to see other people's behavior in terms of a continuum either. Black or white, good or bad, are typically the way you look at things. Either side is an awesome responsibility."[19] Various sections in the book describe the common characteristics of adult children of alcoholics:

Adult Children of Alcoholics...

- Guess at what "normal" behavior is

- Have a hard time completing a project from beginning to end

- Lie when it would be just as easy to tell the truth

- Judge themselves without mercy

- Have a hard time "letting go" and having fun

- Tend to take themselves too seriously

- Have a hard time developing and maintaining intimate relationships

- Tend to overreact to changes that they have no control over

- Constantly seek approval and affirmation

- Usually feel that they are different from other people

- Are either "super responsible" or "super irresponsible"

- Are extremely loyal even in the face of evidence to the contrary

- Are impulsive – These individuals tend to lock themselves into a course of action without giving serious consideration to alternative behaviors or possible consequences. This impulsivity can lead to confusion, self-loathing, and a loss of control.[20]

I had spent a lot of time guessing at what normal is. My H.E.B.S.G. observations of humans, and psychology research in junior high school were designed to figure out what was considered 'normal.' Like most children from abusive families, I was an expert at reading the room. I could quickly adjust to changing moods and retreat at the first sign of conflict.

I was ashamed to admit I had difficulty having fun. I never understood what the attraction was in playing dolls, board games or games like tag. Other girls in my neighborhood spent hours together with their Barbie dolls, exchanging outfits and having imaginary conversations between their dolls. How did they do that? How did they just pretend, and come up with things for their doll to say? I felt embarrassed for them but ashamed that I didn't understand. It seemed so childish. Maybe it was just another way for the adults to laugh at and mock kids like they often did with their fairytales, stories about talking animals, and the persistent efforts they put into convincing kids that there really was a Santa, Easter Bunny and Tooth Fairy. These efforts convinced me that adults thought kids were stupid. When parents finally came clean with their kids, they laughed as if it were a big joke.

I was certainly impulsive. The concept of planning anything felt threatening, because if I had a plan I would be expected to follow it. If I failed it would be bad, but if I succeeded it would be worse because then people would expect more of me. I knew deep down that I was a fraud and wouldn't be able to keep up the façade.

It was during this time that I started experiencing flashes of memories.

11

intervention redux

Nothing changes if nothing changes. – 12-Step Saying

I told my Alanon sponsor about the phone call with my brother but no one else. That call shattered my First Story. If I didn't remember several years of summers, what else didn't I remember?

I tried to come up with memories besides the black and white glossy photo ones. Where did I live on my 9th birthday? Was there a party? I don't know. I knew I was in Camp Fire Girls because Mom had a black and white photo of me with a bunch of girls on our front porch on in Portland. What did I do in Camp Fire Girls? Blank. When I lived in Hawaii according to Mom, I had to take remedial math in the summer between 8th and 9th grade but there is no memory of it. I was sure I'd never been spanked except that one time. Did we go to church when I was a kid? I had a hazy memory of Mabel taking me to her Presbyterian church, and I remembered kneeling in the hard wooden pews at Mass with Mom. I knew our relationship had some rocky years when I was a teenager but she never hit me (except that one slap) and she was kind and loving and protective. I swear the black and white memories of those summers travelling in the carnival were real.

It briefly crossed my mind that Lee was lying to me but his tone of voice was utterly sincere. Still, I called Pops and asked what he knew about when Mom and Galen were married. He said she never talked much about it but he knew they travelled with the carnival in the summers and left Lee and me at the homes of friends and relatives. I still couldn't believe it.

I asked him if Galen was an alcoholic. He said he couldn't answer that, and Mom had told him Galen got mean when he got drunk but again, she didn't say much to Pops about her life before him. I said, but Mom didn't drink... did she? I didn't remember seeing her drink. "Oh sure, she enjoyed Kahlua and cream and White Russians. I tried to get her to like whiskey, but she never did." It felt like the earth was opening up beneath me. "Did you guys drink at home, like when I was in high school in Boise?" I asked. Pops said, "Sure. We also liked to go to that bar called Charlie Browns." I was stunned. I just never remembered that Mom drank at all. I knew Pops enjoyed whiskey every so often, because I remember the smell.

When we lived in Boise Mom was in a car accident and hurt

her back resulting in a series of surgeries and a year in a body cast. I thought that ever after, she took pain pills called Darvon, and the muscle relaxer Valium. Then I realized no, that wasn't true. She was taking Darvon and Valium before that when we lived in Hawaii, because I stole a few to show my drug-using friends. Mom had back problems before the car accident. When I lived with them as an adult in Hagerman, I saw a bottle of whiskey in the freezer but no other alcohol in the house.

There were apparently about 8 years of my early life missing. My First Story was mostly false. I did take ballet in a free community class. I *was* selected to represent my grade school in the Portland Rose Parade Junior Princess contest but I didn't ride the float because I didn't make it to regionals. In fact, Lee said I never went to the parade because it was raining that day and because Mom had to work. But real memories were still locked tight in those boxes deep in my brain, like a safe I didn't know how to unlock.

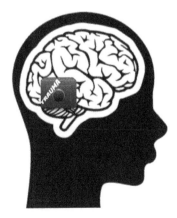

I finally talked about the phone call and the lost memories in couple's group, aftercare, and Alanon groups. The recovery tools of detachment, along with focusing on my own thoughts, feelings and behaviors were what helped me find the courage to move another inch out of the darkness. I feared stepping into the light because I didn't know what I would see.

My life was changing and this time it was too late to step back from the crossroads. I started attending Mass again, sliding into a back pew with my head down, filled with shame and tears. I wouldn't take communion because I knew I didn't deserve it.

I also admitted my marriage was over.

I stupidly decided to tell Walter I was leaving by taking us on a drive. Maybe I thought he would take it better riding in the car. I was wrong. He was furious, and at one point he jerked the steering wheel from me. I lost control and we crashed into a utility pole. When the police came, I was cited for inattentive driving. The policeman seemed to understand that Walter was dangerously angry, because he insisted on driving Walter home, while I waited for the tow truck.

Andie and I moved into a nearby apartment. I wanted to stay close so Andie could easily walk to both her parent's homes. Walter had adopted her legally after our marriage. I took a cue from my Mom's wise example and made sure she knew the divorce wasn't her fault, and that Walter loved her very much. Of course, by then she was a child of an alcoholic father and a child of a codependent and mentally ill mother. I knew she was greatly impacted and felt guilty and responsible.

The black undertow of depression grew stronger, and I again had periods of dissociation. My self-mutilation and rocking escalated. Within a few months of leaving Walter, it took every ounce of willpower to get out of bed in the morning and go to work at the radio station. I often called in sick, something I'd rarely done before. My smoking habit was kicking my butt and I woke up in the morning hacking and coughing. My body ached and my joints became stiff with pain. My skin constantly itched. I was compelled, almost obsessed, with trying to appear normal on the outside.

The lifelong suicide planning started taking over my days. I imagined ways I could die that would look like an accident, so Andie wouldn't be messed up by having a mom who killed herself. In the high desert region of Southern Idaho we lived near the edge of the Snake River Canyon where decades before, Evel Knievel attempted his motorcycle jump. The canyon was over 400 feet deep in some spots and the only way to cross it was a single deck arch bridge built in 1926. Today it's a popular spot for base jumpers but back then the sport hadn't been invented. I knew jumping off the bridge wasn't smart because it would obviously look deliberate. But if I could figure out a way to 'slip' off the canyon edge and fall to my death, that might work.

Meantime the surface of my life looked normal – at least I thought so. I continued being a guest speaker with families at local treatment centers to share my 12-step journey. I sponsored four women in Alanon plus an Alateen group, continued with weekly couple's group (albeit solo), 12-step meetings, and attended several recovery retreat weekends with friends. One popular place for 12-Step retreats was Lava Hot Springs in southeastern Idaho. On one of those trips I asked my friend Dagmar if she would give me a massage. I wasn't sure if I could go through with it but I wanted to try and be present this time. Dagmar was gentle and loving, but after touching my back and arms, I had enough. It was a baby step for me.

Along with depression, paranoia crept in again. My second story apartment's kitchen windows overlooked the other front doors and parking lot, so I kept the curtains closed in fear someone would look in. When I was there alone, a knock at the door sent me into panic and I'd crouch down and crawl on my hands and knees to the nearest closet. If I was in the kitchen I hid under the table and rocked. If Andie was home, I froze and prayed whoever was at the door was someone I knew. All my friends and family knew not to just drop in unannounced.

I don't remember what I was so frightened by; I felt overwhelming shame and guilt combined. Someone told me in a 12-Step meeting that 'guilt' means I did something wrong, but 'shame' means I AM something wrong. In retrospect, I thank God and the village for helping me take care of Andie. I tried hard to act as usual and not let her see my depression and anxiety. I know now that of course she did.

I was friends with a man who also worked in radio, and after I left Walter, our relationship moved from just friendship. I began obsessing about him and tried to become who I thought he wanted me to be, in the same codependent way I'd done with Jeremy in high school. We had sex a handful of times but there was a big barrier for both of us: he was married. Our affair was emotionally toxic for me, and deep down I knew it. I watched at my kitchen window every morning, hoping to catch a glimpse of his car driving by. I had no expectation that he would leave his wife, and I knew his issues with her had nothing to do with me. There was this underlying truth: I didn't want him to leave his wife because I knew our relationship was unhealthy. The biggest evidence of that was I didn't tell anyone about it at the time, not even my Alanon sponsor.

My depression and anxiety continued to worsen, along with my lifelong self-mutilation. The shame I felt about my affair made me sick. I thought I had let go of living with secrets long ago and worked hard to stay honest in recovery. But clearly, I wasn't being honest, not even with myself.

Fortunately, this time I wasn't alone. I had a wealth of friends in recovery who unbeknownst to me were already concerned. One night I arrived at couple's group and the atmosphere seemed different. We sat around in our usual circle and this time; JC opened the conversation saying he was worried about me. Dagmar told me she loved me but was scared that one night I just wouldn't show up for group. I knew what they were talking about and felt mortified to be 'seen', and a little relieved at the same time. My loving, knowing friends were staging an intervention. That night, I agreed to seek help.

There was no doubt in my mind I was codependent with others. By then I'd been attending Alanon (and more recently Adult Children of Alcoholics) meetings for almost five years. I knew I wasn't healthy, but I still tried to act and be who I thought others wanted me to be. I did work hard to uncover my faults – but more so I could stop doing them, or at least hide them from sight so others wouldn't judge me. I was still loathe to let anyone see the flawed struggling, imperfect, emotionally and mentally sick person I was. Yet my dear friends certainly saw through my façade.

I called the Walker Center and spoke to the administrator Gail Ater whom I knew from when Walter was in treatment. Gail listened and heard my anguish. He said, "When the pain of your codependence outweighs your fear of doing the work, then it's time to come in."

They didn't have a bed ready for another week, which gave me time to make arrangements with Walter for Andie and tell my boss at work. Walter was confused and angry. "But you're not an alcoholic or drug addict! You don't even drink!" he insisted. "You don't qualify to go to the Walker Center." I tried to explain but had no words.

The Walker Center was in an arm of a hospital and was a lockdown facility. The staff member who checked me in carefully went through my luggage to look for contraband like drugs. She took my antihistamine, which I used not only for allergies, but because it helped me sleep and lessen the itching I had all over my body. I scratched throughout the day and night, and often bled from scratching my skin raw.

The next morning, I saw the medical doctor and provided samples of my blood and urine, then had my first group therapy session with the other patients. They all introduced themselves as drug addicts, alcoholics and sex addicts. I identified myself as a codependent.

I also took the Minnesota Multiphasic Personality Inventory (MMPI), which is a psychological test that assesses personality traits and psychopathology. It is "primarily intended to test people who are suspected of having mental health or other clinical issues." 21

My MMPI results were sent to a clinical psychologist named Dr. Charles Kaufmann and then I met with him for a long interview. No longer wanting to hide I told him about my depression, anxiety, dissociation, suicide ideation, rocking, rhyming and counting, and how I used to scratch myself and pull out my hair. That's right --- I didn't admit I was still self-mutilating or mention the array of physical symptoms I had. I was scared the Walker Center would say they couldn't help me and send me straight to the state mental hospital. At the time of my admission, I was told that I was only the second patient to be admitted for codependency without other accompanying addictions like drugs and alcohol.

Dr. Kaufmann asked me if my parents drank, and I admitted for the first time I thought Galen had been an alcoholic. He asked if I'd been physically or sexually abused and I firmly told him what had become my mantra: *Oh no, thank God I was never abused!*

Later I learned the diagnosis he gave me from the Diagnostic and

Statistical Manual III (DSM-III), was Mixed Personality Disorder. There are ten types of recognized personality disorders, clustered into A, B, and C:

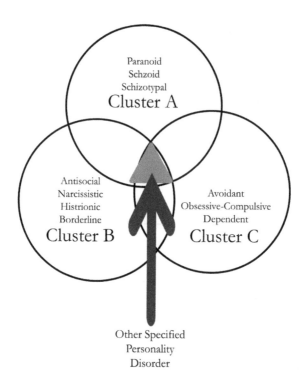

Paranoid
Schzoid
Schizotypal
Cluster A

Antisocial
Narcissistic
Histrionic
Borderline
Cluster B

Avoidant
Obsessive-Compulsive
Dependent
Cluster C

Other Specified
Personality
Disorder

Mixed Personality Disorder should be used when the individual has a Personality Disorder that involves features from several of the specific Personality Disorders but does not meet the criteria for any one Personality Disorder.[22]   (Note: The current edition of the DSM-V changed the name to "Other Specified Personality Disorder".

What did that mean? It meant I exhibited enough symptoms from different personality disorders, but not enough from any one or two of them to land on a single or dual diagnosis. In Cluster C, I knew I was obsessive-compulsive about many things (hello counting and rhyming and relationships!), and despite wanting to see myself as independent and not needing anyone else, I knew I was overly dependent on certain people. The avoidance rang true, particularly around avoiding intimacy, my social anxiety and my fear of criticism and rejection. In Cluster B I related to being histrionic, marked by unstable emotions, a distorted self-image, and knew that even when I tried to avoid attention, I also craved it. The Cluster A type of paranoid hit home, but I told myself that was only when I had my first breakdown. I completely denied my more recent paranoid behavior. Obviously, I met the criteria for the diagnosis of depression and anxiety.

What bothered me the most was reading that personality disorders are almost impossible to cure; symptoms can be managed, and treatment can relieve them, but the patient will likely be on a lifetime program to manage their illness. I told myself it was no different than an addict or codependent who needs to work a therapeutic program for the rest of their life, whether in a 12-Step group or other recovery program. Still, it was hard to accept because even then I needed to believe if I just worked hard enough, prayed long enough, read the perfect book, or found the perfect therapist, I could overcome all of my issues. In other words, I still wanted to think I was in control.

12

inpatient

You gotta resurrect the deep pain within you and give it a place to live that's not within your body. Let it live in art. Let it live in writing. Let it live in music. Let it be devoured by building brighter connections. Your body is not a coffin for pain to be buried in. Put it somewhere else. – Ehime Ora

On my third day at the Walker Center I met my assigned counselor, Elberta Askew. Her office was bright and colorful with tall file cabinets along one wall. She asked me about my family of origin. Did we move a lot? Did my parents drink or use drugs? How did they get along with each other? Was I physically abused? How many siblings did I have?

Then Elberta asked if I had ever been touched in a way I didn't like. I felt my body tense up and assured her, "Oh no, thank God nothing like that ever happened to me."

She pressed forward saying, "I've been learning about how abused children exhibit similar responses as coping mechanisms. For example, a child who has been sexually abused might dress in layered clothing – more than just fashion, and often inappropriate for the season or conversely dress in provocative clothes beyond their age. Or blame themselves for being molested. So I think it's important to ask." A flash of that day in Lee's bedroom rose in my mind but I didn't want to tell her. I'd never told anyone and barely remembered the incident. Besides, that wasn't sexual abuse because all he did was feel my breasts and kiss me, right?   I mumbled, "My brother touched me once that's all."

"How did he touch you? Can you tell me?" she asked.

I don't remember anything else except Elberta standing over me calling my name. I was out of the chair, curled up in a fetal position in the corner by her file cabinets, rocking and shaking, my head in my arms. I felt exhausted, raw, and naked – like my clothes had been ripped off and my bowels slashed open.

I attended afternoon group therapy and an ACOA meeting that night but remained silent, shaking my head no when asked if I wanted to share anything. Elberta met with me again the next day, and shared what she witnessed the day before. She said I started to shake and rock. I pulled my knees up to my chest and kind of fell to the floor. I "shimmied" my body away from her and backed into the corner of the room. I was holding my arms tight against my chest.

I told her that surprised me because I honestly didn't think what Lee did was bad. Elberta thought otherwise, and the fact that I'd reacted to the memory meant *something*. Later, when more revelations came tumbling out of my darkest, most secret places, I realized that this memory of Lee was the first inkling (that I consciously remember) that I had been molested. Just that knowledge alone freaked me out and altered my childhood memories, even more than finding out that I did not actually experience those idyllic summers traveling with the carnival that I thought I did.

I quickly and easily adapted to the structure of the Walker Center's treatment program. Each morning we had group exercise, moving our bodies to the rhythm of music. Then breakfast followed by morning group therapy. After that we were tasked with working on our Steps from Alcoholics or Narcotics Anonymous or in my case, the Alanon 12 Steps. After lunch we had a private session with our assigned counselors, followed by another group therapy session.

In the evenings we were either taken offsite to a specific 12 Step group meeting, or encouraged to meet with whatever 12 Step group was using the Center that night. I attended Alanon and ACOA meetings and if neither were available, I went to other open meetings. On Sunday afternoons our family members could visit us, but we couldn't leave the hospital premises. The Center also provided us with educational sessions to learn about the disease process and progression. One counselor explained that most addicts start drinking or using drugs as teenagers, causing their emotional development to be arrested at that point.

It occurred to me that's why we all related to each other so easily.

Differences in age and background were irrelevant. We were all about the same age emotionally. The first few days I thought of myself as different because I was the only patient who couldn't identify themselves as an alcoholic or drug addict, but during each group session I heard my own fears, guilt, shame, anger and denial echoed in the words of others.

I was so co-dependent that I tried hard to fit-in, be liked and show the counselors what a "good" learner I was. They saw right through me. To my peers, I was that person who would happily listen to and support them while they navigated their own journeys. One day a fellow patient named Dennis found me in my room and asked me to help him write a letter to his wife – a letter he could share with her during his upcoming family session. He told me that he wasn't any good at writing and didn't know what to say. I jumped in to help him, even suggesting how he could phrase things.

Apparently, the incident was relayed to the counselors because the next day during group therapy the administrator Gail joined us. He talked about how alcoholics rely on codependents to lie, excuse and do things for the alcoholic that he/she should be doing for themselves. He said he wanted to illustrate the relationship between an alcoholic and a codependent. He put an empty chair in the center of the circle and told me to get down on all fours next to it. I was nervous, wondering what was going to happen. Then he told Dennis to climb onto the chair and balance by putting one leg on my back and the other one on the chair.

Dennis was reluctant at first. He was afraid of hurting me, but Gail insisted. Gail asked the group, "Who is in control?"

Several of my peers pointed to Dennis. Dennis was standing on me and thereby keeping me down. I was sure that I understood the point – an addict steps on the codependent, leaving him or her stuck in one spot.

Then Gail said, "You're wrong. Dennis isn't in control at all. Think of it this way, what happens if Catherine moves out from under his foot?"

Ahh... Then, it hit me. If I moved out from underneath Dennis, he would fall. I was actually the one in control. I was propping him up. This was a real moment of clarity for me. How could I blame Walter or Galen for my codependency? I always insisted that I was no one's victim but in reality, I acted like I was one and was 'stuck' in whatever situation.

All the rooms at the Walker Center were double occupancy. My roommate was an old woman named Louise. She was at least seventy years old, hard-of-hearing, and in constant need of an oxygen tank. She also chewed tobacco, spitting it into a disposable cup throughout the day. She was at the Center because of an intervention from caring friends, and she introduced herself in each group by yelling, "I'm Louise! I like beer!".

One morning Louise turned on her small transistor radio and flipped it to the radio station I worked at. "Do you like country music?" she asked. "I love this station because my favorite DJ is on it, but she hasn't been on for a few days." I got a sinking feeling and asked, "Louise? Are you talking about Catherine?" Louise's face lit up, "Oh yes, I just love her! I hope nothing has happened to her. I hope she's coming back soon."

I wasn't sure how to respond. On the one hand it seemed deceptive not to tell her who I was, but on the other hand, my identity had nothing to do with her recovery. I also realized that at some point, Louise would probably recognize my voice on the radio as her "friend" and if so, I would either have to admit it or lie about it. I decided to tell her who I was, and immediately regretted it. Louise was a true, diehard fan and could not believe her favorite radio personality was sleeping in the same room with her. She insisted on bringing me coffee and food every day. She followed me everywhere in the center and sat next to me during group therapy.

I asked Elberta what I should do, and she sardonically said, "Oh, let me get this straight; you have someone who is being codependent with you, and you don't like it?" Point taken.

The Walker Center's family therapy sessions occurred twice during each patient's four-week stay. I knew no one in my family would come to the first family therapy session except Andie if I could arrange a ride for her. I didn't try because I thought she was too young. Lee lived out of state. My Pops did live in the area, but he was not a particularly sentimental person. When I called to invite him, I let him know that the session would most likely be "touchy-feely." I also assured him that it wasn't mandatory for him come. Pops replied, "Well, honey, it sounds like I wouldn't be much use in something like that." I was relieved.

JC and Dagmar came instead as my family. During the sharing session, the patient sits in the middle of the circle and listens to their loved ones give 'gifts of truth.' During this session I felt as if I were stripped naked in front of both of my friends, who lovingly and honestly addressed me.

For my second family therapy program, Gail wanted Walter and Andie present. I protested, insisting she would not understand.

Actually, I felt too ashamed to have her there. I conveniently ignored that Andie had been in attendance at Walter's family programs.

I'd left Walter a year before, and I didn't see the point of having him come either. Nevertheless, I followed Gail's orders and called Walter to invite him. He flatly refused but agreed to bring Andie to the sessions. Gail was not happy – he wanted Walter too. Gail spoke to both Walter and Walter's AA sponsor to apply pressure. It worked. Walter arrived with Andie, his face simmering with anger.

Andie was true and honest in sharing her feelings, blaming me for the divorce, and listing all the ways I "ruined" her life. Although hard to hear, I listened with an open heart. I ached for her while also feeling proud of her openness and honesty. When it was Walter's turn to express how he felt, he pulled out a piece of paper from his pocket that I assumed was a letter for me.

Walter looked at me and curtly said, "If you come home right now and forget all of this, then I won't press charges against you for forging my name." He held up a copy of a loan document. My stomach clinched and my face turned red. When I left him, I couldn't get an apartment without a $500 deposit which I didn't have. I didn't want to ask my Pops for it so I went to a quick loan company and signed both of our names on the application. I was desperate. I felt sick with shame and guilt when the truth came out during the session. I was trapped sitting in that chair in the middle of the circle with all eyes on me, definitely in the hot seat. But before I could answer, Gail interrupted. He bluntly confronted Walter for trying to blackmail me.

During the four-weeks of treatment, patients are required to complete the first five steps of their 12-Step program. Every therapy group session or 12 step meeting, we were encouraged to introduce ourselves and name our addictions. For example, "Hi I am John, and I am a drug addict and sex addict." Some people would add other labels like being eating disordered, a relationship addict, etc.

At first, I was reluctant to share anything but being codependent, but I finally I came clean about my food, relationship and work issues. There were so many 'titles' that I came up with an acronym to remember all of them:

- Relationship Addict

- Incest Survivor

- Eating Disordered

- Workaholic

- Adult Child

- COdependent

The first letters of each word coincidentally spelled out RAISED WACCO. That made me laugh.

In my 12-Step program, I got stuck on the 3rd step – "*Made a decision to turn our will and our lives over to the care of God as we understood Him.*" I had attended so many different Christian churches with the majority of them being affiliated with the Roman Catholic Church – the religion I was raised in. I have been a student of the world's primary religions for a long time, so I knew what every other seeker knew – there are strong and similar foundations in each faith, for instance, *Do unto Others*.

I believed in God and prayed yet I still struggled and resisted the idea of Jesus being like a family member like my father or brother. And if "*Jesus loves you just like Grandma Mabel*" was true, no thanks. I viewed Jesus like a controller who was intent on dictating my life. If so then all of humanity's suffering is because He or She ordained it. I also hoped Jesus might be a loving Creator who looked after me. I so wanted to believe the latter, but every frame of reference I had for divine love was *tainted*. I began praying for the willingness to be open to His or Her presence in my life.

One morning just before sunrise I sat outside on the Center's back patio alone, gazing up at the glory of the early morning stars and cradling a warm cup of coffee. I was back where I had been before, broken into pieces and acutely aware that I had exhausted every path forward. I felt completely helpless to figure out what else I could do to recover. AA has a wonderful saying, "Your best thinking is what got you here." A constant reminder from Elberta was, "Stop trying to figure this out and start getting in touch with your feelings. Stay out of your head." I knew in my heart and soul there was nothing else I could do but surrender completely. In the infinitesimal-second that followed, it felt like time stopped and the sky changed.

A shimmering kind of web appeared, linking everything ever

created. My life flickered through the worst moments of my childhood. I saw each time I thought I was alone. Only now, God was there with me, wrapping around me, supporting me and helping me through it. Suddenly I knew why I was missing all of those years in my memory. It wasn't denial or insanity, rather it was my protection until I had the strength to face the truth.

God was there in the dirt basement as Galen experimented, while I left my body to find the hole in the wall. God was there in the poodle bedroom when Mabel used her special hairbrush on me. God was at that California truck stop as I slipped in-and-out of reality, desperate to protect my baby. God was beside me when Mom and Galen yanked my hair, screaming at each other and jerking me back-and-forth.

A profound feeling of awareness and gratitude flooded through me. Yes, I said aloud. *Yes.*

Gail suggested I attend the SA meeting held at the center. SA stands for *Sex Addicts Anonymous*. He echoed what Elberta had said about how sexual abuse survivors often have issues around sex, including adopting unhealthy behaviors such as promiscuity, prostitution, and/or avoidance. I wondered, "Am I a sex addict?"

At that point in my life, I'd had sex with five men, none of whom I'd call 'casual sex.' I knew I avoided any physical activity that focused on my body. For example, I'd never had a massage, played a sport, or used girly lotions on my skin. Even brushing my hair and teeth felt icky, like I was doing something *wrong*.

The SA meeting was well-attended with both familiar and unfamiliar faces present, however nearly all of the group members were male. There were a large number of chairs placed in a circle. I waited until the last possible second before entering the room and taking a seat. The leader of the meeting sat across from me. He opened with, "Let's introduce ourselves. My name is John, and I am a sex addict." The man adjacent to John replied, "Hi. I am William and I am a sex addict and child molester." Next to William sat Jose, who also announced that he was a sex addict.

I didn't realize until it was my turn that I had pushed my chair back so far that I was completely out of the circle. I froze in place, as if I was pressed up against a wall facing a firing squad. My arms were wrapped around my knees. "Hi. My name is Catherine and I'm codependent. I was also... touched as a child. My counselor said I have to be here, so I am," I whispered. The voices around me raised in unison, "Hi, Catherine."

Next, the woman to my right said, "Hi. My name is Carly and I am a sex addict and a relationship addict." During that meeting I heard the words "molester" and "sexually abused" more in the first hour than I'd heard in all of my life. What surprised me was learning how many in the group were sexual abuse survivors.

Back in group therapy, I also learned that addicts and codependents have learned how to anesthetize their emotional lives with alcohol, drugs or like me, behaviors. We were all emotionally stunted, and our feelings presented as four basic emotions: happy, sad, angry, afraid

I related to all of them, except for anger. Anger was forbidden.

During my teen years my mood swings were extreme. When I

became angry at my parents or outraged by injustice, a rush would infiltrate every cell in my body, exacerbating the helplessness, and powerlessness I felt. I was often ordered to my bedroom "until you can put a smile on your face." Showing anger was not allowed. Over the years I'd learned how to dampen my emotions and mute my anger, burying it under layers of fear and shame.

Finding out that my First Story about my childhood was not true *still* rocked me.

Over the years I'd written and sung songs based on those 'memories'.

Mama was a carnie when I was just a child,
Midnight suppers on the midway, popcorn, and a smile.
Daddy worked the derby, copper horses up and down,
And me, I spent my hours on a Ferris Wheel going 'round.

Another song was titled, "*Carousel Riding Again.*" Whenever I sang the lyrics, I saw the glossy, black-and-white still of my mom working in the Hoop joint. I can still hear her saying to a passerby, "Come on! You want to win a prize for your girlfriend! Step right up and let's see how lucky you are!" My mom was not shy.

I 'remembered' a birthday party in which my mom invited all of the kids in my class. Each kid went home with bags of leftover carnival prizes. I realize now that probably never happened.

I trusted the answers would eventually come as long as I continued my recovery journey. I learned a truth while staying at the Center – a truth also expressed by author Sarah Wilson, in her memoir about dealing with anxiety. She writes about how people tend to feel like they must fix what's wrong with them, and that the fixes we seek are almost always *outside* ourselves. This really resonated with me.

I'd read many books throughout the years looking for the perfect solution for my problems. The implication was the answers are *out* there. The truth is the answers are *within*.[23]

Something else happened to me as I moved through my stay at the Walker Center. For years, my body itched intensely, my muscles were always tense, and I had daily headaches and back aches. All of that diminished as I opened up and faced more truths about myself. My physical recovery is grounded in fact. Dr. Ruth Lanius teaches and conducts clinical research at the University of Western Ontario in Canada, and she edited a book about how untreated early childhood trauma impacts physical health and disease.[24]

To graduate from the Walker Center's treatment program, I had to complete the 5th step – *"Admitted to God, to ourselves, and to another human being the exact nature of our wrongs."*

The facility had a list of locals who were willing to hear a patient's 5th step. Some were local pastors of various denominations and others were recovering addicts. Since I was only the second fully-codependent patient admitted to the Walker Center, they didn't have a roster of Alanon members yet. When Elberta tried to show me the list of candidates that were available, I told her that anyone would be fine. It felt like I was taking a major step forward in my quest to let go of control.

On the scheduled day I went to the lobby to meet the person who would hear my 5th step. He was a man who looked a bit younger than me. He felt genuine and kind. He was dressed in jeans and a plaid shirt. He introduced himself as Father Tim Richey, and I almost laughed at the irony. A Catholic priest! Elberta and I had never discussed religion and I'd left it blank on my intake form.

I told the priest *everything* from my 4th step self-inventory. My head was low as I stared at the floor. I told him that I was intolerant, controlling and manipulative. I told him how I always had to be seen as the good guy but was in fact judgmental, impatient, self-righteous and irresponsible. I tended to live in the past. I knew that my character faults were shields to keep people at a distance, and to keep myself from being honest and intimate in all of my relationships. If things were going okay, I self-sabotaged. I cried in shame when telling him how I was scared of my father, and extremely relieved when he died. I felt so guilty about that.

Fr. Tim listened patiently for over two hours. Then he gave me an unexpected gift – one that knocked the air out of my lungs and made my knees buckle. He granted me absolution. It was as if a force flowed through me, and for the first time since I left therapy at 21, I felt completely clean and whole again.

This time I was determined to stay that way.

13

healing pieces

There is no one way to recover and heal from any trauma. Each survivor chooses their own path or stumbles across it. ~Laurie Matthew

After leaving the Walker Center, I followed through on my aftercare plan. Ninety 12-step meetings in ninety days along with 2 years of weekly group aftercare, as I'd done with Walter. Elberta also suggested that I try to be open to opportunities that could help me heal, like attending group therapy for sexual abuse survivors. She added there were other avenues I could try, such as regressive hypnosis, but only if it felt right.

There were just three Alanon meetings and one ACOA meeting

each week in the area I lived, so I attended open AA and SA meetings, and an open NA (*Narcotics Anonymous*) meeting to reach my 90 in 90. I also rejoined the couple's group. Attending these meetings and listening to hundreds of people's struggles, reinforced what I discovered at the Walker Center – addicts and codependents share the same underlying disease – one that at the time I suspected was fueled by codependency and shame.

I embraced complete honesty. In the 12-Step program, this is referred to as "rigorous honesty." I marveled at the paradox of surrender, that by being honest and vulnerable, I was freer and stronger than I'd ever been before.   One of the most beautiful gifts in my recovery is how I began to see and appreciate people for who they are, not for who I wanted them to be. By accepting and forgiving my whole self, warts and all, I could share, listen to and connect with others on a more human level. And even though I had a long way to go in learning to love myself, I embraced being fully present and loving others. Much of this was thanks to the unconditional acceptance I found in 12-Step communities. In the thousands of shares I'd heard across the years, and regardless of how recent or far along in recovery the person was, nearly everyone was *trying* to come clean with themselves and others. We all accepted a fundamental truth - parts of us were broken.

I returned to the Walker Center as a regular Alanon speaker for their family therapy programs, but this time I understood my codependency better and could admit how it had negatively affected my relationships throughout the years.

Adults Molested as Children Group Therapy

About four months into my aftercare plan I joined the group Elberta had mentioned for sexual abuse survivors. There were six other women and a counselor. Listening to the other women share their stories of sexual and other types of abuse made me realize how much we had in common. There were little things that I never thought about before like not knowing how to take care of my fingernails. When you live in a stressed environment things like teaching your daughter how to manicure her nails are not high on your priority list. Nor is teaching her to cook, to explore interests or to nurture her dreams. Many of the women had unhealthy or strained relationships with their mothers. All of us wondered if our moms knew about the sexual abuse. At least one woman knew the answer was yes because her mom was complicit in her dad's molestation. Another woman wondered if her dad knew that her mom was abusing her.

I felt a kinship with these women and briefly pondered talking about Grandma Mabel but was still too ashamed to admit it even to myself. I wanted to believe that my mom didn't know. I told myself that in those days people didn't think of child abuse like they do now. Back then it was perfectly legal to discipline a child however a parent saw fit, including beating them black-and-blue. Back then it was inconceivable that a grandmother would physically, much less sexually abuse a grandchild. At that point in my recovery, I was not ready to admit that Grandma Mabel's behavior was abuse.

I learned that sexual abuse encompasses much more than

penetration. There is the overt kind of abuse where for example, a father or son makes sexual comments about his daughter's or sister's body. Sexual abuse also includes unwanted touching.

But there's covert kinds of sexual abuse: a father slips his arm around his teenage daughter's waist, letting his hand graze the bottom of her breast or slide down to cup her bottom. A parent tells sexual jokes in front of their son or daughter. A mother or father who uses their child as an emotional spouse – a confidant, the "little man or woman" – is sexualizing their behavior and is covert abuse. A parent who laments their child's growth and maturity in a way that sends a message they don't want the child to change or grow-up, especially if sexual undertones are present. "Oh no, you are growing up! Next thing I know you'll meet someone and leave me all alone."

We had specific assignments and stages to progress through before we could graduate. One of the assignments was to fill out a police report form. The counselor explained that filling it out reinforced the validity of the abuse and taught us to be our own advocates.   I was unable to finish, having frozen just seeing the questions.

None of the women had reported the original incidents, including incest and rapes that went back to childhood. My body was spasming and jerking as I tried to write down the stark facts, but I was still in denial. All I remembered at that point was what happened with Lee, so I wondered why I was even in the group. I discounted Galen's and Mabel's abuse completely. Denial. Denial. The counselor helped us process our feelings. She also instructed us to write a letter to our abuser(s) with the proviso that we would not give it to them. At home, I tried. But I couldn't get past the opening of "Dear Lee," without freezing with anxiety, my body trembling and shaking.

One woman was angry. She wanted to confront her father and uncle in front of the family at an upcoming gathering. For her it wasn't a question of not having the courage to confront them. The counselor urged all of us to consider focusing on ourselves first, stressing that our mental and emotional health were paramount. We talked about the differences between confronting someone and seeking revenge. Most of us feared that our abuser(s) were still acting out with other kids in the family and wondered if we should get the police or child protection services involved. We were empowered to intervene if we had credible knowledge.

For some of us like me, confrontations were either too frightening or they were not possible. Galen and Grandma Mabel were dead. But Lee was still alive. I wanted to minimize the impact of the incident on me. I sensed I'd been abused more than once – I just had no memory of it then. There was an echo and an icky feeling when I heard certain family member's names.

Another assignment involved getting a massage. Getting a massage can be therapeutic for abused adult children. It helps them reconnect to their bodies. Many of us had learned to sexualize all types of touches. Some of us had a sexual history involving several partners and even prostitution. Others like me, went to the opposite extreme of avoiding intimate touch. We had learned to treat our bodies like they are our enemies. All of us avoided true intimacy on emotional, physical, and sexual levels.

One of the women in the group was named Lorna and she also happened to be in my aftercare group from the Walker Center. She asked me if we could go get a massage together, explaining that she didn't want to be alone with a stranger touching her. Going together sounded safer to me too. I knew I did not want a male masseuse. I also refused to take off my pants. We found a female masseuse in the phone book and called to make the appointment. As suggested by our counselor, I explained that I was in therapy to recover from childhood sexual abuse, and I would bring a friend with me for moral support. Once there, the woman assured me that I could leave my clothes on. She gently touched my upper back with her hand, resting it there for a minute or so. Then she pressed her other hand on my back and began to massage it. I remember trying to stay present in the moment but it was too hard. My muscles had tightened so much that they hurt with the slightest pressure. After about five minutes I could no longer take it and told her to stop.

Back in the sexual survivor's group, I learned that the hypersensitivity I'd always been told was a fault, actually functioned like an early warning radar system. I had visceral reactions to certain people without knowing why. And while I knew about 'triggers' – i.e., objects, locations, sounds, smells, and/or people who spark traumatic memories – my personal warning instincts were...*different*.

For example, there was a man in my 12-Step community whose wife was a good friend of mine. I felt guilty for my negative reaction to him because I had no concrete reasons to dislike him. He and his wife asked me to housesit for them while there were on a vacation.

While there, I rummaged in a desk drawer for a pen, and found a stack of pornographic paperbacks. These books were not the adult variety kind, rather they were stories and drawings of children having sex with adults. As I flipped through a few pages, I felt horrified.

Other group members had similar internal radar detectors. Gradually I learned to trust my gut feelings when I met someone who felt icky to me. I came to understand that my radar wasn't just tuned to sexual offenders, but to people who struggled with addictions and other internal wounds.   I think the popular term, 'acting out' is *sanitizing* the truth. To say a child molester is acting out, dilutes the severity of his or her actions. The truth is a child molester is a person who sexualizes and/or rapes a child for his or her own sexual gratification. I believe *any* form of child sexual exploitation is a form of sexual abuse.

I was not allowed to graduate from the group until I completed the section on anger. My anger was crammed tight into my iron boxes, and once in a while one of them would pop open, with my anger spilling out. I hated myself when that happened. I realized that I was out of control, but was powerless to reel my emotions back in. The idea of deliberately opening one of those boxes filled me with dread. What if it unleashed a tidal wave? What if I drowned in the raging tsunami of anger?

My fellow group members each completed therapy and left. The counselor told me to practice letting go of my anger at home and to continue working on it during a private session with her. I had witnessed what she meant by "work" in group therapy sessions.

One-by-one, each person in group had started to slowly build up anger as they thrashed a pile of pillows. Some screamed their rage, while others collapsed onto the pillows sobbing. Each time the sheer rawness of their pain swallowed me, triggering an intense desire to flee.

At home, once my daughter left for school, I looked for an instrument to use as a bat. I settled on an empty pot to beat my pillow with but I felt foolish and silly. I tried to force my anger to appear by vocalizing my feelings and imagining Galen and Grandma Mabel. But here's the thing: it takes a certain amount of self-esteem to be angry about something, and I wasn't there yet. I still blamed myself. I still believed that what happened was my fault and I didn't deserve to be angry at anyone. Plus, placing responsibility on someone else seemed like admitting that I was a victim. I hated, hated, hated that.

I debated not returning to see the counselor but knew I had to. Not because I thought it was the healthy choice, but because I didn't want anyone to know I'd quit. One thing I learned while completing my recovery work is to keep trying no matter what. To do less is to *fail*. Because of the 12-Step community, I witnessed hundreds of examples every week from people who kept *trying*. Some people tried to take it one-day-at-a-time, while others (like me) tried to make it one-hour-at-a-time. I reminded myself that this felt scary because it wasn't the old, familiar way I had done things. I was stepping into an unfamiliar place of light.

The next week I talked to the counselor and told her my fears, but added I was willing to do whatever it takes. She said to me, "Doing what we want is different than doing what it takes. We always look for the easiest, softest ways to grow, but usually it takes the hard stuff that we don't want to do."

I beat the hell out of that stack of pillows. And afterward I did feel a sense of release. I knew that one exercise wasn't going to be enough. There was a lot more work ahead of me.

Hypnotherapy

I still worked in radio, and along with my on-air and production shifts I was the station's public service coordinator. Per the Federal Communications Commission, radio station licenses require owners to provide a certain number of minutes each week for public service announcements (PSAs) and/or programming. Local non-profit groups could request a 30-60 second PSA. One day I took a call from a man who said he was a local hypnotherapist and counselor at a non-profit organization. He explained that he was hosting a free conference for area counselors to discuss hypnotism as a potential psychotherapy.

He was also looking for a volunteer to demonstrate his ideas. He asked me, "Are there any 'issues' you want to work on?"

Uh...

I asked if he used regressive hypnotherapy. I told him a brief version of my inpatient stay at the Walker Center. He seemed delighted to have me as a volunteer.   When I arrived at his office there were about ten counselors waiting. The man gave a brief presentation and then introduced me. He explained to the counselors, "Today, I'm going to use hypnosis to uncover some hidden memories from her childhood, and then demonstrate how the process can work to heal those memories." He added the session would be videotaped.

All I knew about hypnosis was what I had seen in movies, where the person doesn't remember anything afterward. But actually, the hypnotist has to specifically instruct you to forget. In my case I remember one part of being under very clearly – once I was relaxed, the hypnotist instructed me to go back to a period in my childhood when I felt threatened. Grandma Mabel appeared.

The hypnotist asked me to describe what I was seeing, and suggested I could erect a thick glass wall between Grandma Mabel and me. He assured me that she couldn't get through the wall. Then he called on my higher, adult self to be "present," and to comfort the scared child within. He suggested that my inner child could speak directly to Grandma Mabel and tell her whatever I wanted. He assured me that I was safe. I heard my voice shake and sound like a child's as I looked through the thick glass. I told my grandma I did not like it when she dressed me, bathed me, and *touched* me. I told her I didn't want to hear her talk bad about my mom, and I hated it when she said I should be ashamed of myself for staying with my mom. Inside even as I was speaking, I could feel a weight lifting from my stomach.

He did another demonstration while I was under, but I only heard about it later from one of the counselors who had been there. The hypnotist thought it would be fun to demonstrate how the power of suggestion can make people agree with statements they would never agree with if not hypnotized. He led me through a series of rational statements to get me to conclude that there was no God, and that nothing divine existed in the universe. When

I learned what he did, I felt angry and used. I contacted him and asked him to give me the videotape. He claimed he didn't have it anymore, but I didn't believe him, and accused him of unethical behavior.

If someone was to ask me today about regressive hypnosis, I would happily share the positive aspects of my experience but also offer a strong caution to double check the practitioner's licensing and reputation.

Choosing Healthier Environments

A few months later I left my career in radio. Broadcasting, like other forms of entertainment, tends to attract people with problems. At both stations I worked for, many of my co-workers struggled with untreated codependent behaviors and/or alcohol, addiction, sex, or food issues. This environment could be deceptively toxic for someone who is trying to stay clean. My boss Bobby* acted like a sex addict, such as blazingly watching porn at work.

Bobby was fascinated by what I'd learned about sex addicts during my stay at the Walker Center. I suggested he read Dr. Patrick Carnes' book, *Out of the Shadows*. The book discusses and defines the three basic levels of sexual addiction. Bobby laughed and declared that he must be a sex addict. I didn't laugh with him. I replied, "Seriously Bobby? If you want to explore sex addiction there are Sex Addicts Anonymous meetings on Wednesday nights. You should attend."

A few days later, Bobby suggested that I wear short skirts and high heels – a ludicrous request, given that my male co-workers wore jeans and t-shirts to work. I was the only woman on the air staff. Next, he left a woman's magazine on my desk with a note saying, "Page 53 should be of interest to you." On that page was an article titled *Sleeping Your Way to the Top*. I confronted him about his behaviors, but nothing changed.

Eventually I reached out to a female attorney named Kristina, who I knew from the 12-Step community. She told me I had a solid case to sue my boss for sexual harassment but then she asked me a fair question, "What do you want?" I thought about that with rigorous honesty. I wasn't interested in money. I just wanted to go to work and dress like everyone else. I wanted equality and I wanted to stop keeping an eye out for Bobby. Ultimately, I wanted Bobby to stop leering, commenting on my appearance, insinuating and harassing me.

Kristina replied, "It sounds like you want your boss to change his behavior." I agreed. She asked, "What happens to us when we try to force someone to change?" I felt like I was talking to my Alanon sponsor and saw her point. If I took Bobby to court, I would be focusing my time and emotional energy on trying to make him change his behavior, when my energy would be better spent working on my own recovery and serenity.

This realization made me admit that the toxicity in my work environment was endemic, and I was already slipping into old patterns of angry self-righteousness, railing against someone else's bad behavior, taking their inventory, and spending way too much time trying to get them to change. I was acting the same way with Bobby as I had with Walter before I found Alanon.

Did I believe my boss met the criteria of a sex addict? Absolutely.

Did I believe I could *force* any addict to change? I knew better than that.

It wasn't fair, but 'fair' is a word children use when they are trying to navigate the world. I was heartsick and angry that I chose to leave my profession, but deep down I knew I made the right decision for me. Staying in radio wasn't worth my recovery.

Bobby tried to talk me out of quitting, promising that he would change his behavior (while at the same time rolling his eyes that I "couldn't take a joke"). But it wasn't just about his behavior. I had reached a higher level of mental wellness and recovery, and no longer wanted to work in an unhealthy environment. It's akin to an alcoholic who stops drinking and realizes that it's stupid to keep hanging out at bars. At that point in my career, I was hosting the morning show. I finished my final air shift and said goodbye to my listeners.

The Healing Piece

I read and heard about 'body memories' and how our bodies can react to certain events or triggers years later, even if we don't remember what happened. One morning my car wouldn't start, so a friend came over to jumpstart it. He told me to sit in the driver's seat and he would tell me when to turn the key. I watched him pull jumper cables from his truck. He walked to the front of my car and attached the cables to my car battery.

At this point I physically froze. Terror washed through me, causing my body to shake and jerk. My hands were numb, and my mind went blank. Sometime later, my friend tapped on the driver's side window trying to get my attention.

"Start the engine!" he yelled. I tried to force my hand to grasp the car key, but I couldn't move. Finally, I opened the car door and bolted out of the car – not stopping until I was almost a block away. Why? I don't know. It was the same panic and fear I felt when I tried to put a plug into an outlet. I guessed the jumper cables triggered a body memory.

I heard about a local project called *"The Healing Piece,"* coordinated by the local Suicide Action Prevention Network. Childhood sexual abuse survivors were invited to submit representative art, poetry, music, dance, sculpture and other mixed media for a public show. Each piece could be submitted anonymously, with the owner's entry numbered without a name. At first I hesitated, wondering if my privacy would be respected. I also wondered if I qualified as an 'abuse survivor.' Seriously. Even at this point my denial was still in charge.

I'd met people who were sexually abused as children and buried their memories, which is what I did by double-and triple-locking them in black iron boxes. Previous researchers theorized that the defensive coping strategies employed by sexually abused children likely stem from denial. Once recovery efforts begin, there appears to be common stages that occur such as emerging awareness.

I decided to submit a series of poems I'd written to The Healing Piece, each one featuring a different stage in my process: denial, emerging awareness, shock, anger, grief, and hope. When I arrived at the building where the displays were showcased, a kind woman assured me that I didn't have to give my name or address. She wrote a number on a sticky tab and told me to place it on the back of my entry. Number 103. Then she gave me a corresponding ticket with the same number.

Inside I saw a long table with other entries being prepped for the show. An old, worn, handmade rag doll with only one button eye held my attention. The woman who took my entry explained, "You can tell how well loved she is, can't you? This entry was on the doorstep in a shoebox this morning. There was a note inside from a woman who said she was 84-years-old and had never told anyone about being abused. This doll was her comfort, and she wanted us to have it. I just wish she could have brought it in so we could make sure it was returned to her." My heart ached. But I understood the old woman's desire to hide her identity.

On opening night there was a special panel featured, including a juvenile court judge, a doctor, a child protection services caseworker, and my friend JC. There were also musical and dance presentations, some that moved me to tears. Later I was asked to record my poems for inclusion in the planned video of the show. I should have felt excited and accomplished, but instead I felt raw and exposed in the recording studio. I was determined to speak from my heart.

Spiritual Steps

After leaving radio I did some freelance ad writing and production work, then was hired in sales for a new company handling business graphic design and printing needs. Once a week I visited the town where the Walker Center was located to develop clients. As it turned out, Fr. Tim's parish was also there. I attended his noon Mass whenever I was in town. Afterward we'd sit in his office and visit for a few minutes.

During one of our discussions the subject of vocations came up, and I admitted there was a time when I felt God was calling me to religious life. Fr. Tim suggested that I look into the Oblate program at Ascension Priory in a nearby town. He referred me to a Fr. Boniface. I didn't even know there was a monastery of monks in the region, but I found my way there on a Sunday morning. I told Fr. Boniface I was interested in learning about Oblates.

At that point I had no idea what an Oblate was, or what kind of program it was. I didn't even know what the word meant. I was acting on faith. Fr. Boniface was dressed in a full-length black habit, and he looked somewhat forbidding but kind. He explained Oblates are lay people who study the Rule of St. Benedict, which guides many monastic communities. The individuals take vows to the house they are attached to, which in my case would be Ascension Priory, a Benedictine community.   What?!

I panicked and said, "Oh my God, no, no. Listen, I'm not a good person." Fr. Boniface lifted his eyebrows and replied, "Really?" I continued, "Oh yeah listen, I swear sometimes. And I smoke...cigarettes."

He gave me a small smile, and said, "Oh I see. Well, those habits don't prohibit you from serving as an Oblate. We happen to have an inquiry weekend coming up, where people interested in learning more can come and stay in our guest rooms, have meals with us and pray with us. Would you like to attend?" I felt deeply that I needed to do just that.

As I packed for the inquiry weekend, I brought packets of sweetener in case the monks didn't use sugar. I wanted to bring my pillow, certain that I'd be sleeping on a bare pallet on the floor. I worried about getting cold because I figured there would be no heat, except on Sundays. I felt pretty foolish when I arrived and met Fr. Joel, the Oblate Director. The modern building was toasty warm, my room had a comfortable twin bed – and pillow – and at lunch the meal was hot and delicious. There was also a variety of sweeteners.

The schedule consisted of morning prayer followed by a conference and then lunch, then an afternoon conference, Vespers in the chapel with the monks at 5pm, then dinner. At 8pm we joined them again for Compline, after which was Grand Silence until the following morning.

Vespers is an evening prayer of praise and thanksgiving in the Roman Catholic, and in other Christian liturgies. It is part of the Liturgy of the Hours, which forms the set of prayers "marking the hours of each day and sanctifying the day with prayer."[25]

The morning prayer is called Lauds, followed by morning Mass. At noon is Sext or mid-day prayer, and then Vespers followed by Compline or night prayer. "From ancient times, the Church has had the custom of celebrating each day of the liturgy of the hours. In this way the Church fulfills the Lord's precept to pray without ceasing, at once offering its praise to God, the Father, and interceding for the salvation of the world."[26]

Once in my room on the first night, I opened the small booklet I had been given, titled *The Rule of St. Benedict*. The pages fell open to a section about the '12 steps of humility'. There was enough similarity to my recovery program that I fell to my knees, my fear evaporating, and realized that God had brought me here.

The next day the group met with Brother Sylvester, who taught us about St. Benedict. Benedict was a sixth-century Italian holy man. He attended school in Rome but was dismayed at the paganism there, so he decided to live alone inside of a cave in a place called Subiaco. Afterward he established multiple monasteries and wrote his Rule.

The Rule is divided into chapters that guide all aspects of monastic life. Today, many lay people seek wisdom from the Rule, and from living in a community with others. Oblates try to live the Rule as much as possible in their lives. They also volunteer if possible, at the monastery they are attached to. Oblates can join either male or female monasteries.

That fall I enrolled in classes at the local community college. I was scared but determined to try. It didn't occur to me that older students have an advantage, with better work ethics and life experience. Many also have a family and a steady job, which they maintain in addition to their studies. It shouldn't have surprised me that I made all As in the classes. My English professor assigned us an "I-Search" paper each semester. I-Search papers are similar to research papers, except the subjects are any topic that means something personal to the student. I chose to write about becoming an Oblate, and since I had a year of novitiate before making my vows (promises) at Ascension, I dove deeper into why

I felt called to do so.

I knew there would be no future romantic relationships. By then I had been celibate for over ten years and had no interest in dating. There was a time when I explored joining a convent and I attended a few vocation retreats, but community life scared me.

First, I think of myself as an introvert.

Second, my social anxiety was still a problem.

As long as I had a job to do it was easy to be in the forefront, but just being social for the sake of being social had always been hard. Growing up, I was often told I was too serious, too sensitive, and "why do you see everything in extremes?" At the same time, I was purposely the clown, joking around with friends. I was naïve about a lot of things, which I learned was a source of amusement to others.

I admitted that my core intention to become an Oblate stemmed from a longing for God and a deep desire to serve in whatever way possible. The Rule of St. Benedict was both simple and complex, and I accepted that being part of a community would present challenges. The vows that Oblates take are the same as other Benedictines: *Stability, obedience*, and *conversatio morum*. The vow of *stability* is to the particular monastery the Oblate professes but more so the stability of perseverance in prayer, and faithfulness to God's call. *Obedience* of course to God, but also to the prior or abbot of the monastery. *Conversatio morum* has been translated differently through the centuries but the best explanation it and the other vows came from a wonderful passage by Ester De Waal:

My Yes means that I try to listen to God in all the many ways that he speaks to me; that I hear and respond – so this is the Yes of obedience. My Yes means that I accept the present and do not try to run away from myself, but remain where I am, firmly rooted and accepting myself – so this is the Yes of stability. My Yes means that I live open to the new and that I am ready to journey on, to move forward whatever the cost – so this is the Yes of conversatio morum.[27]

The idea of stability was unnerving, since up until then I'd never stayed anywhere longer than a few years. But I wanted to try.

After a year of study and prayer I made my final oblation during Mass, taking the name Mary Magdalene. There is one theory that the Mary Magdelene in the bible refers not only to the fallen woman, which I related to, but to the faithful Mary who was sister to Martha. Mary Magdalene was also the first to witness the empty tomb of Jesus and to proclaim that He was risen.

Over the next several years, I volunteered at Ascension when I could. Brother Max taught me the proper way to scrub toilets and wash linens, and Father Andrew and Father Joel were happy for my help in their respective offices.

Genograming

One thing my years in 12-Step groups reinforced was that diving deep with another human and being rigorously honest and true in my relationships felt right and whole to me. I struggled against a natural bent for leadership, still not confident in who I was becoming. It took an incredible amount of work to stay in the *now* each day. Using the new therapeutic tools and exhibiting positive behaviors every. hour. of. the. day. was exhausting.

The good news was my rocking habit was decreasing. The self-mutilation continued, along with a brewing fear of someone breaking into my apartment. My physical health had significantly improved since leaving the Walker Center. There was absolutely a mind-body connection.

The next year of college I had the same professor, and decided to write a paper on genogramming, using my family as an example. I expanded the genogram to include my family members' religion, profession, economic status and so forth. I didn't know much about my mom's or dad's upbringing, and they were both dead, so I reached out to the few relatives I remembered, most of whom hadn't seen or heard from me since I was a child. Galen's brother Archibald told me about how Grandma Mabel's first husband (their father) left them when the boys were young. Mabel took her sons and lived on her father's farm in Oregon for a time. According to Archibald, my great-grandfather was a very, very strict Presbyterian who was swift with physical punishment.

I also learned that Grandma Mabel had been institutionalized at least twice for her mental health, which was something I'd heard but not confirmed. I spoke to my mom's brother and learned that my maternal grandfather had been a cook in the army. My grandma Bea cleaned houses for a living.

By the time I was done with my paper, I saw emerging patterns through three generations. Issues with alcohol and overeating were prominent, along with physical abuse, and out-of-wedlock pregnancies. My ancestors were predominantly blue-collar workers, such as farming, factory and restaurant work, carpentry, and cleaning. Early death was a common factor in my family. There were two prominent religions: Catholic and Presbyterian.

Creating the genogram the same way the group therapist had done in the sexual abuse group, proved too difficult with the various threads I wanted to show, so I devised transparent film overlays with different colored inks to trace specific patterns. Today with computer programs, it's much easier to create a complete genogram tracing any number of factors.

Sharing the Progress

For several years I attended an annual women's retreat and one year was asked to share my story. The retreat attracted a wide range of counselors, along with women in various recovery programs. The three-day event featured small conferences, break-out groups, keynote speakers, bodywork, and meditation. I agreed to speak, even though I was still missing eight years of childhood memories. I knew the reason why I hated brushing or combing my hair and taking baths – that had to do with Grandma Mabel. I also suspected there was a reason I avoided putting objects in my mouth, including toothbrushes – and why I kept tearing the inside of my mouth -- I just didn't know why.

About a hundred faces stared at me from the podium. The support and love I encountered in 12-Step groups was abundant in the room. I was shaking with stage fright and taking deep breaths to calm myself. Even though I'd worked in broadcasting for many years, there's a big difference between talking to a live audience in the open and talking to a live audience from behind radio booth walls.

Besides, I wasn't there to be a radio personality. I wanted to share my story with honesty, openness, and willingness – the H.O.W. of recovery. My counselor Elberta from the Walker Center was in the audience. After I finished my talk, she came up to me and gave me a great hug.

"You know so much more now!" she said. Then she said something I still remember to this day: "You are a miracle, truly. I wouldn't have been surprised if you had wound up in a long-term institution, but you've worked very hard and I want you to hear me when I tell you, that you are a miracle."

14

ropes

Traumatized people chronically feel unsafe inside their bodies: The past is alive in the form of gnawing interior discomfort. Their bodies are constantly bombarded by visceral warning signs, and, in an attempt to control these processes, they often become expert at ignoring their gut feelings and in numbing awareness of what is played out inside. They learn to hide from their selves. ~Dr. Bessel A. van der Kolk

A counselor who had heard me speak at the retreat contacted me. She was facilitating a therapy group for young male sexual offenders, ages 14-to-18. She asked if I would share my story with these young men. She explained that the boys were court-ordered to participate in the sessions, but when it came time for the boys to write 'amends letters' to their victim(s), none of them truly understood or accepted the severe injuries their actions caused. The counselor believed that if I shared my experiences, it would help the boys understand the gravity of the situation. I was extremely apprehensive about it but felt like I had to say yes.

The group met in the counselor's small, carpeted office. There were about a dozen teenage boys sitting in chairs in a circle. They stared at me suspiciously.

The counselor said, "We have a guest speaker today, who wants to talk to you about what happened to her and how it has affected her life. Please give her your respect and attention."

I drew a deep breath. With a shaky voice I told the boys my First Story. I spoke about how I initially believed that I had never been abused. Next, I shared my symptoms with them. Lastly, I shared the negative coping strategies I used to get through the day. Even though I didn't remember the abuse per se, my body and buried memories did remember. I also told the boys about how my brother touched me inappropriately and how maybe that seemed minor to them, but the effects were devastating for me. I reminded myself to be vulnerable, knowing that my strength lay in speaking truth.

As I finished talking, tears were sliding off of my nose. Silence permeated the room. When I looked up, I noticed a few of the boys were crying, hiding their faces in the sleeves of their shirts. None of the boys returned my glance. Finally, one of them spoke.

He stared at the floor and said in a low voice, "All I did was put my hand down my sister's pants. It's bullshit that the judge made me do this because that's all I did! It's kind of like what your brother did to you... all he did was feel your boobs..."

Then the boy choked up and asked, "Do you think my sister is going to end up like you, because of what I did?"

I didn't know how to answer his question.

Later I ran into the counselor at a 12-Step meeting, and she thanked me again. She said my story had a real impact on most of the boys, especially when they realized how their actions *could* impact others.

She added, "Of course some of the boys tried to laugh it off. They are still in denial."

I understood. My own journey was filled with denial – false stops and starts, spirals and staircases, and boxes.

During SA meetings several people would identify themselves as relationship addicts and/or romance addicts. I had also identified myself as a relationship addict while inpatient care, but I was unsure of what that really meant or even if the title even fit me. Maybe I was a sex addict but in a reverse way.

There is a sad similarity among sex addicts – most were sexually-abused as children. As a result, many sex addicts have been conditioned to use sex as a *tool* to manipulate and control others. Many sex addicts become overly sexualized themselves, starting in childhood. Many pedophiles were also sexually-abused as children.

One of the people in my SA group suggested that if I wanted to know for sure, I should complete the *SA First Step Inventory*.

The SA First Step Inventory is not only precise but difficult to complete. Once done, the person shares their inventory in front of an SA group. These individuals openly admit that they were unable to effectively manage their addiction and as a result felt powerless.

Some of the questions include:

- What is your earliest recollection of sex?

- How old were you, and what did you feel the first time you masturbated?

- What about pornography – detail your use and abuse.

- Describe a time when your sexual behavior was dangerous to you and/or others.

- How have you used people for sexual gratification?

- How has your addiction caused financial stress?

There were also other questions about my sexual history and I answered each one as honestly as possible.

When I read my inventory aloud at an SA meeting, there were 30 or so people in attendance. I don't remember looking up, because I felt naked, exposed and ashamed.

I detailed how I *chose* men who were emotionally and/or physically unavailable or unwilling to be truly present (i.e., Jeremy, Walter and Galahad), and how I kept them at arm's length, while simultaneously obsessing about them to the point of ignoring the rest of my life.

I'm pretty sure that I gave off a signal that said, "Come close. No, stay back." And if a man (or woman) wanted more from me, I fled. In other words, I created chaos in every relationship, because chaos and fear were my comfort zones.

I also detailed the sexual abuse incident with my brother. I talked about how Grandma Mabel used to 'bathe' me.

There was also an incident involving a priest. The first time Pops was sent to Vietnam, we moved to Idaho and attended a tiny local Catholic church. Only thirteen families worshipped there. The priest showed up on Sunday mornings and had a number of churches to cover in the region.

At the end of Mass, he greeted everyone at the door as they left. But he'd often pull me back against his chest while he talked with my mom. The priest would wrap his vestment around me so no one could see what he was doing. He slid his hands up my dress, cupping my young breasts and squeezing them. I felt sick and helpless.

After a couple of months someone told the priest that my mom had divorced my father before marrying Pops.

We arrived at Mass the following Sunday and the priest spotted us in the pew. He walked over to quietly speak with Mom. I couldn't hear what he was saying to her but whatever it was, it caused her to go rigid. Then she grabbed my hand and stood up. Lee stood up too, and we walked out of the church.

I found out years later that even though Galen was dead by then, the priest told my mom that she could not take communion, and... something else, which made her and Lee feel so humiliated they never went back. I had to take Catechism, but Mom made sure I took a bus to the next town, where it was taught by nuns. Lee took confirmation classes but refused to be confirmed, saying he was done with the church.

Mom asked me if I wanted to be confirmed, but I knew that I'd have to make a confession first, and it would probably be with *that* priest. The idea of confessing to anyone horrified me, because it was drilled into my bones not to talk about things that happened. I told my mom that I didn't feel ready to be confirmed.

In my SA inventory, I also included examples of covert sexual abuse, which is even more common than overt sexual abuse.

One Easter while in the 5th grade, I received my first bra. Lee's Easter basket was filled with candy and something he had been wanting. My Easter basket had two small, unwrapped boxes with photos of ladies in their bras. I was embarrassed and confused.

Mom said, "Happy Easter! We got you two bras because you definitely need to be wearing bras from now on. It is apparent that you need something, especially when you wear a t-shirt. Go on and try them on!" She was so...delighted. And I was so...mortified.

Lee laughed and Jim said, "Well, you can model them for us."

"Yes, go on, and try them on. Then you can show us," my mom said as if it were no big deal. I took the basket, ran upstairs to my room, crawled under the covers and rocked. It was a long time before Mom came in and sat on my bed.

"Did you try them on?" She asked. "It's okay, you don't have to model them if you don't want to. Jim and Lee were just joking around."

The next day at school as I was changing into my gym clothes, the other girls started laughing and pointing at my bra. I was the only 5th grade girl in school who wore one. After that I made it a habit to change in a bathroom stall before and after gym class.

I usually wore layers of clothing because I felt safer, even in Hawaii's sweltering, tropical heat. One day I slid on a long-sleeved gold turtleneck and went for a walk on the base's beach. At the far end of the shore were a group of young Marines in khaki uniforms. It looked like they were having a picnic. I steered clear of them.

That night Jim and Mom had a private discussion in their bedroom. Then Mom took me aside. She chastised me for wearing form-fitting clothes like the turtleneck. She told me to never wear it again.

Mom explained that Jim was at a troop-outing on the beach and that several of the young Marines were whistling and joking about my breasts and figure. There was an unspoken tone in

Mom's voice that suggested it was my fault. Those types of insinuations were not new to me or any girl in American culture. As a female I was flooded with insinuations that reduced strong, capable women to sexual objects. These messages are still rampant in advertisements, sitcoms, movies, magazines, overt jokes featured on sitcoms, and sexual comments about women.

I admitted to the SA group that I dissociated from sex. I also shared with them how ashamed I was that I wasn't a better lover. I studied books like *Joy of Sex* because I was desperate to learn how to fake it. I had been sexual with five men in my life – two of whom I was sleeping with during the time frame of a couple months. I told the group that I still didn't know who my daughter's biological father was.

I said I clung to unhealthy relationships, playing conversations over and over in my head trying to figure out how to be whoever I thought my partner wanted me to be. Even worse? I wanted to control him with the right words.

When I finished my SA inventory, one of the old-timers was the first to respond.

He said, "I don't think I've ever heard a First Step Inventory be so detailed and honest. In my opinion you're definitely not a sex addict, but you sure sound like a relationship addict."

A sea of heads nodded.

In addition to Andie's normal teenage adjustments and hormonal shifts, she still harbored unresolved anger about the divorce. I knew my mental health problems were affecting her too. I decided we should enter family therapy. A friend recommended a counselor named Howard who had advanced training and professional experience in anger management.

Andie did not want to go but I insisted, and it was definitely the right decision. During one of our earliest sessions with Howard, he uncovered how my codependency issues were triggering my daughter's anger. I learned that I had a habit of making excuses, blaming myself, and trying to control Andie's feelings. No surprise there. Over time, I learned how to develop (and enact) better boundaries with my daughter. I began to lean on my 12-Step friends and the couple's group, which often meant emergency late-night calls stemming from fears, worries, and doubts about my parenting methods.

On my one-year anniversary after leaving the Walker Center, I was invited back to spend the day with the other patients. My former counselor Elberta and the director Gail met with me to plan my day. In addition to attending therapy with the current group of patients, they said I would participate in a newly added Ropes Course.

I'd heard about it – a specially-designed square built 30 or more feet off of the ground that included ropes and wires. It was a form of experiential therapy that has been proven to be effective as an "adjunct to inpatient therapy,"[28] particularly for anxiety.

I must have looked aghast because Gail leaned in and gently patted my shoulder.

"Surrender," he said with a smile.

The square was formed with four large upright wood poles anchored in the ground. Each side of the square was connected by a specific type of rope and wire. I was put in a climbing harness and introduced to a patient who would be my 'belayer' - the person on the ground controlling my safety rope. If I fell, my belayer would provide counterweight so I wouldn't crash to the ground. I climbed the ladder to a small platform. Then, the counselor instructed me to walk across it to the next pole. But first, I had to verbalize my fears.

Given my fear of heights, and my disconnection to my body, my legs were already shaking. I could feel myself detaching.

But one advantage to being a full-on codependent is that sometimes the non-stop quest for perfection, and unrelenting urge to people-please comes in handy. I was determined to show everyone how far I'd come since my inpatient stay.

The walk to the second pole was over a sturdy timber log. The counselor clipped my harness to a thick top wire. I held back, frozen in place from taking that first step. I thought about every step I'd taken during my recovery and remembered that every time I had felt the same fear, I still did it. I stepped off of the platform, clenching the wire above me as I crossed over.

From the second platform, there was only a thin wire to traverse ahead of me. I had no idea how I would get across it.

The counselor asked me what I was feeling. I struggled to

find the right words, besides *terror*. He asked why I was afraid, relentlessly pressing me to dig deeper.

"Of falling!" I whispered, tears streaming down my flushed cheeks. "Of falling!" I said again, louder this time.

"Okay, what will happen if you fall?" He challenged. "Do you trust your harness? Do you trust your belayer?"

I was sobbing, "I don't know... I mean, yes, I trust my harness."

"What will happen if you fall?" he asked again.

My knees buckled, and I slid against the second pole with my arms wrapped tightly around it.

"Get up. You can do this," he said.

I took a deep breath and felt trapped.

I was aware that there was not an out, except with that wire. I felt helpless. Slowly I stood up, and stepped onto the wire, as it sagged a bit from my weight. I slowly inched across until I was in in the middle, equidistant between the poles, still holding on to the top wire.

"Catherine, I want you to let go of the top wire," the counselor said. I froze and shook my head in defiance, "Nope, cannot do that."

I started crying. "What are you afraid of?" The counselor pressed.

"I don't know!" I insisted.

"Sure, you do. Let go of the wire now!" he demanded.

I felt red-hot anger wash through me and raised my voice to him, all kinds of words rushing out in a type of word vomit. "I told you that I can't! If I let go, then I'll fall and if I fall... then, I'll lose control...and I'll be bad!"

In that microsecond I let go of the top wire and fell, dangling from my harness in mid-air. A warm, wet trickle of hot urine ran down my pantlegs.

"Okay, that was good, Catherine! Look, you fell and it's okay. What are you feeling?" He asked in a gentler tone.

All the air was nearly gone from my lungs. A wave of peace and surrender washed through me as I realized the truth – I had lost control, and it was okay. I was not a bad person after all.

"You can stand up now," the counselor instructed.

My muscles felt weak and unsteady from utter exhaustion, but I managed to stand on the wire by using the top wire for balance and made it across to the third platform.

I don't remember now what the course design was between the third and fourth platforms. Maybe I blocked it out.

The final leg of the course involved walking across small boards attached by ropes. The wind made the boards sway. I barely remember getting across them until I was back on the first platform.

Immense relief flooded through me. I'd had made it.

"Okay, now for your final task," said the counselor. "I'm going to unclip your harness from the safety wire. Then I want you to jump off the platform to the ground."

I looked at the counselor like he was insane.

"Catherine, you have to trust your belayer on the ground to break your fall," he explained.

I looked down the 30-or-40 feet and saw the stranger holding the rope below. I looked back at the third leg of the course and felt a deep strength that I'd never experienced before.

I closed my eyes, let go and jumped.

After Andie graduated high school, she left for a summer internship with an out-of-state theater company. I was close to completing my associate degree. My advisor at the college urged me to apply to her alumni, Amherst College in Massachusetts to enter their renowned writing program. I felt intimidated, certain that if I somehow managed to get accepted I'd fail because I'm not a great writer. Competent, yes.

Also, there was the hard reality of costs. I was forty years old at the time and had zero savings. I qualified for the U.S. government's need-based federal subsidy program, the Pell Grant. But the highest amount awarded barely covered my tuition at the local two-year community college. While going to school, I'd been working thirty-hours each week in an office for a heating and air-conditioning company, and another ten hours per week in the college's work-study program as a student assistant in the writing lab. Between those hours, raising Andie, volunteering at Ascension Priory, and maintaining a full-time credit load, I knew there was no way that I could afford a traditional four-year college.

I was also afraid.

I'd worked hard to arrive where I was at, with good mental health and healing taking place.   I was part of a huge village of others making their own journeys and we supported each other. For the first time in my life, I felt stable and sure of my footing. I also felt the Oblate vow of stability and wanted to live close to my monastic brothers at Ascension.   I had the courage to leave, but not the willingness to strike out on my own. After Andie returned in the fall, she enrolled in the same college I went to and shared a large apartment with several other girls who were students there.

Early one morning I sat on my second-floor apartment steps, watching the mist rise over the fields and considered my options. Whatever my career field, I wanted to be an instrument of good. My spiritual life was leading me more in all things. Then I realized something and laughed out loud– I hadn't asked God how He or She wanted me to serve. That seemed like a no-brainer but clearly, deep down I just wanted to be in control.

I quieted my mind and heart and asked. I immediately received an answer.

I didn't like it. Not at all. As loudly as someone standing next to me with a megaphone, I heard and saw the path forward. I would move to Mt. Angel, Oregon, where Ascension's mother house Mt. Angel Abbey was located, and where I could attend their four-year seminary.

It felt like I was being called.

The tiny town of Mt. Angel is known for the large abbey on the hill which has its own zip code and postal name, St. Benedict, Oregon. The Abbey was founded in 1882 by Engelberg Abbey in

Switzerland. It is part of the Swiss-American Benedictine Order.

Mt. Angel also boasts the largest annual Oktoberfest in the Pacific Northwest. Its 3500 population have strong connections to Germany and are primarily Catholic. Mt. Angel is unusual in another way – until fairly recently, the only church allowed to build within city limits was the Roman Catholic Church. I was also surprised to learn the local school was named St. Mary's Public School.

I knew some of the monks who lived at Mt. Angel Abbey, because a few of my brothers at Ascension had either studied or transferred there. Brother Max and I were friends, and we coordinated an annual ecumenical retreat weekend at Ascension Priory for people who were HIV+ or who had AIDS. Fr. Boniface asked me to take one of the young monks with me when I left, who was starting his first year of seminary.

There is a beautiful Benedictine saying, *"We come with empty pockets to serve the Lord."*

I moved to Mt. Angel with only some clothes, books, my guitar and a few dishes. I gave away everything else I owned, including my extensive library of science fiction books.

I found a room and bath rental owned by a vibrant older woman named Beverlee. I signed up for the seminary choir but couldn't pull together the financial resources needed to attend additional classes. I didn't have a paying job at that point. During my three years in Oregon, I worked a number of part-time jobs including office positions, advertising voice and production work, and ironically considering I couldn't pass basic algebra, I was a teaching assistant for a math class at Chemeketa Community College.

I was also hired as a coordinator for a community-building project directed by Dr. Sharif Abdullah of the Commonway Institute. He had a grant from the Rockefeller Foundation to work in three communities that were undergoing massive shifts in demographics. One of these communities was Woodburn, Oregon located near Mt. Angel.

Over the previous ten years, Woodburn saw a huge shift in population from temporary, seasonal Latino farm workers to permanent residency with families accompanying their working loved ones. The majority of workers and families were monolingual Spanish speakers. Around the same time, a 150-home tract was built for predominately retired white middle-class senior citizens. Already living there since the 1960's was the largest contingent of Orthodox Russian Old Believers outside of Russia, with many speaking no English. They lived apart from the mainstream and have preserved their religion, culture, rituals and dress from the 1700's.

Dr. Abdullah's project involved bringing stakeholders from the traditionally enfranchised communities – people like the mayor, community leaders, school and church leaders, etc. – to the same table with the traditionally disenfranchised people – i.e., non-English speakers, low-income individuals, and groups identified as *other*. There was no dominant language in the room because we used three-way simultaneous translation equipment to better understand each other. Everyone wore a headset and spoke in their preferred language. In my personal life, I also served on the local church parish council and co-taught the parish senior confirmation class.

Once a week I drove thirty miles to meet with Brother Adrian, a monk from Mt. Angel who had taken a leave of absence and was living in Portland at the time. Br. Adrian and I first met at the HIV+/AIDS Idaho retreat. He was diagnosed HIV+ after he had been professed as a monk at Mt. Angel. We became friends, and the more I heard about his past the more determined I became to write his biography. We met every week to unpack the stories of his life. His disease had progressed to full blown AIDS. It was a joy and honor to record his memories and reflections.

After I had been in Oregon for a few months, my depression began to worsen. I tried over-the-counter remedies like St. John's Wort, but it didn't help. I also went to local Alanon meetings, stepped up my exercise routine, and tried to get plenty of sleep. But the black nothingness sucked me further down.

I needed help.

I had failed again.

15

new pathways

We cannot become what we want by remaining what we are. – Max Depree

I had no health insurance. I was working three jobs but they were part-time. The money I made was enough for my rent, food, gas, and a few extras. I knew the free health clinic did not offer counseling services. The black undertow was stronger than ever.

I was fragile, barely making it through most days. I felt utterly hopeless.

Then I heard an ad on the radio – *"Depressed? The Lily Drug Company is seeking people who are moderately to severely depressed for a clinical study. You will receive medication and counseling."*

I was being thrown a lifeline.

The screening process was thorough. In addition to a full physical workup with a doctor, including an electrocardiogram and a stress test, I spoke to a psychiatric nurse and then a counselor. The counselor diagnosed me with major depressive disorder (MDD) and enrolled me in the study. I made regular trips to Portland to pick up the study medication and meet with the counselor. I also took a weekly telephone assessment.

This drug study involved measuring the efficacy of fluoxetine alone versus fluoxetine combined with a low-dose blood pressure medication. The hope was that the fluoxetine and blood pressure combination would work more quickly and be more effective. It usually takes antidepressants between two-to-four weeks to start working and for a patient's depression to substantially lift.

Important Note: Throughout this book are references to research, history and current information about trauma, mental illness and/or addiction. All the research I found is predominantly from Europe and North America; readers should not infer a global application. This is because most epidemiological and historical data from North America and Europe were conducted using subjects who were overwhelmingly Caucasian, and often only male. For example, the famous alcohol use screening tool of 20 questions was developed by Johns Hopkins University in the 1930s, targeted for English speaking white males.

According to the Mayo Clinic, researchers have connected depression to all of the following[29]:

- **Biological differences.** People with depression appear to have physical changes in their brains. The significance of these changes is still uncertain but may eventually help pinpoint causes.

- **Brain chemistry.** Neurotransmitters are naturally occurring brain chemicals that likely play a role in depression. Recent research indicates that changes in the function and effect of these neurotransmitters and how they interact with neurocircuits involved in maintaining mood stability may play a significant role in depression and its treatment.

- **Hormones.** Changes in the body's balance of hormones may be involved in causing or triggering depression. Hormone changes can result with pregnancy and during the weeks or months after delivery (postpartum) and from thyroid problems, menopause or a number of other conditions.

- **Inherited traits.** Depression is more common in people whose blood relatives also have this condition. Researchers are trying to find genes that may be involved in causing depression.

I also learned that depression can be a common adverse reaction to trauma and loss. I recall one addiction treatment specialist saying, "I have never met an addict who was not profoundly depressed."

Brief History of Depression and Treatments

For more than 2,500 years, both research and records from people with depression have given similar symptoms and descriptions. First, there has always been a recognized distinction between normal, emotional sadness, and disordered depression, and most often the difference was accounted for by context. This contextual approach did not focus merely on symptoms, "but emphasized that to be considered as disorders, depressive reactions must be of disproportionate duration or severity to the situation in which they emerged."[30]

In the past, various cultures believed that depression is caused by demons and evil spirits. Treatments consisted of burning, beating, starvation, etc., individuals who were depressed. Christian beliefs during the Middle Ages reinforced this theory. Common treatments used to involve exorcisms and committing depressed people to insane asylums.

In 1621, *The Anatomy of Melancholy* was published. The author explained that symptoms without cause are referred to as "disordered depression."

The author wrote, "without a cause is lastly inserted to specify it from all other ordinary passions of fear and sorrow."[31]

Treatments included getting plenty of fresh air, exercise, enough sleep, and good food.

Over time the definitions of depression evolved to include two major types. "The first condition was characterized as deep mental anguish, hopelessness, complete joylessness, stupor, and suicidal thoughts and/or actions." People with disordered depression were referred to specialized healers, who treated their "insane conditions."

The second condition belongs to a brand-new category called, "nervous disorders" with the causes found in physiology, such as brain lesions.[32]

In the eighteenth and nineteenth centuries, depression was commonly seen as a weakness in character or temperament and couldn't be changed.

"Treatments during this period included water immersion (staying underwater for long as possible without drowning), and/or using a spinning stool to put the brain contents back into their correct positions. Additional treatments included diet changes, enemas, horseback riding, and/or forced vomiting. Benjamin Franklin is also reported to have developed an early form of electroshock therapy during this time."[33]

In the late nineteenth century, German psychiatrist Emil Kraepelin and Austrian neurologist Sigmund Freud took very different positions on the topic. Dr. Kraepelin strongly believed that the context, including a person's history, should be examined to distinguish "disordered depression" from "situational depression."

Freud thought otherwise. He said, "Although grief involves grave departures from the normal attitude to life, it never occurs to us to regard it as a morbid condition, and hand the mourner over to medical treatment."[34]

In the late nineteenth and early twentieth centuries, lobotomies and electroconvulsive shock therapy were sometimes used in cases of severe depression. Between 1920 and 1950 behavioral psychology pushed the idea that depression is a "learned behavior" and as a result it could be "unlearned." New treatments arose from this theory, including cognitive behavioral therapy developed by Dr. Aaron Beck in the 1960s. His goal was to treat depression.

In the 1950s the first major pharmacological breakthroughs happened. This included the discovery of tricyclic antidepressants. Researchers continued to debate theories and discuss the classifications of depression.

"Similar to the other major diagnoses in psychiatry at the time, opinions regarding the classification of depression at the end of the 1970s featured an extraordinarily broad range of unresolved conflicts on how best to measure this condition."[35]

Dr. Kraepelin's diagnostic work influenced the Diagnostic and Statistical Manual of Mental Disorders. In the 1980s, the third edition (DSM-III) was published to provide "a definitive set of symptomatic criteria for depression that has remained stable until the present."[36]

But the DSM-III criteria did not stop the discussion, nor has the current DSM-V, which still puts normal sadness and depression disorder into the same diagnostic criteria.

"The wholesale, and largely arbitrary, adoption of one among a number of competing ways of defining depression perhaps accounts for why – more than 30 years after its promulgation – research on depression has yet to yield any major breakthroughs in the understand of the etiology, prognosis, or treatment of this condition."[37]

In 1987 a game changer was approved by the U.S. Food and Drug Administration (FDA) for treatment of depression – Prozac (fluoxetine). Fluoxetine is just one in the classification of drugs known as selective serotonin reuptake inhibitors (SSRIs). The FDA has approved fluoxetine for the treatment of the obsessive-compulsive disorder (OCD), major depressive disorder, bulimia nervosa, and other anxiety disorders.

In adults, "SSRIs have been shown to have powerful and broad-spectrum therapeutic results in OCD."[38]

My own OCD was not as pronounced as it was in my youth, but I still had to check doors, windows, and stove every night, and once again, I was rocking. The habit of counting and rhyming was still part of my daily life.

Once approved, the pharmaceutical industry made billions off of fluoxetine and by the year 2002 the number of prescriptions had risen to 33,320,000.[39]

In the past, researchers believed that fluoxetine worked by regulating serotonin levels in the brain, leading many to equate major depressive disorder (MDD) with a chemical imbalance. That supposition has recently been challenged.

"At its simplest, the hypothesis proposed that diminished activity of serotonin pathways plays a causal role in the pathophysiology of depression. ... Simple biochemical theories that link low levels of serotonin with depressed mood are no longer tenable."[40]

In other words, SSRIs can be very effective in some cases but it's still unclear why they work for some people but not others.

First, people with severe depression tend to respond most meaningfully to antidepressants, while people with mild-to-moderate depression typically do not. Second, for a majority of people who do respond to SSRIs, serotonin is crucial. Some (not all) depressed people have low levels of serotonin in their brains. SSRIs are designed to increase serotonin levels. Thus, depleting serotonin in depressed patients can and often does cause relapses. Third, there is a "brain-as-soup" theory, which hypothesizes that the depressed brain simply lacks serotonin, and although that is true for some depressed people, it is naïve to say this is true for all depressed people. In fact, clinical trials show unequivocally that only a *fraction* of severely depressed people respond to serotonin-enhancing antidepressants, like SSRIs.[41]

Twenty-plus years after I participated in the clinical drug study, I learned that research had made further breakthroughs in understanding and treating depression. A research paper published in 2019 concluded that there is an association between low-grade peripheral inflammation and altered brain structural integrity, which are interrelated biological correlates in patients with MDD.[42]

Older treatments like electroconvulsive therapy are still in use, along with newer ones like transcranial magnetic stimulation, vagus nerve stimulation and/or deep brain stimulation, as well as certain psychedelics such as psilocybin. Talk therapy is central to nearly all proven depression treatments. In my opinion, too many doctors prescribe antidepressants without a proper workup or referral.

I felt guilty about taking pills because my 12-Step background had convinced me that a drug is a drug. I had long refused various doctor's recommendations to take an antidepressant. I think it was about control. If I worked hard enough in therapy, attended enough 12-Step meetings, read enough self-help books, and didn't slack off on using recovery tools, I wouldn't need drugs.

I called my friend JC and talked to him about my concerns, expecting him to talk me out of taking the pills in the clinical study. Instead, he said, "I don't know anyone who works as hard as you do at recovery. I believe that there are some people who have clinical depression, in which the chemicals in their brains don't work right. I say trust the doctors and counselors and take the medication."

The results were undeniable. Within two weeks I felt the black undertow recede. My energy and focus returned, and the dark grey fog lifted. I felt physically stronger and healthier. Colors were more vivid than I had ever seen and lights were definitely brighter. My rocking stopped completely! I had never felt this calm. I discussed this with my assigned counselor and she explained the science behind clinical depression vs. situational depression or psychological depression.

In some people the brain's neurotransmitters, which are chemical messengers in the brain, are imbalanced. As a result, no amount of therapy alone can help. I learned that I could not control a biochemical process on my own. It wasn't not my fault.

At the end of the study I was given a six-month supply of fluoxetine. I later learned that I'd been in the control group, which meant I only took Prozac.

My work with Br. Adrian continued and he eventually returned to live at Mount Angel Abbey. For the last several months of his life, Br. Max and I became his primary caregivers in the abbey's infirmary. About a week before he died, Br. Adrian let go of his core secrets, which changed the entire scope of his biography. I knew then that my purpose for being in his life was to help him come clean, and it didn't surprise me when he died a few days later.

I continued to see my family and monastic brothers on visits home. I sent group letters to everyone. Email had been invented by then and one of my close friends from Ascension Fr. Linus* was studying in Rome. We frequently emailed each other and shared on deep spiritual and emotional levels.

A few months after Dr. Abdullah's inclusivity project ended, I got a front office job at a private college and continued doing voiceover work.

Then Pops called me,

He'd been diagnosed with the same damn blood disease my mom had, myelodysplastic syndrome. But in his case, I suspected a mutagenic acquisition either from using pesticides on his parent's farm or from the chemicals he encountered during his Vietnam tours like Agent Orange. (Years later the truth about the contaminated water at the Marine Corps base Camp Lejeune was confirmed, and MDS was a known outcome from exposure. Pops had been stationed there at the time.)

I moved back to Twin Falls, visiting Pops in Hagerman and working as an employment consultant for a contractor at Idaho's Department of Health and Welfare. My job was to meet with clients receiving food stamps and/or cash assistance, and work with them to find employment, get their GED if needed, and/or enroll them in short-term training programs. The end goal for these folks was to transition off public assistance. I taught them classes in resume writing and household budgeting. Clients were also required to gain job skills through volunteer work.

I felt happy to be back near Ascension. I volunteered in the ecumenical ministry center with Fr. Joel, and in the business office with Fr. Andrew. I continued to help coordinate the annual HIV+/AIDS retreat.

As part of my paid job, my boss sent me to a workforce development conference at the Disneyland Anaheim Resort in California. On the last day of the conference, I turned the television on while packing in my hotel room. It was September 11, 2001.

A tower at the World Trade Center in New York City had been hit by a plane. At that point the newscasters were assuring viewers that it was a tragic accident. Minutes later I saw a second plane approaching the smoking tower, as if in slow motion. I went hollow inside, silently praying no, no. The world seemed to shift around me as the second plane hit.

The United States was under attack. No one knew if this was the start of a massive incursion or a terrorist incident. I went to the lobby, which was packed with guests staring at four mounted television screens near the hotel bar. Two of them were tuned to the same national broadcast while the other two were tuned to local stations. All but one had the sound turned off, with written words streaming across the bottom of the screens.

Over the next few hours, I watched the local news coverage of Los Angeles's empty freeways, except for military trucks rumbling along. Airports, train, and bus stations all shut down. According to rumors, a fourth plane was already airborne and enroute to LA. Speculation was that the next probable target would be the "happiest place on earth" aka Disneyland. The theme park was immediately evacuated. My hotel was only blocks away.

I rushed back to my room and called Pops. He was his usual calm, reassuring presence with a lifetime of military experience.

He said, "Stay put. Do whatever the authorities tell you."

I told him about seeing tanks and military trucks on the local news.

"Good," he said. "That means they're already deployed and have a plan."

Hanging up, he reminded me to "keep my head down." Then he told me he loved me.

The conference wrapped up early and most of the attendees went home in their personal vehicles. I had flown in from Idaho and knew I was stranded until the airports reopened. The desk clerk extended my reservation but moved my room to a lower floor as a precaution. I looked again at my return plane ticket dated for that day.

Three days later Los Angeles airport reopened. The atmosphere at the airport was tense. Hastily assembled security measures were employed, while mostly silent passengers moved slowly through the corridors. Like Americans everywhere, we were still in shock.

My Pops and me.

Back home, I focused on my professional and volunteer projects, helping Pops with his medical appointments, and attending Sunday Mass at Ascension. I strove for an emotional, mental, physical and spiritual balance. For me, balance is key to my mental health.

Over the years therapy, treatment, 12-Steps and other healing tools became easier to navigate. I no longer had to remind myself every hour (or minute) to stay present and focused and honor my feelings. But along with wholeness, came the understanding that some people in my life did not accept the person I was becoming, while others were mired in their own illnesses and struggles and just wanted me to keep them company.

These individuals let me know in (subtle and direct ways) that they expected me to react like I used to – codependently. My recovery and healing journey threatened their own personal denial.

As a result, some people tried to shame me back into the false me - the one they *used* to know. I let go of those people. My mental health and serenity were too important to me. I tried to leave with kindness and honesty.

I'd finally quit smoking but still ripped the inside of my mouth everyday. Living alone again meant the recurring fear of break-ins and/or attacks. I checked the doors and windows at least twice before bed.

My startle response was still hyperactive. Br. Inigo at Ascension loved to sneak up on me and watch me jump. He did it as a sign of brotherly affection and always laughed. I didn't have the heart to tell him the cause(s) of my lifelong anxiety. I still had trouble falling asleep on my own and used an over-the-counter sleep aid. My depression was well managed with fluoxetine.

A year after September 11, the contract I worked under ended and I applied for a job as a coordinator for a federally funded demonstration project that focused on juvenile offenders. It was an exciting challenge. Twice a year I flew to one of the partner cities to join workers from the other 28 sites for a weeklong training conference in youth development and leadership.

My first trip was to Dallas, Texas. I always enjoyed flying but felt weirdly tense and anxious at the airport. I was hypervigilant to every aircraft noise or hum. I didn't realize that I was experiencing trauma around my last airplane ride – the one coming home after September 11. When I got to the Dallas hotel, I called a friend to process what I was feeling.

All in all, my life was good.

I had no interest in dating and enjoyed living by myself. I felt I'd been called to a single life. On weekends I treated myself to a movie and meal out, sometimes alone and sometimes with a friend or my Ascension brothers. The College of Southern Idaho catalogs arrived in my mailbox twice a year, and I found a class that I thought would be interesting, *The Twelve Core Functions of a Counselor*.

I was delighted to find my instructor was Howard, my family counselor with Andie. I took the class hoping it would help me become a better listener and friend, and because I'd always been fascinated by the field of psychology. I once briefly thought about becoming a licensed counselor, but I knew that was not my path.

Howard was an excellent teacher. Our class learned the basics of patient screening, intake, assessment, and case planning. He also introduced other therapeutic modalities such as experiential therapy, which I had been exposed to with the ropes course forty feet up at the Walker Center. He decided that part of our semester final would involve participating in a therapy application. We would rappel off the nearby Snake River Canyon rim to the Snake River below, a height of about 400 feet.

Most of us looked at him in horror. I immediately thought back to my Ropes Course experience.

On the appointed day the skies were clear and blue, a common occurrence in the high desert life of southern Idaho. Howard met us at the college, and we followed him to the canyon rim. After hooking up the harnesses and some basic instructions, the first of us turned her back to the empty space and stepped backward off the edge, facing the cliff wall.

She was shaking. She slowly rappelled down to the ground, growing smaller in the distance.

Then it was my turn.

I was shaking too, afraid of heights and losing control, and even more because being on a tether meant a passing bee could hold me hostage.

It took a long time for me to take that first step. I prayed to God for the courage to do it and the willingness to remain emotionally present. After the first few small jumps, I felt brave enough to look down. BIG MISTAKE. Now my whole body was shaking and jerking, and I stared hard at the rock in front of me trying to regain my inner balance and conquer my fears. I jumped a bit further off the rock and down another ten feet or so.

Then my worst nightmare came true. I heard the thick, saw-like sound of a large bee near my head. I panted and froze again, struggling to breathe through the panic. My flight, freeze or fight response was screaming, so I kicked hard off the rock and let the rope slide quickly through my hands, dropping a good twenty feet in the process. I wet my pants but kept quickly descending until I finally felt the ground beneath my feet. I fumbled frantically to remove the carabiner. Then I ran hard about fifteen yards to get away from any more bees that might be lurking.

My favorite monastic brother at the monastery was Fr. Linus. Through the years, our friendship flourished and we kept in touch through email when I left for Oregon, and he left to study in Rome. Once he finished his studies, he returned to Ascension Priory. It was a joy to have him home. One day he surprised me at my workplace and asked to talk outside. He said he had decided to leave religious life.

Immediately I felt like I was drowning on the bottom of the ocean floor, trying to move as the water pressure slammed me down. The air in my body seemed to leave with one exhale. For about a week I was unable to sleep. Every cell of my body stayed in a state of panic. I was locked into intense grief. I couldn't keep food down and I lost weight.

I struggled to show Linus the calmness and support he needed but I was losing my best friend, the person I had the deepest connection with spiritually, emotionally, and intellectually, a friend I considered my soul mate. I was certain he would fall in love and get married to someone, and I wouldn't see him or talk as often.

Linus moved to a city over a hundred miles away, but we visited each other on occasion. My feelings for Linus were changing but I was in denial...until one Saturday morning.

He arrived at my place, and we hugged each other as usual. But this time we both felt a shift we couldn't explain. I pulled away, surprised and scared. The last thing I wanted was to screw up our friendship.

Soon after, we shared our first kiss.

I told myself if Linus felt anything it was only because of his new circumstances. In my mind, there was no possible way he could love me in a romantic sense. All my old self-doubt, fear of sexual intimacy, rejection, and abandonment roared back to life. We talked about our feelings. I reacted like a skittish wild animal, while Linus remained calm and certain. He kept moving closer. I realized that despite all the healing and recovery work I'd done, I'd been single and celibate for fourteen plus years. Who I was now had zero experience with romantic or physical intimacy.

We agreed to be celibate for at least two months. We also kept our new relationship private; he had enough to deal with transitioning to secular life, a new job and a new city. I told myself that this new direction in our friendship could easily fade away, and prayed with a prayer group that Linus would return to Ascension. I meant it. He had a true vocation to serve God.

One weekend I drove the long miles to his city, and we went to see a play at a local theatre. During intermission he spotted his cousin in the crowd and stiffened.

"Linda's here with her daughter," he told me.

I felt very uneasy. Linus had expressly said he didn't plan to tell his family about us yet. Just then I heard his name being called and his cousin was coming toward him. I turned away, pretending not to know him.

When we took our seats again an awkward space was between us. His cousin was sitting just a few rows in back of us, and I wondered had she seen us holding hands earlier?

That night back at Linus's apartment, I couldn't sleep. It was the middle of the night, and I paced the living room in a panic, convinced that I was unworthy of his love and certain he would leave me eventually. I had to cut and run. It didn't matter that my relationships – not just with him – were healthy and true. It didn't matter that I recognized I was letting old tapes to play in my head; I couldn't stop the overwhelming urge to flee. At the same time, I couldn't just leave without letting him know. That would have betrayed my own healing and disrespected my relationship with my best friend.

I woke Linus up to tell him and reassure him my reason had nothing to do with him. Because I did that, our relationship reached a serious turning point. He seemed dazed at first, unwilling to let me go without talking. He knew about my fears of abandonment and my pre-recovery history of running. We talked it through, and I agreed to stay. I knew it was the right decision. Back home a couple days later, I wrote to him:

Dearest Linus,

Above all else this past weekend, I will never forget and will always be grateful for your loving perseverance with me Saturday night. I was momentarily overwhelmed with fear, fragility, old tapes playing, and a lack of sleep. My reaction to leave was warring with my recovery in an intense internal struggle. I did not want to hurt you in any way, nor worry you. I did not want to leave you but felt so raw and vulnerable I wanted to hide.

Emotionally, the past month has been a revelation, and a grace in the gift of our growing love for each other. But with that, for me, has come some old fears. Not just fears about possible loss, but old, recurring echoes: am I good enough, strong enough, healthy enough, and loving enough for you?

I confess, seeing your cousin at the play was also a small part of what was going on for me. Linus, that was not your fault. Under the circumstances you have described in your family, your decision makes good recovery sense. You aren't ready to deal with the likely toxic response from your family once they find out we are together.

For my own behavior, I'm reminded of a reading in one of my daily meditation books, pointing out that feelings can remain the same, but the response is new. After all these years of work, I'd say 95% of my responses are new and healthier these days. Saturday night fell into the 5% and brought a replay of the old reliable response to fear – flight.

I also must not deny that our mutual commitment to a two-month period of celibacy gave me a gift of insight into how strong one old tape still is. It's one I learned as a child, that my true worth to a male person is tied to being sexual. It does make sense that even though I've healed in significant ways, I have not actually been in a sexual relationship in many years.

On the positive side, I recognize that my need to let you know, and to reassure you that you didn't do anything wrong, was even stronger than the fear response to simply leave. Then, your response to me was so utterly accepting and loving. Linus, you tried so hard to help me stay with my feelings and stay present with you, while at the same time I knew you were struggling to stay present to your own feelings. The next day, when you said you knew our relationship would suffer if I left, I realized you were right. I look back today as a result of your insight and recognize the places and people I lost along the way when I took flight in other relationships.

I am grateful God was present, and that you loved me enough to not only accept my fears and be willing to let me go, but to try

*and help me stay and reach the shore again when I felt like I was
drowning. I've never felt so completely naked and yet so completely
accepted and loved.*

I couldn't imagine a life without him, even if he returned to the
monastery and we remained plutonic friends. That night's shift in
our relationship felt like the final piece of a beautiful mosaic that
had dropped into place. It felt right and true.

Slowly, I began to trust that truth.

Several months later we planned our wedding, but only told
Andie and Pops.

It bothered me that Linus didn't want his family to know or
attend our wedding. Linus's reasons seemed sound. He'd spent
a long time learning and healing from family dysfunction to
finally reach a healthy place between honoring his parents and
maintaining his personal boundaries.

I talked with a counselor about my concerns and told her
some of the examples Linus had shared with me about his family
dynamics. She said she respected Linus's decision, then said she
wanted to talk about my abandonment issues, which surprised
me. I honestly believed that I had never been abandoned despite
being left multiple times as a kid, despite both of my parents dying
before I was 26 years old, despite Galahad's abandonment, despite
... despite.

Counselor and author John Bradshaw believes that childhood
abandonment is much more than a parent's death or desertion.

According to Bradshaw, the meaning of child abandonment should include "various forms of emotional abandonment, such as stroke deprivation, narcissistic deprivation, fantasy bonding, the neglect of developmental dependency needs, and family system enmeshment."[43] He added that any form of childhood abuse is a type of abandonment.

I told the counselor that if I did have abandonment issues, they were minimal compared to my lifelong depression. She looked thoughtful for a moment. Then she explained her work with child protection services, where she evaluated infants and toddlers who were abandoned by their parents.

"I can always tell the ones who are depressed," she said, "because they survive. Depression can act like a protective layer to abandonment for infants and children – and adults. The babies who are not depressed are the ones who die," she added.

Her words pierced my heart, and I started crying like a lost child.

It was a breakthrough moment. I accepted that I had abandonment issues. I'd been convincing myself for years how independent I was, how I didn't need people around, how I liked being alone, how I didn't need to physically stay in someone's life, and how terrifying it felt when any adult said that they loved me, especially men. The revelation enlightened and worried me.

After all of the therapy, 12-Step, and other work I'd done to be mentally and emotionally healthy, how could I delude myself about an issue so central in my life? What else was I deluding myself about?

Linus transferred to the local branch at his workplace, and we got married and moved into an apartment in Twin Falls. I was still working on the federal demonstration project. Our relationship was based on years of trust and friendship and for the first time in a sexual relationship, I felt present and alive.

Our transition to living together was seamless. Our love for each other continues to grow, and every day I am grateful beyond words being married to my best friend. The usual transition stuff for newlyweds never happened, I think because we knew each other so well.

I helped Pops stay in his house by doing laundry, cleaning, shopping, and taking him to doctor's appointments. He and Linus shared a special bond, and they were both happy to watch television together while I cleaned.

Pops died on a grey day in January.

Even though it was expected, I was overwhelmed by grief. He'd made his final wishes known to all of us. He also had a will. My stepsister was the appointed executor of his estate. She decided that meant that she was also in charge of his funeral arrangements, obituary, etc. When my stepsister took over, I felt like I'd been stabbed in the stomach. It triggered my past feelings of being excluded from family decisions.

Lee was in Thailand when Pops died, but he came back after the funeral to help sort through the estate. By then I was barely holding on. My pain and grief were combined with rage – rage that Pop's wishes were not being respected. I tried to use the tools I had learned in therapy and 12 Step programs. I allowed myself to feel my feelings, often in the safety of Linus's loving and supportive arms.

I lost my ability to speak up for myself and worse, to speak up for my dad. It took a few years to understand that my anger was also fueled by years of simmering resentment over the way my stepsister had treated my mom and Pops.

When I first moved back from Oregon to help Pops, I made a conscious effort to mend my relationship with her. She had always loved Andie and they had a close, warm relationship. I wanted to support that wholeheartedly, so I tried my best to be friendly with her.

After Pop's death, I felt deeply betrayed by her actions. I didn't realize then how my own feelings contributed.

Linus looked into getting his master's degree in library sciences. He found an online program and then got a job as an assistant librarian in a Massachusetts town named Athol.

We looked forward to the adventure of moving to an area with a different culture and environment and leaving the dusty Idaho deserts behind.

16

progress, not perfection

Your truth doesn't have to be proven, validated, or accepted by others. It may have been denied in your abuse, but it never wavered.
~Jeanne McElvaney,

New England culture is different from the culture in the western United States. Where an antique shop on the Oregon coast might sell a wood sailor's trunk from the early 1900s, a shop in Massachusetts would have one dating back to the 1600s. Where Boise, Idaho became a city in 1863, Athol, Massachusetts incorporated a hundred years earlier. The industrial revolution also had a stronger impact in the East. Athol was a manufacturing and mill town best known for being the headquarters of L.S. Starett Company, maker of high precision tools. Today, most of their manufacturing is done outside the United States. Another large employer called the Union Twist Drill Company closed their doors in the 1980s. The town became depressed after that loss, along with the closing of a handful of key mill companies, all of which showed in the town's struggling infrastructure.

When Linus and I arrived, we learned that despite a population of over 11,000, the nearest grocery store was a town away. There were also no hotels or motels and only a few jobs were available. Linus started his online master's program while employed at the Athol Public Library. I landed a job with the local community coalition, working with a universal health care access program.

Our apartment complex contained six units in each building and a washer/dryer in the basement for tenants. One day I carried a basket of laundry downstairs and saw a pair of small legs sticking almost straight up from the top loading washer.

"Do you need some help?" I asked, startling the young boy. He wiggled his legs down and his head popped out; his arms held a wad of damp clothes.

"No thank you. I couldn't reach everything to get it out," he replied, as he transferred the clothes into the dryer. His name was Caelan and he was six years old. He lived with his mom in the upstairs apartment, and over time they grew to trust us. I looked forward to Caelan's regular visits, usually announced with a knock and the question, "Do you have any snacks?"

My job at the community coalition was to help people access free health care. This was in the early days when the concept of universal health care was being discussed on the political level, and Obamacare had not been approved by Congress yet. Massachusetts decided to launch its own initiative, and the local coalition was engaged in that program.

From my first day on the job, I felt tension from the two other employees – the office clerk and my new boss. I normally could assimilate easily into any job but there was an invisible barrier at this workplace. For example, the coalition coordinated an annual dental health fair. I offered to assist, knowing the only staff were my coworkers. I also had a lot of experience in crafting community projects and events. But my boss made it clear that she didn't need or want my help, which seemed odd. She repeatedly told me, "You don't understand the people who live here like we do. This is a depressed area."

One day Linus arrived at my job to take me to lunch. Just as I was ready to leave, my boss asked for a quick word. She said, "You sound *too happy* when you answer the phone. You need to tone it down, because people around here don't like that." I was taken aback and simply nodded. Linus overheard. We were both stunned. I debated telling my boss about my voice work in Oregon, where I was paid to provide voice-automated telephone services – because of the friendly way I answered phone calls.

In all fairness, physical changes were happening to me – physical changes that were affecting my ability to think clearly. My brain was foggy and I was exhausted by the end of each day. I pushed hard to be focused and present at my desk but often felt like I was trying to break through a thick wall. I'm sure the quality of my work was impacted.   I saw a doctor and had bloodwork done. My thyroid and the endocrine system were out-of-whack, and a routine chest x-ray uncovered two small 'aliens' in my lungs. The heart glitch that showed up on my ECG during the clinical drug study caused my doctor to send me to a cardiologist for an echocardiogram and stress test. The cardiologist had me wear a Holter monitor for 24-hours to monitor my heart rhythm. Next, I was sent to an endocrinologist for more tests. Nothing led to a definitive diagnosis. The heart glitch was benign bigeminy. And with changes to my diet (i.e., eliminating soy) my thyroid readings began to stabilize. But I was still exhausted.

The endocrinologist suggested that I remove as much plastic as I could in the home. He explained there were no accepted studies yet tying plastic to the endocrine system, but his patients had related enough success stories that he thought it was worth a try. Gradually over the next six months, my energy returned, and I began to feel more like myself again.

Later I had another CT scan, and the aliens in my lungs hadn't grown in size so that was a relief.

I was keenly aware of an old adage which said, "When the soul is in pain, the body cries out." Even after all the healing paths I had taken and how happy I was with Linus, I still carried a tightness in every muscle in my body, and I still felt an undercurrent of fear that at any moment my amazing life would be snatched away.

Then one morning I was fired from my job. My boss told me I was let go because she decided I'd broken a HIPAA rule; I supposedly violated a client's privacy. I knew I had not but didn't fight her excuse. Despite acknowledging that I was unhappy in that job, despite knowing the environment was not a good fit for me, and despite being confident that I'm a capable worker, I was still devastated. My self-esteem smashed into pieces. I felt like a failure.

A few months later, I was hired at a Methodist church in a nearby town. I worked in the quiet office preparing the weekly bulletin and handling other tasks the pastor needed. It was the perfect job for me at the time and included a loving and welcoming group of congregants, and a gentle and wise pastor.

I also met a new friend named Mary, and again experienced the universal truth among fellow travelers: those of us who are true to ourselves and who seek and find the divine in others, will meet and know each other immediately on both a heart and soul level. It's spirit meeting spirit.

After two-and-half years Linus completed his third master's degree and began looking for a job out West. We felt out of place on the east coast. He was hired by a regional library system in Washington State. Before we left, we made Caelan a calendar complete with marked days each month so he would know when we would call him, when he could look for a letter or a package from us. That ritual became an annual tradition for many years until he became confident enough not to need the calendars.

Right before Thanksgiving, Linus and I flew to Seattle. We took the rental car and drove to the small town where Linus had been hired as a library manager. The town sits at the base of the Cascade

Mountain range. The main road runs into a dead end.

Driving into town that morning, I saw fields and mountains covered with fir trees. The skies were cloudy; this area north of Seattle gets about the same amount of rain. We went up a small hill onto the main street with Mount Pilchuck rising tall over the vista. I choked up and felt something new. Linus asked, "What's wrong?"

I wiped the tears from my cheeks and said, "I think...I think I'm finally *home*."

We purchased a small, comfortable house in the heart of the town so Linus could walk to work. We decided that I'd offer my skills and time to our new community in whatever ways were needed, instead of getting a paid job. Besides, we were consciously reducing our carbon footprint and had become a one car family.

It was the beginning of the Great Recession, and many people were losing their jobs and even their homes and cars. I created a website that listed local neighbor to neighbor resources for those in need. In the process, I met with many professional and volunteer service providers. From my own experiences and what I'd learned from low-income clients in the budget classes I taught in Idaho, I wrote a guidebook outlining no cost and low-cost avenues for finding housing, food, health care, transportation, clothing, insurance, youth activities, and so on.

I was asked to join a board of directors for the local public safety foundation and eventually became CEO. I volunteered to write the town newsletter and oversee scheduling at the new civic center. I designed a welcome brochure for newcomers, and produced a video about the area, inviting citizens to submit their favorite photos. And because it was so much fun, I was one of the announcers for the annual town festival and parade. Linus and I both planted deep roots in our new community.

I struggled with the fact that for the first time in my adult life, I wasn't earning a living. It took a number of years before I was truly okay with that, because I felt shame and guilt about not contributing financially. Echoes of those negative messages that I am only valuable for what I *do*, rather than for who I *am*.

Linus joined the local community coalition and the Chamber of Commerce. We'd never been so connected to where we lived, and for me it felt true, as if I was meant to be here.

My relationship with Andie also improved along with my mental health, but I still struggled with my codependency with her. One Easter I went to Boise to visit, and she had a frank and impactful talk with me. I wrote about it in my journal...
Andie's "gifts of truth" hit home with me.

Projecting – I had been projecting again, concerned about how she would react, think, and project unrealistic scenarios, such as blaming me for our family issues. She informed me that "she says what she means, and nothing more." Truthfully, I was glad to hear that confirmation because she was right --- me taking things personally comes from me projecting onto her.

Dwelling on the past – Again, so much of my dwelling arises from me projecting and trying to manage an assumed impression that I put on Andie. She was right --- when I talk with her; I sometimes bring up stories about the past. I pointed out that I noticed that I tend to do this around all of my relatives, not just Andie. But in any case, it was yet another avenue for me to honestly view my behavior.

Putting myself down – This one is huge. I have a history of putting myself down. I believe it stems from my childhood, and learning early on to dumb myself down, and then later from living with survivor's guilt because I was no longer mentally ill, poor, abused, homeless, uneducated, etc. The truth is I have a habit of putting myself down to lift others up (this is disrespectful not just to myself, but especially to the other person).

Putting what others say back onto myself – i.e., backward projecting, turning things back onto myself, and/or self-centeredness. This is another way I tend to take things too personally, project, etc. I would say this one is a behavior arising out of the others.

I resolved to do better and use all of my tools and lessons learned during my healing and recovery, not just in a crisis. Consciously observing my own behavior again, I saw how right Andie was. It was disheartening how far I'd slipped back into old habits and patterns. Recovery is definitely a journey. The goal is progress, not perfection.

Even though we stayed in regular touch, it had been years since I'd seen the women I walked with during the early years of my recovery from codependency; my "sisters of the heart." I reached out to Barbara, Dagmar, and Cheri, and we set up a getaway reunion in Idaho. It was glorious and just what my heart needed. Three days and nights of listening, nurturing, and laughing with hugs and tears, and the joy of being true with each other. I also saw Karen, who is now the person whose known me the longest. She is my oldest, best friend.

Back home with Linus I returned to volunteering. With much thought, I decided to step back from the foundation I ran. Coming to terms with aging brought me to another truth about my family: the average age of death is 55 years old. My father died at 33. My mother at 48. My only sibling at 59. Grandfathers at 47 and 62, and grandmothers at 67 and 68. As I write this, I am 68 years old, so I figure I'm living in bonus time.

I reflect on what I wanted to do with my time left. The answers come immediately.

1. Love better. Love the people I love better. Love my neighbor. Love them with my best self.

2. Hug people where they are and love them where they are at. Love the people I do not want to love. Which brought me to:

3. Let go of my judgments. Ask myself, "Does this really matter?"

I once heard people should ask themselves, "If I die next week, does 'this' really matter?" Ditto with my stewing and steaming about what other people are – or are not – doing that I disagree with. My opinions can influence my behavior and the choices I make, but frankly no one needs my judgments. Judging others is another way I keep them at a distance, making it much harder to accept, embrace, and love them exactly where they are. It prevents me from being true with them, and I think, with myself.

17

suffer the children

Each child belongs to all of us and they will bring us a tomorrow in direct relation to the responsibility we have shown to them. – Maya Angelou

When I was a kid I asked my parents, "What are we?" Mom said I was a mixture – part Irish, but she didn't know what else. She added, "It doesn't matter anyway because everyone in the United States is a mixture of something. We're all immigrants from other countries, except for Indians because they lived here first."

Fast forward 50+ years and I discovered online genealogy research and DNA testing. I started researching Caelan's family tree along with my own, and for his twelfth birthday I privately published a 200-page book detailing what I'd found. I included stories I uncovered about his ancestors.

I did the same thing for Andie, and with the results of my own

DNA test discovered I was much more than just part Irish. I am 99.2% Scots-Irish. I'm also a direct descendant of men who fought in the American Revolution and the Civil War. One of my great+ grandfathers was a founder of Concord, Massachusetts, where Louisa May Alcott lived and where the famous cemetery named Sleepy Hollow is located.

Andie's family tree only showcased her maternal side, since I still didn't know which of the two men was her biological father. I strongly suspected it was Jeremy, my friend from high school. One time when she was young, I reached out and offered to pay for a paternity test to settle the matter, but despite several years having passed Jeremy refused to take one. He thought I wanted something from him. I felt hurt at the time because I still thought of myself as the noble martyr. It took years of working on myself to see his perspective.

When Andie was 17, she had a strange lump in her breast that needed surgery. The doctor stressed how important it was to know if breast cancer ran on either side of her family. I had no idea where Jeremy lived, so I contacted his older sister and explained that I needed to know if breast cancer was an issue in her family. She of course asked why, and I replied, "Look, you're talking to a mom who's scared right now so it doesn't matter why I am asking. Just tell me!" She said breast cancer did not run in her family, which was a huge relief.

My brother Lee and I stayed in touch with each other throughout the years. We finally had a closer relationship, and I know it was because of my healing work. As a codependent I wanted my family and friends to behave in a certain way and was frustrated and angry when they didn't. Like so many other relationships in my life, the changes started once I kept my focus on myself and stopped trying to change other people's behavior. I learned (albeit slowly) to detach from my expectations for them and instead accept them for exactly who they were, and where they were at in their own journey.

A couple years after Pops died, Lee began a long medical quest to find out why he felt so tired. At first the doctors thought he had lung cancer. But eventually his oncology team at Vanderbilt University Medical Center diagnosed him with neuroendocrine cancer which is a rare disease (under 200,000 cases are diagnosed each year in the U.S.). Lee also had a few symptoms that puzzled his team, and his doctors presented his case at an oncology conference in the hope of gaining more information about it. Surgery was not an option, so he started chemotherapy and radiation.

I'd never been to Lee's home in Tennessee, but I wanted to go and spend some time with him. Andie said she'd come too.

That first night Lee was full of surprises, talking easily about our past without any prompting. He recalled how he rescued us from a couple of the places where we were dumped during the summers – places with abusive people. Lee also told me how he snuck out of Grandma Mabel's house after we were kidnapped and found a way to contact our mom. Lee talked about Galen too – the fights he and Mom had and how much he hated the man. I heard immense pain behind his words and realized how his trauma had held him hostage his whole life.

When Andie and I retired to the guest room she looked at me

in surprise and said, "Wow! Uncle Lee is certainly chatty all of a sudden!"

I didn't know why. Perhaps it was because of his illness. Maybe he wanted me to know all of his secrets before he died. I no longer cared. I just wanted to hang out with him. I was powerless to stop his cancer, so instead I gave him neck and back rubs, brought him ice water, and gave him more hugs than he had ever allowed before. Saying goodbye, I hugged him, and my tears came. I couldn't stop heaving and sobbing into his chest. He held me tight and whispered, "Hey, you know something, right?" Then he tapped my heart and said, "I'm always going to be right here, Sis."

Brief History of Child Abuse and Protection[44]

As a child, I believed that an evil transformation took place when people grew up. I believed that becoming an adult turned humans into heartless creatures, who hurt (and probably took pleasure in hurting) babies, children, animals, and other weaker beings. As a curious adult, I discovered that much of what we consider "child abuse" today was ignored, tolerated, encouraged, or praised as good parenting.

The justifications have varied depending on cultural norms and religions, but an underlying belief remains – children are the property of their fathers. This belief permeates almost every culture and religion, as far back as archeologists, anthropologists, historians, and historical records indicate.

What we term child abuse today wasn't even recognized until

recently. For thousands of years around the world, a parent had the right to kill their child with impunity. In all cultures, infanticide was a common practice designed to control the population, ensure an inheritance for existing sons, get rid of babies born with deformities, get rid of female babies and babies considered to be worthless, and/or to lessen financial burdens on families. Illegitimate children, babies born of incest or rape, and babies the father suspected were sired by someone else were often killed.

Discipline was historically harsh, and in many cultures, reflected in laws. "If a son strikes his father, his hands shall be hewn off," read one Babylonian law. For more than 400 years in the Roman Empire, the father decided if his child lived or died. The most common method of death was exposure by placing a newborn outside in the elements to die. In ancient Greece and Rome, babies were "discarded in rivers, dunghills, or cesspools, placed in jars to starve, or exposed to the elements and beasts in the wild."[45] Exposure is still the preferred method of killing babies in some cultures today.

Infanticide was also common in medieval and Renaissance Europe. In all these places, more girls perished than boys. Often families would kill every daughter born to them until they had a son; subsequent daughters were allowed to live. [46] Children who misbehaved could be branded or burned. During the Middle Ages in Europe, child abuse was not considered a crime against a person, but rather a crime against property, because children were designated as the property of their fathers.

Although Christianity was one of the first religions to expressly forbid murdering a baby, the decree was not enacted until

400+ years after the crucifixion of Jesus. Today, infanticide is outlawed in most industrial nations, but it's still practiced in some non-industrial cultures. In addition to killing an infant, there have always been more passive ways to deal with older, misbehaved and unwanted children. Beatings, mutilation, selling children, abandoning them and so on is prevalent in every country today.

Until recently, children were expected to work the same jobs and hours as adults. In the Middle Ages and well past American colonial times, children were often deemed "apprentices" for a master, with zero protection from horrific treatment. At that same time the laws allowed parents to beat recalcitrant children to death.

Child sexual abuse has also extended across every culture in time. From as far back as 200 BC, it was an accepted and common practice in Rome and in Greece for men to sexually-abuse or sexually-exploit young boys. Interestingly, it was frowned upon as an "unmasculine act" for an adult man to have sexual encounters with a boy once the child had entered puberty. During the Middle Ages, Europeans also "sometimes treated young children as sexual playthings. A striking example involved the future King of France, Louis XIII. According to a diary kept by the royal physician, members of the French royal court fondled his genitals, and ladies-in-waiting played sexual games with his tiny fists."[47]

In New York City during the 1820s, more than 75% of the rape victims were under the age of 19. An 1894 textbook, *A System of Legal Medicine*, reported that the rape of children "is the most frequent form of sexual crime."[48]

In the 1880s, states began raising the age of sexual consent for girls. During early colonial times, the age of consent was 10. As recently as 2001, at least one state's age of sexual consent for children was 14. Today, most countries in the world set the sexual age of consent between 16 – 21.

When a family had too many mouths to feed, children were often given away or sold. In 1948, Lucille Chalifoux of Chicago made national news when a photo showing her four children next to a "for sale" sign, became public. The news media at the time presented the situation as "tragic," because Lucille and her husband, Ray, could not afford to keep their kids. But nearly two years after the photo was released, all four children had been sold. A fifth child was also born during this time. A July 2013 follow-up edition in the *New York Post* included interviews with some of the surviving children.

Adoption was rarely considered in the U.S., until the Tennessee Children's Home's operator, Georgia Tann, received accolades for her unlicensed adoption agency placements. She opened her informal agency in 1924. She sold an estimated 5,000 children until a state investigation closed her doors in 1950. Many of the children were obtained through fraudulent means such as kidnapping. Barbara Bisantz Raymond published the book, *The Baby Thief* in 2007, based on Tann's schemes.

Fundamentally speaking, children were not considered to have inherent rights or privileges. Beyond the primal urge to continue the species, children existed only to serve adults emotionally, physically, and/or sexually.

During the Industrial Revolution, young children provided employers with cheap and easily controllable labor. By 1911, more than two million American children, under the age of 16, were working – the majority of them 12 hours or more, six-days-a-week. Often, these child workers toiled in unhealthful and hazardous conditions and always for minuscule wages. Young girls continued to work in mills, even though they were in danger of slipping, and losing a finger or a foot, while standing on top of machines to change bobbins; or of being scalped if their hair got caught in the machinery. And, as ever, after a day of bending over to pick bits of rocks from coal, breaker boys were still stiff, and in pain. If a breaker boy fell, he could be smothered, or crushed by huge piles of coal. And, after a breaker boy turned 12, he would be forced to go into the mines, and face the threat of cave-ins and explosions.[49]

Extreme forced child labor continued legally in the U.S. until the Fair Labor Standards Act of 1938. Yet even today, problems exist. In 2020 the wage and hour division department fined employers $3,579,570.80 in child labor civil money penalties, involving more than 3,300 kids.[50]

The *World Health Organization* defines child maltreatment as "the abuse and neglect that occurs to children under 18 years of age. It includes all types of physical and/or emotional ill-treatment, sexual abuse, neglect, negligence, and commercial or other exploitation, which results in actual or potential harm to the child's health, survival, development, or dignity in the context of a relationship of responsibility, trust or power."

The first true legal remedies for kids in the United States came about through child labor reforms that only applied to employers but *not* to parents. Then in 1874, Mary Ellen Wilson's case came before the U.S. Supreme Court. Mary Ellen was a child living with foster parents, who physically brutalized and neglected her. Eventually, the American Society for the Prevention of Cruelty to Animals (ASPCA) became involved. The society argued that under the law, animals were better protected than children. The court agreed, removing the girl from the foster home. Soon after, with assistance from ASPCA, Mary Ellen's attorney set up the *New York Society for the Prevention and Cruelty to Children*, becoming the first child protection agency in the world.

It still took a hundred more years for the federal government to pass legislation to protect kids. In 1974, President Richard Nixon signed into law the *Child Abuse Prevention and Treatment Act*. The impetus was in part due to a 1962 paper published by pediatrician Dr. Henry Kempe and his colleagues, titled *The Battered-Child Syndrome*. The paper helped shift the recognition that child abuse is widespread and significantly impacts society.

It would be wonderful to believe that current federal and state laws adequately protect children, but that's not true. According to the World Health Organization "nearly 3-in-4 children, aged 2-4 years, regularly suffer from physical punishments and/or psychological distress at the hands of their parents and caregivers, and 1-in-5 women, and 1-in-13 men report having been sexually abused as a child." According to *Child Abuse America's 2019 statistics*, 1-in-6 adults have experienced 4 or more adverse childhood experiences.

From earliest recorded human history, children have been and continue to be abused worldwide. Science, medicine, social welfare researchers, and educators now understand the long-lasting trauma of verbal, emotional, physical, and sexual child abuse. I believe that the core belief that children are the *property of their parents* is what needs to change, before real progress can be made.

My brother was 59 when he died. I reminded myself that the stages of grief can come and go, and I wasn't too concerned when my depression deepened over the ensuing months. I finally made an appointment with a counselor to help process my grief. She was immensely helpful and after 5 or 6 sessions, I was back-on-track. She reminded me to work on my mental health every day, not just when I felt overwhelmed. There was another reason why Lee's death hit me so hard. Lee was the last person alive who knew me as a child. He was also the last person in my immediate family to die. I was the only one left.

One day I checked my email and there was a message from someone I didn't know. It was a man named John, who wrote that he was Galen's and Archibald's half-brother on their father's side. I had an uncle I didn't know about! I felt nervous and anxious. It had been many years since I'd made contact with my father's side of the family. I sometimes emailed or spoke with Archibald on the phone, and he was a good person. He and his wife had moved to Alaska when I was young and raised their five children there, far from the rest of his family in Oregon. Like Galen, Archibald was extremely intelligent. He pursued several interests such as astronomy and music. I called him to ask about John and he reassured me that this new uncle was a good guy.

I decided to meet him. Unlike Archibald, John looked strikingly like Galen. They shared the same dark hair, eyes, and build. I was taken aback and held tight onto Linus's hand. But John was definitely not Galen. John and his wife were delighted to meet me, and over the next few years we occasionally got together. I liked having another uncle, although every time I saw him, I had to consciously let go of the automatic uneasiness knotting up my insides, because of his resemblance to Galen.

John wanted to gather stories about the big brother he had barely known as a child. Archibald compiled several short remembrances and sent me a copy. I was stunned by what I read. After my paternal grandfather left Grandma Mabel, she moved with her two boys to her father's farm in Oregon. Archibald wrote how Galen took great pleasure in tricking him into touching the farm's electric fence, laughing when Archibald got shocked. Reading those words, I felt both horror and relief. The hair raised all over my body, and deep down I accepted for the first time, that I wasn't imagining the experiments Galen did in the basement. Now I understood why I was so scared of electricity.

I noticed that something was physically wrong with me again. I started to have hand, head, and neck tremors. Icepick headaches involved piercing jolts of pain that lasted longer than usual. On two occasions, I'd completely forgotten that I had been cooking food on the stove until the burning smell alerted me. I had a hard time remembering plans and events, and wondered if it was all normal aging stuff.

My doctor sent me to a neurologist, who gave me an MRI. That was normal but my electroencephalogram (EEG) results were abnormal in the awake, drowsy, and sleep states, due to a "mild-to-moderate slowing" in my bilateral frontal temporal regions. This slowing was more prominent on the left side as compared to the right one. The findings were nonspecific, but they suggested that a focal pathology involved my bilateral frontotemporal lobes. There were no epileptiform discharges seen or subclinical seizures. The doctor said the findings were "unusual" and suggested that I test again in a few months. The second EEG had the same result. Next, the neurologist wanted me to have a lumbar puncture. She also sent a sample of my blood to the Mayo Clinic for a paraneoplastic antibody panel, designed to locate and identify neurological disorders of unknown origins. This test can also detect cancer.

There were no findings. Then I was sent for a neuropsychological evaluation by a neuropsychologist. When I scheduled the appointment, I was told to bring a sack lunch because the testing process would last eight hours. Along with a clinical interview with the doctor, I took eighteen different tests. I was given memory, verbal learning, dot counting, and manual dexterity tests, and an intelligence test, all in addition to assessments for depression, anxiety, and personality disorders. A few weeks later, Linus and I went to get the results from the doctor.

She told me that I had scored well on everything, but there were some indicators that I hadn't done my best. That sounded like my old behaviors of impression management, that on some level I wanted the results to indicate something wrong. I owned the truth in that. I didn't want to have wasted anyone's time if there wasn't something organically or psychologically wrong with me. In her notes she wrote, "the current findings likely underestimate her maximal ability level in some areas."

According to the test results my IQ was 122, reflecting superior intelligence, while my verbal comprehension index was 132. That meant my verbal IQ was higher than 98% of the general population. My recall and visual recognition on the other hand, were on the low end of the average. But my working memory was in the superior range. I also tested as ambidextrous, which I already knew.

Finding out I'm officially intelligent and have great verbal skills forced me to change my perception of myself. I could no longer tell myself I wasn't very smart. When I shared the news with some family and friends, they laughed at my surprise.

My inattention or inability to concentrate was greatly helped after trying the psychologist's recommendations. The physical tremors were still present, but at least I knew I didn't have an organic problem. I was living as they say, my best life. Every morning after opening my eyes, I gave thanks. I'd come so far in my healing journey. My hyper startle response was still in charge, as was my compulsive need to double check that doors and windows were locked, and the old undercurrent of fear that someone would break into my house. I didn't realize at the time that my anxiety about being in purely social situations was also tied back to my childhood.

I honestly believed there was nothing more I could do to manage the few remaining negative behaviors.

I was wrong.

18

eating the elephant

We think that boxes take everything that's bad and they lock all that nasty stuff out when in reality they take everything that we are and they lock all of those great things in. ~ Craig D. Lounsbrough

When I first learned about false memories, I felt a sense of relief. If I had false memories then I hadn't been abused, right? I eagerly shared the news with my therapist, who nodded and agreed that there were instances of false memories.

But if that were the case with me, then how did I explain my behaviors from pre-school to the present? Why did I often wear pajamas under my clothes starting at around 8 or 9 years old? Where did my self-mutilation and body-hatred come from? Why did I hate being naked, even when bathing? Why did I feel so relieved – then guilty – when Galen died? And Mabel? Why did

I remember spending several summers traveling in the carnival when I didn't? Why did my body shudder and shake for decades before recovery, just seeing or hearing the words 'molest,' 'incest,' and 'sexual abuse' during general conversations or in movies or books?

Were my memories false?   I wanted them to be.   Were my memories repressed or suppressed? That's a more interesting question because scientific and psychological debates are strong on both sides. Research into the existence of repressed memories suggests that prior to 1786, repressed memories were unheard of and undocumented in fiction or non-fiction.[51]

Yet when I was in Elberta's office that day and experienced a flashback to that incident in my brother's bedroom, I wasn't shocked that it happened. I remembered that it happened, but I thought I'd tucked that memory away in a corner of my mind. There was no sense of "Wow! How did I forget that happened to me! And now I'm remembering!" Instead, it was just a recognition that the memory was now forward in my mind. And then there was my reaction – my extreme dissociation and 'coming to' on the floor?

Where did my phobia of electricity come from?   I also experienced visceral, bodily reactions when my friend tried to jumpstart my car and when my mom told me to plug in an iron.

The Science of Memory

Presently, the study of memory involves an interdisciplinary

link between cognitive psychology and neuroscience or cognitive neuroscience. One of the first surprises I discovered was this:
The brain in general, and memory, in particular, has a distinct negativity bias. It pays more attention to, and highlights unpleasant experiences. The brain typically detects negative information faster than positive information, and the hippocampus specifically red-flags negative events to make doubly sure that such events are stored in memory. Negative experiences leave an indelible trace in the memory even when efforts are made to "unlearn" them. This is probably an evolutionary adaptation, given that it is better to err on the side of caution, and ignore a few pleasant experiences, than to overlook a negative, and possibly dangerous event. [52]

Today I understand so much more about how one response to intense trauma is to protectively suppress memories and dissociate from the events.

In 1889 French psychologist and physician Dr. Pierre Janet studied dissociation and found that what we call PTSD is a psychological defense mechanism against traumatic abuse. Although it's normal to change and distort one's memories, "people with PTSD are unable to put the actual event, the source of those memories, behind them. Dissociation prevents the trauma from becoming integrated within the conglomerated, ever-shifting stories of autobiographical memory, in essence, creating a dual memory system."[53]

In other words, the 'boxes' I'd buried deep in my underwater cavern were just another way for me to dissociate from what really happened. The memories were suppressed until I was emotionally and mentally ready to deal with them. During the early years of my recovery, I was always amazed how every time I thought I was done and couldn't possibly get better – it was then that deeper buried issues and memories would start surfacing.

Today, there is international consensus by scientists that "1) traumatic events are usually remembered in part or in whole, 2) traumatic memories may be forgotten, then remembered at some later time and 3) illusory memories can occur."[54] I experienced all three of those states at one point or another.

It seemed that as I became strong and healthy, something at my core allowed the darker things to come to light. I've learned from listening to thousands of other people who shared their healing journeys, that the same pattern holds true for everyone. Today when I'm faced with a shock to my system, I still start to dissociate, but am able to easily pull myself back and be present and active again.

But there is another major defense against loving myself. Food. Tied into loving and supporting my body is eating.

I wondered, *Does it have to be that way? Is there a kinder, gentler, more self-loving way of facing my eating issues, and connecting with and loving my body? Just because each step in my recovery requires uprooting mountains, diving deep into undersea caverns, and exhausting efforts to open those iron boxes – was that the only way for me?*

I no longer thought so. All the work I've done over the years has led me here today. There are no more boxes to open and unpack, no more buried secrets or blinding self-revelations. The path is well-trodden, and I know the way.

I tend to sit with my feelings around food. Not eating itself, just food in general. Echoes of guilt resound deep inside, primarily because my brother and I used to be punished with the withdrawal of food. "You go to bed without your supper, young lady!" As a result, food became a sign of danger.

Every September after the summer carnival season, my mom left us in Galen's care while she worked at the Puyallup Fair in Washington State. This was the last fair before Aunt Holly and Uncle Max brought their joints home to Portland for the winter. Mom was gone for about two weeks at the fair, which always fell on my birthday. When she came home, she brought leftover game prizes and stuffed animals, and threw me huge birthday parties with everyone in my class invited.

Wait … I don't remember seeing any pictures of my birthday parties and now that I think about it, I don't actually have memories of those parties either. It was just what I had told myself and others for as long as I can remember. So those parties probably didn't happen.

The first few nights after Mom left for Washington, Galen took Lee and me to the Portland dog race track. We wouldn't return home until way past my bedtime. He warned us not to tell our mom about it, and laughed as if it were a special secret. I thought it was fun, even though I was cold sitting in those outdoor stands.

I still remember the tune that was whistled over the loudspeakers as the dogs walked around the track before each race. Usually within a night or two, my father had gambled away the money my mom left us for food.

At that point, Galen started getting creative with the few staples we had on hand.

One time he made a huge pot of plain macaroni noodles with no sauce. When I complained, he said he would put some of his own special sauce on my pasta. He poured a generous amount of spicy hot Tabasco sauce on top and told me to dig-in. After one bite I spit it out and reached for a glass of water. Galen thought my reaction was hilarious, belly-laughing at my torment. He insisted that I could not get up from the table until I'd finished every flaming hot bite.

That was a firm rule in our house.

For breakfast we often ate a bowl of wheat flake cereal with milk. Sometimes Lee and/or I would complain about the sogginess and not want to finish it. "You can finish it now, or it will go into the refrigerator, and you can eat it for lunch," my mom always said.

If Lee kept complaining, she'd get mad and threaten him. "If you don't finish that I'm going to rub it in your hair!"

One time Lee called her bluff. She turned his bowl upside down on his head – milk and soggy flakes in his hair and on his face. We both learned to finish the food put in front of us.

That is ... until Lee taught me a trick. He told me to back my chair up to the wall grate (where the heat came out). He showed me how to surreptitiously remove a grisly fatty piece of meat, or a hated vegetable by moving it to my hand, and then leaning back just far enough to push the morsel through one of the grate's small openings. That worked for about a month, until the smell of rotting food tipped off my mom.

Thanksgivings were spent at Grandma Mabel's twin sister's house.

Myrtle* was Mabel's identical twin and was married to an attorney. They lived in a sprawling home in a fancy Portland neighborhood. The large dining room table seemed to groan under the weight of all of the food. I was overwhelmed by the quantity of it and fought an animalistic urge to throw myself into the large serving bowls of mashed potatoes, gravy, dinner rolls, the huge stuffed turkey, and glazed baked ham. We only saw these foods when we were there, or at Grandma Mabel's house for the Christmas gathering.

I remember sneaking extra rolls into my coat pockets to take home, and the frantic urge to eat as much as possible. But Mom's rules about food and politeness kept me from following through on my urge.

"Don't be a pig. Save some for others. Sit up straight with your hands folded in your lap until I say you can start eating. Mind your table manners."

I felt ashamed of my hunger.

Sneaking food was associated with lying, and an intense shame because of the way my mom handled one situation when she was still married to my father. We lived at the end of a street in a duplex apartment. Behind the houses grew a huge patch of wild raspberry and blackberry bushes, a common sight in the Pacific Northwest. Lee and I were under strict orders not to pick the berries or play in the bushes because if we got stains on our clothes, she could not get them out with her old wringer washer. Nevertheless, we often carefully ate the berries when we were hungry.

Of course, the inevitable happened.

I think I was five or six years old at the time. Reaching for a higher branch laden with fruit, I fell into the ripe raspberries, crushing them against my t-shirt, and leaving a splotchy red stain. I panicked.

Then we heard the familiar whistle from mom that meant it was time to come home for dinner. Lee ran ahead, while I plodded slowly toward the house. By the time I got there, I had figured out a way to get out of being punished.

I went into the house calling, "Mommy! Mommy!" When she appeared I said, "I wasn't playing in the raspberry bushes, but this boy on a bike came riding by me and threw a handful of berries right at me. Then, he laughed, and said hah-hah! You're going to get in trouble! Then, he rode off."

Silence greeted my story. She looked at me with a stern frown, and said in a steely voice, "You're lying to me. I despise people who lie."

I persisted, "No, no, there really was a boy, and he threw the berries right at me. He knew that I would get in trouble!"

"Oh, you're definitely going to get in trouble, young lady," she said.

My father came in, and I told him the same story, but this time with more emphasis. I hoped that he would believe me.

Mom shook her head in disgust and said, "Well, since you keep on lying you can stay in your room. Every time someone comes into this house, whether it's a neighbor, or your grandparents, or anyone at all, you are going to stand in front of them, and tell them that you lied to your parents. You are going to tell them exactly what you lied about. You'll do this every day for the rest of this week."

That evening, and all the next day, I listened in fear for a knock at the door. When it finally came, it was our upstairs neighbor. My mom invited her in, and they went to the kitchen, where they talked in low tones for what seemed like forever.

I was so ashamed that I hid under my bedcovers until I heard, "Cathy? Come into the kitchen right now." I started crying. I pulled the blankets over my head, so no one could see me. Then I layered Lee's blankets on top of those until I must have looked like a small, moving pile of bedcovers. I felt my way from the end of my bunkbed to the kitchen and stood there, shaking in shame and crying. I don't remember what I said, but Mom told me to go back into the bedroom. I think she lifted my punishment at that point.

But her desired goal was met. After that, I did not lie to her. As I grew older, I learned how to obfuscate and omit as protection. But if I tried to outright lie to my mom, my face and ears would get red and I would be unable to hold eye contact with her.

My overeating started when we lived at Camp Pendleton Marine Corps Base in California. Pops had returned from his first tour in Vietnam, and we lived on base for a short while before he was transferred to Hawaii. I don't remember much about the school I attended there, other than the gym teacher who forced students to walk naked in an open shower while she watched. I do remember the small Quonset hut near our house. Military families who lived on base during the late 1960s and into the 1970s didn't have a lot of options for on-base shopping. The PX was open for limited hours, so every few hundred homes had a small convenience store inside a Quonset hut. Ours sold a multi-flavored frozen ice treat that I loved.

But my hunger was never satisfied.

I discovered that I could sneak a cup or two of brown sugar into my room and eat it while I read a book. At the dinner table with my family, I felt conscious of how much I ate. I was silently judging myself with every bite.

One day a letter arrived for me. It was from Galen's estate. Mom sat me down and said, "Your daddy wrote you a letter before he died, and even though it says to hold it for you until you turn 16, I think you should have it now."

I was about to turn 13, and it had been just over two years since my father's passing. Mom continued, "I hope you won't be mad at me, but I opened it and read it." I felt deeply violated. It hurt to realize that I still had nothing of my own. She explained, "Honey, your dad's illness affected his mind in some ways, and I just wanted to be sure he hadn't written something that would hurt you. But it's a beautiful letter and you should have it."

Sixty+ years later, I realize that my father's letter was a beautiful goodbye to his daughter. He hoped that I was not still grieving him and was happy. He wrote, "Now that you are 16 years old, you are growing up. Your mother and I decided that you could start wearing lipstick and dating boys at this age." He ended the letter by reminding me that he'd had "a wonderful life" and that he loved me.

I felt like Galen had written it for someone else – not me. The same uneasiness and fear that arose whenever I thought about him, tugged at me deep inside.

I understand now that my overeating coincided with my turmoil about the letter, what I felt about becoming a teenager, and the continuing transformation of my body. I felt ashamed of my steady weight gain. Other girls my age wore makeup and curled their hair. I wanted nothing to do with that.

I hated the idea of anyone seeing or commenting on my body, so I wore long pants and long-sleeved blouses. I lost myself in books and food, curled up on my bed with the door closed. I purchased books at yard sales, scouring for science fiction and non-fiction books about science and space.

By the time we moved to Hawaii, I'd added psychology textbooks to my reading list. I hoped to find an answer to a question that had risen in my thoughts. Was I crazy?

Galen had been sick in the mind. I was pretty sure Grandma Mabel was sick too. Maybe I was too.

My sneak-eating expanded from frozen ice treats and brown sugar to devouring packages of saltine crackers and rolling up bits of white bread into small balls to chew on. I discovered I could butter a piece of bread, cover it in brown sugar and squeeze it all into a ball. Maple bars and mashed potatoes were my weakness, and Mom seemed happy to oblige my request for a pastry whenever we went shopping.

I also felt survivor's guilt about accepting the comforts of our new life. The older I got, the more I punished myself with food. My panic rose if there were vegetables or a salad on my plate. I didn't deserve healthy foods. As a young adult I joked about living on instant mashed potatoes and maple bars, but that wasn't far from the truth. There were a couple exceptions. When I was pregnant with Andie I lost nearly 30 pounds before her birth, simply because I was eating healthy foods. At one point, my OBGYN sent me to a nutritionist because I wasn't gaining enough pregnancy weight. The nutritionist asked me to track every bite for a week. Since I didn't bother with portion control, my log looked something like this: Lunch – a can of tuna, can of green beans, piece of bread with margarine, and a glass of milk.

I craved red meat and pickles dipped in chocolate frosting. My taste buds changed too; suddenly I liked onions and bell peppers, rice, broccoli, and salads. The nutritionist looked over my food log and said, "You're actually getting plenty of nutrition, so I don't understand why you're not gaining weight." She asked me if I usually ate this way.

"Oh, no ... I used to hate vegetables and meat. I lived on instant mashed potatoes and macaroni and cheese. I'm also exercising now, which I never did before." Ahh... As the baby grew and gained weight, I lost weight. When Andie was born, I'd only gained two net pounds.

After her birth I stayed on the healthier diet because I was nursing her. But once Andie was weaned, I went back to punishing myself with excess food. I also stopped exercising. Of course, most of the weight came back. The second time I lost a significant amount of weight was during my year and a half of cognitive-behavior therapy. I ate whatever my mom put in front of me, which included vegetables and fruit.

When I read Geneen Roth's bestseller *When Food Is Love*, it struck a chord because I saw the obvious connection between the way food was given to me – or restricted from me – as a child. Naturally I equated food with love, and since eating could be a form of loving myself, I felt unworthy and ashamed to eat healthy options.

I once went to an *Overeaters Anonymous* meeting shortly after I left treatment at the Walker Center. I looked over the list of 15 questions and knew I was being rigorously honest with my answers. I wasn't bulimic, anorexic, a binge eater, or any of the other common signs of people with eating disorders. I definitely connected food with emotional comfort, but my poor eating habits centered around my belief that I didn't deserve to nourish my body. My body needed to be punished.

Later, I realized the wisdom in one of Roth's later books – food is not the problem – it's only the middleman. "It is the vehicle, the means, the transport for the internal sense of self – of value and worth, of deficiency and scarcity – to express itself."[55]

Linus introduced me to his world of food with its rich diversity, and flavor. He taught me about wine, and how to appreciate it paired with certain foods.

Today, the deep pang of empty hunger that is never satisfied has almost completely healed. Because of that, I'm no longer punishing my body through food.

It took three more years to implement my transition plan to leave the foundation where I was CEO. After nearly ten years and the practical limitations of my aging, I knew it was time. Afterwards, I felt an immediate sense of weight lifted off me.

I had a long history of saying "yes" to projects to keep myself from moving forward in the healing process, along with the lingering echoes of workaholism. Within a few weeks, the temptation was rising. The "I need to do this! I could do that; it wouldn't take long. Oh, this group asked if I could help out" mentality consumed me, and the urge to commit was strong. Even though every box of secrets in that underwater cavern had been dredged up and opened (or so I thought), the old messages continued to echo, "Taking care of yourself is selfish, and don't rock the boat because the life you have now is the best ever..."

I quieted those voices and leaned into peace and solitude.

One of my sisters-of-my-heart, Barbara, called to tell me that she had lung cancer. I flew over and spent a week with her in Idaho. So much of our healing journey had been shared together. We'd been through losing our parents together, relocations, marriages, divorces and job changes and years of painful, personal growth. When I returned to Idaho after Pops' diagnosis, I lived with Barbara and her family for a few months until I found work and could get my own place. At one point, I ritually burned all of my childhood journals in her fireplace.

As close as we were as friends, we were even closer as "sisters." I cherished those days with Barbara until the presence of one of her actual sisters triggered old wounds that still weren't healed. I'd worked hard to resolve my feelings toward my stepsister.

Eventually I recognized how I muted my voice, and how by trying to force a friendship with her, I'd been untrue to my feelings.

The few times we saw each as children, we didn't get along. I didn't like the way she treated my mom and Pops, and I carried that grudge into adulthood. I also couldn't shake an underlying feeling that I was somehow second-rate. My stepsister was Pops' *real* daughter, and I was the one he had to accept as part of marrying my mom.

Now a similar scenario was playing out with Barbara and her sister. It frustrated and infuriated me how she was treating Barbara. It reminded me of how my stepsister treated me and Pops. I went to see Cheri and poured out my feelings to her. She wisely reminded me that my recovery and healing must come first. She asked me if taking the sister's moral and emotional inventory was helping me. Okay ... it wasn't. I returned to Barbara's home and practiced detachment with her sister, which made my time with Barbara much richer.

When it was time to say goodbye we clung to each other tightly, both of us sobbing. Barbara died a couple months later, and I felt like a hole was left in my heart.

What surprised me was with each loss, my grief deepened. I guess I thought at a certain point, losing people would become easier. But like so many other paradoxes in becoming whole, the pain felt deeper and more profound because I was truer with my feelings.

I view death as a friend. Not in the dark, sucking undertow of depression, but because I accept my life will end. Maybe part of that is because so many of my friends and relatives have died. Plus, depression and suicide run in my family. Five of my cousins from both sides of my family committed suicide. My niece killed herself with an overdose. It's impossible to say, "never again," but I no longer see suicide as an option.

I came to understand another behavioral response learned from trauma – anxiety. I laugh aloud at the incredible depth of my denial to avoid admitting it. One time in my early 20's, a male friend was telling me his girlfriend was "high maintenance." I asked what that meant. "You know, she's a bit like you – high-strung," he said. An immediate wave of denial hit. I was absolutely not high-strung! I was Zen mother earth, calm and serene. A person who didn't expect *anything* from anyone, and who was always an understanding, laid-back friend, right? He made it worse by adding, "Well you know, you're nervous. You get anxious about a lot of things."

Today when I hear, read, or see something that triggers my anxiety, I pay attention. I need to touch it, own it, and trace where the feelings are rooted.

Symptom-wise, my depression was well-managed. Physically I was in good shape, though not the shape I wanted to be in. Losing weight was still an issue, and it was driven for the wrong reasons. The truth is, I still hadn't become friends with my body. My diet and personal hygiene were on task, but I didn't like looking in the mirror or weighing myself.

In our cozy, quiet home my husband often startled me. He

might pad softly from the kitchen to the study and poke his head in to ask a question. My response was to emit a high shriek and jerk my body up. Shortly after purchasing our home, Linus reinforced the door jams and had a steel security screen installed at my request. We also installed a home security system and put wood dowels in the windows to prevent them from being opened. I turned our walk-in closet into a safe room with an extra phone, flashlight, reinforced door, and the gun my dad had given me.

I occasionally wondered if my actions were 'normal' or overblown. I wondered if there was anything else I could do therapeutically. I knew there were no more secrets and no more boxes left unopened. So why was I still afraid? Why did my body keep reacting to a danger that wasn't there?

I remembered when I approached my 40th birthday with feelings of dread, it surprised me. I talked it over with a friend, who was a licensed family counselor. He asked where my anxiety was coming from, and I drew a blank. He suggested a psychological technique he had learned in graduate school. I sat in a chair facing him. He told me to close my eyes and relax. Then, using both his forefingers he lightly tapped my eyelids, alternating eyes between taps. He asked me a few important questions like, "What do you see happening once you turn 40?" Within a few minutes the answer was clear. I cried.

"My mom had everything bad happen in her 40s," I replied. "She was in a car accident which led to numerous back surgeries and severe chronic pain. After four surgeries and a year in in a full body cast, she was finally able to function normally again. She was tired and weak though, which then led to her terminal diagnosis of myelodysplastic syndrome. She died at the age of 48."

Once I identified the origin of my anxiety, it was easier to understand and manage. Would it be possible to do something similar to address the pervasive fear and anxiety I often felt?

19

going back

Our maps of the world are encoded in the emotional brain and changing them means having to reorganize that part of the central nervous system. ~Dr. Bessel van der Kolk

A revised form of that therapy technique is in use today, and widely practiced among trauma counselors who specialize in treating post-traumatic stress disorder (PTSD). It is called eye movement desensitization and reprocessing (EMDR.)

In 1987 psychologist Francine Shapiro developed EMDR through a chance encounter. She was walking in a park one day and noted that moving her eyes side to side appeared to reduce negative thoughts and memories. Over the next few years, she developed a theory, that EMDR "processing is thought to occur when the targeted memory is linked with other more adaptive information. Learning then takes place, and the experience is stored with appropriate emotions, able to appropriately guide the person in the future." [56]

By 1995, EMDR was an accepted treatment practice conducted by trained clinicians. It has a success rate that surpasses traditional therapy approaches, including antidepressants like fluoxetine. Dr. Bessell Van der Kolk writes about how the physical changes in the brain are apparent in brain scans taken after treatment:

> "We arranged (with a neuroimaging specialist) to have twelve patients' brains scanned before, and after their treatment. After only three EMDR sessions eight of the twelve had shown a significant decrease in their PTSD scores. On their scans, we could see a sharp increase in prefrontal lobe activation after treatment, as well as much more activity in the anterior cingulate and the basal ganglia." [57]

To date, researchers are still trying to pinpoint exactly how the therapy process works, but I think what happens during EMDR is that both sides of the brain are engaged in reprocessing memories.

In 1994 Stephen Porges, Ph.D., introduced the *polyvagal theory*, which provides a deeper understanding of what's biologically happening in humans facing trauma. In short, Porges' theory "made us look beyond the effects of fight or flight, and put social relationships front and center in our understanding of trauma."[58]

Dr. Van der Kolk posits that feeling safe with other people is vital to our mental health, and certainly for our children's well-being. Porges himself believes we 'co-regulate' through face-to-face positive social interaction, and it is a biological imperative because "our survival as a species relied on the ability to identify and cooperate with trusted others..."[59] The critical issue is reciprocity or being truly heard and seen by the people around us.

The need for social engagement is so ingrained that Porges' counts it as the first level of response to a threat – we call out for help from others but if no one comes, we learn that no-one will help. Our more primitive reactions kick in, namely the fight/flight/freeze response.

Research using rhesus monkeys shows that environment and genetics play important roles in one's development. Of the various personality types, there were two that were identified as "causing problems." Some monkeys were anxious, fearful, withdrawn, and/or depressed. Others were highly aggressive. Abnormalities in the monkeys' brain chemistries could be found early in the monkeys' lives (within the serotonin gene with long or short alleles).

The problem was the monkeys' alleles were short. More specifically, when a monkey from either group gave birth, its offspring appeared to inherit the short alleles except ... when the newborn was removed from its birth mother and given to a supportive foster mother. Then the monkey behaved normally! Humans share the same serotonin gene as rhesus monkeys.

"Similarly, New Zealand researcher, Alec Roy, found that humans with the short allele have higher rates of depression than those with the long version, but this is true only if they also have a childhood history of abuse or neglect."[60]

EMDR therapy has become more accepted and practiced, but finding an available, qualified counselor can be hard. Fortunately, when I met with Catherine Pasley, I felt an immediate comfort and connection and knew I could work with her.

At our first appointment we talked about my expectations and the EMDR process. I was surprised to learn that I wouldn't start the process until after my intake. The immediate goal was to create a safe, calm place within myself. Catherine wanted me to visualize a 'container,' a place inside of myself where, if needed between sessions, I could 'store' whatever was coming up until I saw her again.

Of course, I immediately thought of a box. A square box like an iron safe, heavy, and secure. I visualized the box but still felt anxious. So in my mind, I bound the safe with steel chains, then stored it inside a large metal shipping container with locks. Then I moved the shipping container off an imaginary pier and onto a deserted island. Afterward I covered up the container with palm leaves, so it couldn't be spotted from the air or sea. That was my container.

My 'calm place' was easier.

I practiced meditation from time-to-time over the years and have used guided imagery in group therapy and on my own, to help overcome my fear of dentistry. My calm place is a deserted beach in the tropics with ocean waves gently lapping the sandy shore, and diamonds of water sparkling in the sun. Two palm trees provide shade over my comfy lounge chair. I sit, relax and listen to the seagulls, while the ocean waves and dolphins splash about. The warm air surrounds me and fills the silence between the spaces.

Before my first appointment with Catherine, I put together a three-page synopsis of my childhood and therapeutic journey. I wanted to bring her up to speed and not waste time verbally reviewing my life. I also included the results from Dr. Reilly's cognitive and intellectual tests.

I asked Catherine if she had received the information I emailed. She told me she had but hadn't read it because she wanted to meet me without knowing my history. Although disappointed, I was still prepared to tell her my story. She held up her hand and explained that with EMDR therapy, the client *does not need* to talk about their past. I was astonished. I'd never been in a therapy where I didn't have to dig down and talk about my past or current feelings.

Catherine instead suggested that we do a "trauma inventory" using just a word or phrase that I associated with a specific event. She wrote down what I told her – summers, kidnapping, and electricity. These keywords reflected (what I thought were) the core events that influenced my abandonment issues, codependency, and deepest safety fears.

What follows was taken from journaling about my sessions with Catherine.

May 17
First session yesterday with EMDR beyond the calm place and

container exercises. Started with Catherine asking me to place myself in my feelings of being left in those summers. Sense of heaviness in my stomach... feeling unwanted, confused, hurt, stupid. I talk about being at Uncle Joe's, that I don't remember anything except seeing the movie The Three Lives of Thomasina at the cinema. And reading the story of Beautiful Joe, an abused, abandoned dog who is taken in and given love, and dies. And I wonder why mom and Galen just left us. Always a different place. Did no one want me back? And sometimes starting school somewhere, because they didn't come and get us when they were supposed to. The keepers were annoyed, some angry. I don't know who they were, other than Joe... and I think Aunt Jean. Were we left with Aunt Sara and Gene one summer? Some wisp of a memory of a dark place at Joe's. What made David so mad he tracked mom down, and demanded she come get us? Is that why we never visited Joe again or even saw him? He came to Idaho once after Mom died. Pops called me at work to tell me to come down and say hello. I felt a stab of fear and didn't go. I'm wary of him still. We exchange Christmas cards, and that's it.

After several minutes my mind has veered to mom, and why she left us. In particular, me. Why no explanation? Did she think I was too stupid to understand, or did she think it was the kindest way? I felt hot tears, and finally pulled my hands away and held myself, crying. Went to my calm place and took deep breaths. Finally opened my eyes. Initially, sense of relief and release, but after coming home the heaviness hit again. Woke up this morning feeling pretty good, until the heaviness hit again... now there's a hard ball in my stomach and I'm trying to identify feelings, and just be with them. Very difficult.

(later) tried to practice with a beginner yoga video, and about 5 minutes in with the breathing and stretching, started crying. Feeling fragile and vulnerable because I was caring about my body.

May 18
Woke up feeling like I do when someone has just died. That hollow, but heavy weight in my stomach, and numbness, and pain in my shoulders from tension. Heart flutters. Went to Seattle with Linus to see a play and have lunch with friends. Felt normal --- good to have something else to focus on. Tonight, heart flutters and heavy weight is back. Will take magnesium and watch some tv. Still no actual memories, but wow, my body is sure working through something.

May 23
Extended session today. Yesterday my belly was burning, muscles tense, cloudy focus, heart stuff.... didn't get to bed until late, even with trazadone. We didn't do any EMDR exercise today, because I needed to verbally process with free association. Lots of tears about Dave's death, and our visit together before he died. Realizing how left out, disregarded, put aside I felt growing up. I told Catherine about the years I thought I was alien, and the 3x5 cards I used to record my observations of human behavior.

She pointed out, "You really detached, even from the human race." I had not made that connection before. We talked about how my 'mission' to study human behavior not only detached me from being human, but also gave me a purpose, a meaning to why I was alive. That's when I made the connection to my workaholism. Having any meaning as a person was tied to work, to my 'assignment.'

Stomach still rollicky but my muscles are more relaxed right now. She wants me to practice yoga, my calm place, and to keep journaling.

June 8

The session after my last entry was astonishing. Did the EMDR back to those summers of being left, which led to feeling unwanted. As we worked, at some point, the point of observation for me was as an adult, my heart hurting for this child. I wanted to hold her and reassure her she was valuable and worthy, but since I was a stranger to her in the memory, I couldn't just walk up to her on the sidewalk outside Joe's house and start hugging her. Then I realized I could speak to her as just a 'friend of your family', and I told her directly she was talented, and smart, and she was going to grow up to be amazing. I held her in my arms and patted her back and assured her that even though sometimes bad things happen, it's not her fault, and I knew she would grow up to be kind and wonderful. I felt such a lightness, and coming out of the EMDR, Catherine asked me to gauge the level of distress associated with being left. I said, "My parents should have definitely handled it better. They should have just been honest with me and said they were going to work and wouldn't be back until summer was over. But feeling wise, it's like... a recognition that yes, that happened, and yes, my parents should have done better, but it was a long time ago, and it doesn't have a major influence on my life today." Then I felt pure astonishment at the truth of my words. I was worried it was going to be a temporary after effect, but even today I feel that way.

This past Thursday's session was different, because we started down a different memory, this time the kidnapping and when mom *and Galen were screaming over my head, each with a hank of my hair jerking me from one direction to the next. I knew it had nothing to do with me; it wasn't about them wanting me so much as I was a pawn. As the session progressed, I remembered David telling me I didn't belong, that mom and he wouldn't be stuck in their life if I hadn't been born. I remembered the classroom at that school a few blocks from Mabel's, where she enrolled me as a MacNully*. The feeling that I didn't have my own name.*

Since then, I've felt heavy and stressed and sad. This morning, I realized that removing the photos of me from family albums was about far more than the idea I might one day be a spy who needed to hide her identity. It was about erasing myself so I couldn't be found. And the overwhelming drive to disappear as an adult ---- years of fantasizing about just leaving to go somewhere no one would ever find me or know me, like Australia. And during Andie's growing up years, telling myself I just needed to wait until she was a whole, happy adult who would be able to handle my absence.

June 13

Today is rough. We went back to the fight by the car at Mabel's house, with mom pulling one way and Galen the other. I couldn't get attached to it, and my mind kept drifting until I was feeling the fear and powerlessness of being locked in the car while Galen was in the bar for what seemed like hours. I got in trouble for peeing my pants, but I couldn't hold it anymore, and I wasn't allowed to get out of the car. And then to napping with mom, and being told to stay still, don't move, even when I had to go to the bathroom. It all made sense. The years of practicing holding it in, to the point of pain, then to sit on the toilet and keep holding it in while waves of pain shot through me. And the scratching and self-mutilation, and the ripping my mouth, where it always hurt. It was always about control. It's why I hated the word 'victim' and never wanted to see myself that way, because I had to believe there was some kind of choice in all of it, that I had some kind of control. I could have run away, I could have tried to fight back, I could have told someone but didn't, so somewhere in all that I was in control making a choice. I also told Catherine about mom reading my mind, and how helpless I felt at times, and about focusing on building a brick wall, brick by brick when I was riding in the car with her and felt she was trying to read me. That feeling of having nowhere to hide, no privacy, no control. I feel sad. Sad and hurt.

June 30

Thursday's session was really tough. As we talked about where to 'go' next, Catherine suggested the time I told Mabel to leave me alone in the bathroom. I don't feel any particular stress about that, and as I was telling Catherine I said, "I think there might be something in that stupid room she made for me with the poodle pictures on the wall." Then, as I started telling her about those pictures, and the French furniture, my whole body reacted. My legs crossed and clamped together like welded iron. I crossed my arms tight against my chest and my muscles started jerking and twitching. Tears leaked down my cheeks.

I still don't remember what happened in that room. As we did the EMDR, I was sobbing. Details of the room came clearer ---- I remember the venetian blinds, the curtains, the French vanity, an old painting behind curved glass, and I think ... I think there were dolls in the room. I remember the bed was up off the floor and the bedspread hung low, and I hid under the bed.

Afterwards I was heavy and sad and numb, and physically exhausted. I couldn't focus on anything, and I had a splurge of comfort food. Before going to bed I used the container and stored it all inside the safe, wrapped in chains, stored inside the metal shipping container, left on the deserted island.

Writing this now I feel heavy sadness in my belly, and my arm muscles are twitching. Even though I used the container it's been there on the edge. Yesterday my mind wandered back to those poodle pictures, and I impulsively googled 'vintage poodle wall pictures 60's' and then clicked on 'images'. Dozens of different ones filled the screen, and my body tensed, then start jerking uncontrollably as I scanned the images.

(The next entry was written over a month later.)

August 29
We started in on the end of the sessions – the big one, around electricity. No memories, just lifelong effects. Some pieces came back. Galen experimenting with his tv sets and other gadgets. Galen in the basement. The dark basement with dirt walls. It was probably a big cellar at some point. Galen kicking the dog General down those stairs. David wasn't allowed in the basement. Naked light bulb with wires. That's all. That's enough. Body jerking, shaking, sobbing. Exhausted afterwards, and feel tired still, with small ball of sadness deep inside.

September 3
This week between sessions is the most difficult. Had a period of

dissociation, a lot of trouble sleeping (even with the trazadone), and generally tensed up, with waves of numbness cresting into fear and then down again. Body jerky and twitchy. Hard to focus with people. Keeping very busy with tasks, chores, and playing online games – and watching tv.

Linus told me I was "wonderful" the other day, and the tears welled up with shame. I realized, it seems logical that many kids who are sexually abused get told they are "special" and "loved" and probably even "wonderful". So those uplifting, affirming words become attached to abuse, secrets, and shame. I always blamed myself for not being able to take a compliment, for feeling like I wasn't worth it, or that if someone had that impression of me, it put too much pressure on me to live up to it. What would they expect or want from me? Now I see the association and realize, maybe it isn't because I lacked self-esteem. This reaction after EMDR this week is gift and insight. I want all this to be over. I want to be free and strong and confident.

Processed with Catherine at today's session. Feeling calmer, and a quiet sense of acceptance but at the same time sadness for what I went through as a child.

September 10

We revisited the basement again, and this time I was more like an observer from my higher self, feeling compassion and love for me, and a feeling of sadness for Galen. He was the way he was.

Catherine and I came to the conclusion that therapy would be ending soon. I told her that both Linus and I noticed significant changes in my body responses the past couple of weeks.

Linus was amazed at how my startle response had diminished so much and so rapidly. I was too. I got up in the morning and couldn't remember locking and checking the doors and windows before going to bed ... in fact I realized it had been several days since I checked!

Part of me was shocked, like "Oh crap! I could have been attacked!" But almost immediately that feeling was replaced with a new sense of calm and safety. I shrugged my shoulders and realized, "It doesn't matter anymore." I mentioned my epiphany to Linus, and he replied, "Yes, I wasn't going to say anything, but the alarm has been off when I get up; not every day, but it's happening more lately."

I said, "I feel differently now. We take reasonable precautions, like locking the doors and setting an alarm. I feel like, not scared at all, but like I'm being reasonable without worrying."

Wow.

I've lived my life with undercurrents of fear and at times, terror. I wasn't sure I could trust that the fear was truly gone after just a few months of EMDR. But it was.

My body began reacting differently too, along with my diminishing startle response. Before EMDR, I had neck and backaches every day and constant and painful icepick headaches. I tended to hunch my shoulders up to my neck, even while watching tv or reading a book. The twitching and trembling I'd experienced during the past several years had become quite noticeable to others. But after EMDR my shoulders relaxed more, the icepick headaches lessened, and my hand and head tremors declined. I felt more physically whole. And another huge change was my social anxiety seemed to be gone!

Catherine discussed the next steps with me.

EMDR is effective in treating many cases of PTSD, but the years of stored trauma in my body would need another type of therapy. This therapy is called *bodywork*. I remember hearing this term while in group therapy for sexual abuse survivors. There are massage therapists who specialize in the field of trauma.

I felt uneasy about doing any kind of bodywork. I struggled with the idea of liking my body, much less loving it. Every day I promised myself that I'd exercise. But not do it. Getting dressed, and feeling the snugness of my jeans just reminded me that I need to lose weight. Putting on my bra and anticipating the shoulder and back pain from my large breasts, despite finally having the right bra, depressed me. Sliding on my panties (over my flabby belly) only highlighted my huge post-pregnancy stretch marks.

Even though I meticulously used sunscreen and kept my body well-covered, the intense sunburns I received as a child in Hawaii affected me in my 50s.

I'd had a squamous cell carcinoma removed from my back. At that time, I went through two rounds of efudex, a chemotherapy drug that's applied to the skin. The first round of chemo was to treat my forearms, which were covered in pre-cancerous actinic keratosis. The treatment was painful and ugly to look at. The second round was for my neck and upper chest. It also hurt. I stayed indoors, feeling self-conscious about the angry, red raised sores and blotches.

Yet, I'd made some progress towards being nicer to myself

through the years. After each shower I rubbed warm coconut oil onto my legs, arms, and neck. My dermatologist always commented on how healthy my skin looked.

I decided to book a massage. The first person I found with an opening was named Glendy. When I arrived, I nervously asked Glendy to only focus on my back and shoulders.

She asked me what kind of massage I wanted, but I was so tense, I said, "Uh, I want to keep my clothes on if that's okay. I just want my back and shoulders massaged. I'm really anxious about this." I told her, "I've been working with a therapist, practicing EMDR. My therapist told me that I need to do some bodywork, so this is my first step with it." I expected Glendy to ask what EMDR was. She didn't.

She smiled and said, "I actually know what EMDR is. I went through it myself. In fact, my specialty is helping clients with stored trauma in their bodies. In my tribe, I'm a healer." My shoulders relaxed and I began to feel a sense of gratitude. I was thankful that Glendy's door was the one that opened to me.

Glendy had me lie on my back while she covered me with a blanket. This made me feel safer. She explained that she was going to touch me. She gently cupped her hand on my right shoulder, holding it there. She asked me to inhale long and slow, hold it and slowly exhale. After a few breaths, my muscles began to untense and relax. But then I started twitching all over. I apologized, "Sorry, my body's been twitching for the past few years, but there isn't anything wrong with me ... I don't have Parkinson's or anything my doctor could find."

Glendy did not move her hand. She explained that after any

trauma, a person's body "stores" his or her muscle response until the trauma can be safely released. And when a person has experienced long-term trauma (i.e., a combat solider or abuse victim), it can take the body a quite a while to let go and heal.

Glendy's words hit me deeply and my twitching transformed into jerking and spasming, in the same way it had in Catherine's office during intense EMDR sessions. Glendy placed her other hand on my chest, over my heart, and held it there. Tears streamed down my face as the jerking intensified. She reminded me to breathe.

I don't know how long she stood there, simply resting her hands on my chest and shoulder. I tried hard to stay present in the moment. After a while my tears stopped and the jerking slowed down.

Glendy pulled her hands away. She told me to take my time and only get up when I felt ready. Then she left the room, closing the door behind her.

I kept breathing. My whole body was sore the next few days, and I felt as if I'd been pushed physically to the limit.

I determined to do some practice yoga after Linus went to work. This time I consciously breathed, while trying to stay present in my body.

I started shaking and jerking again, like I did with Glendy. I started sobbing. I sat on the couch, while holding myself, and rocking. Again, no specific memories, just my body reacting on a primal level. When would I get through this?

20

the horizon

Our future is our choice. – Dr. Sharif Abdullah

The second time I saw Glendy, my body's reaction was a repeat of our first visit. I lay on her table face up and clothes on, with her touching my neck and upper chest. My body jerked and spasmed, and deep sobs created a steady stream of tears with no conscious memory or understanding of why.

Yet my physical reactions and fears continued to change after my EMDR sessions.

Catherine explained to me how the changes would continue for months. She told me that I might not even notice them at first. Several months after I finished EMDR therapy, Linus and I planned a week-long vacation at a beautiful lake. While looking at the resort website I said to him, "Say! They have parasailing! I'm ready to try that if we do a tandem."

He walked into our study from the bedroom and stared at me.

"You want to go parasailing?!" he asked, disbelieving. I didn't feel apprehension or anxiety. I felt a happy anticipation and thought sure, why not try it? The idea of parasailing would have never crossed my mind even a year before.

The night before our scheduled parasail, Linus asked, "How are you doing? Are you anxious about tomorrow?" I did a quick check-in with my feeling and body and shook my head in disbelief. I replied, "I really am fine. In fact, it's amazing to me that I'm not freaking out."

The next morning, Linus and I arrived at the boat launch and were joined by two other couples. One couple were newlyweds, and the other one was a fit-looking young man and his mother, who wore an Indian sari. I wondered if the mother would have trouble strapping into a harness with a full-length skirt.

The boat captain and his crewmember went over the safety instructions and explained that we would be ascending 400 – 600+ feet up in the sky. The captain asked who wanted to go first, and my arm shot up. Linus looked at me, again surprised.

Once harnessed, we sat at the back of the boat. As the boat sped up, the parachute behind us filled with air and we lifted off of the boat rising higher and higher. I held Linus's hand, expecting my usual terror of heights to flood over me and the dreadful feeling of helplessness with my legs dangling beneath me.

Instead, I felt excitement and a sense of wonder. The sky was bright blue and the water sparkled from the spray of the speeding boat. It was incredible. The boat looked so small below us. I let go of Linus's hand and my harness and spread my arms out. I laughed. I looked at Linus and said, "When we get home remind me to send Catherine a thank-you note!" I laughed again.

A few days later I booked a relaxation massage at the resort. I wasn't ready to take off all of my clothes, but I removed my shirt and bra and lay face down on the table. I told the masseuse what I wanted, and added that I didn't want to talk much.

A soothing blend of new age music permeated the room. The masseuse gently touched my back and started kneading and pressing. I could feel my neck and shoulder muscles tense at this stranger's touch, so I took deep breaths, slowly in-and-out until my muscles relaxed. She also used CBD oil made from cannabis but without the psychotropic ingredient of THC. Her hands felt good and I gradually relaxed.

What is bodywork?

I spell it as one word because I have seen it spelled that way in some books and papers. Regardless, I don't like that word. I don't like placing the emphasis on 'work.'

The goal is to fully integrate my body into myself and to practice kindness and acceptance in the same way.

Some time after completing EMDR, I decided to continue doing the bodywork by committing to massage. Glendy was booked solid, so I found another massage therapist nearby. Her name was Lily. She was about Andie's age. During our initial session when I told her about EMDR and my goals for body work, she knew exactly what I was talking about. I told her I could only remove my shoes and top.

It took me another session before I felt comfortable and safe enough to remove my pants and let her work on my legs. I had decided to try deep tissue massage, because I'd heard it can help clear toxins from the body, and because the pressure used is more intense. Over the first few weeks, Lily eased me into it. There were certain pressure points where she simply held the tissue still, pressing into it. My body would start quivering, then trembling. But I stayed present. Sometimes I cried. But I stayed present, and I kept going back.

Until I didn't. After a few months the dread I felt driving to my appointments felt overwhelming, and I stopped going. Was it because the whole point was to be nice to my body? To practice self-care and even self-love? It had been years since I froze in fear or flashed back into terror at being touched. I decided to give myself permission to take whatever time I needed to process, feel safe in my body, and then be open to trying again.

More recently, I've been exploring the proven treatment approach called Somatic Experiencing®. Developed by Dr. Peter A. Levine, it is described on the Ergos Institute website as "A naturalistic, and neurobiological, body-oriented approach to healing trauma and other stress-related disorders; restoring the authentic self with self-regulation, relaxation, wholeness, and aliveness."[61] One of the first reassuring things I read is that the treatment doesn't immediately focus on the trauma event itself. Moving into the treatment slowly is key. "Titration is the slow release of compressed survival energy. Somatic Experiencing® operates in cycles, where you sense your way through the normal oscillations of internal sensation – contraction/expansion, pleasure/pain, warmth/cold – but only at the level that you can handle without becoming overwhelmed. This repeated, rhythmic process helps you to develop a greater capacity to handle stress and stay in the present moment, *where you belong.*"

I just recently found a locally trained practitioner. My resistance – and yes, I feel it – is ironically that the treatment takes time, and I cannot rush it. A small part of me still wants to believe in quick fixes, despite learning over and over again there is no such thing.

It's humbling to see a geologic time chart. To put that into perspective, imagine all of earth's history boiled down to a 12-hour clock. At midnight our planet formed. Almost an hour later life appeared. By 3:17am, bacteria made their debut. Hours later, at 8:41am, the first multi-celled organisms came into being. At 11:59:59 – about a half-second ago – it was the Ice Age. And, about a quarter-second ago, we modern humans joined the party.[62]

We emerged anatomically modern only 100,000-years-ago. Wow. Just ... wow.

But something catastrophic happened around 70,000 years ago that wiped out nearly all humans. One theory posits a giant super volcano erupted in Indonesia. Whatever caused our near-extinction only 1,000 to 30,000 of the hardiest, strongest individuals survived. It was like pushing the reset button on the human race. Those few people lived throughout the African continent until some migrated to other parts of the world, and then adapted to the various climates and conditions by (for example) developing lighter shades of skin. Thus, every person on Earth today is a descendant of that tiny group who survived 70,000 years ago. This explains why most animal DNA has *thousands* more variations than human DNA. We descended from a tiny gene pool only a millisecond-ago in geologic time.

Science hasn't figured out why we took so long to suddenly learn. In evolutionary terms, it's like we were doing what we'd been doing every day for 60,000 years, then woke up one morning and invented farming, cities, art, and of course beer[63], all before breakfast. Writing was invented less than 4,000 years ago. Once our species started learning, we accelerated at warp speed, and continue to this day. (To me, this seems impossible without outside intervention. I was delighted when I read speculation that people with a negative RH factor like me, are descended from extraterrestrial origins. I chuckled at that, sending a nod to the younger version of myself who was convinced she was an alien.)

According to historians, cultural anthropologists and archeologists, humans were – by our definition today – an incredibly savage, violent species. That part of being human is still prevalent today. It lurks beneath the surface of polite company, although we're apparently not quite as savage as we were in the past. In Steven Pinker's meticulously researched book *The Better Angels of Our Nature*, he provides breathtaking details on how violence has dramatically declined in recent history, despite our perceptions that violence is on the rise.[64]

I look at the progress made in treating addiction, trauma, and mental illness in a similar way. Research has exploded in the mental health field, and new insights are applied almost every day. Much has changed since I was in treatment at the Walker Center.

In those days, the vast majority of drug and alcohol counselors were recovering addicts themselves, and certification with a basic college-level program wasn't mandatory. Insurance companies were paying for in-patient alcohol and drug treatment, typically up to 28 days. In my case, I needed a psychiatric diagnosis to satisfy my health insurance because I wasn't a substance abuser.

Treatment centers varied in their approaches, though most featured an initial detox period followed by individual and group therapy. Most incorporated required attendance at 12-Step meetings and had patients complete the first five steps before leaving treatment.   Many featured a family program, where the identified patient's family spent up to a week learning about the standard addiction model and how codependency with the addict happens and attending group therapy sessions with their patient. The Walker Center's family program involved the patient and family in two sessions of three days each.

In-patient treatment facilities were also introducing experiential therapies like ropes courses, morning meditation and exercise, and addressing other addictions like food, sex, and codependency. There was an emerging awareness that nearly all of us were depressed.

In the 40+ years of 12-Step meetings and other therapies, everyone I've met has substantial issues around shame. Several professionals believed shame was at the core of addiction.

Today, the treatment landscape is markedly different. To receive Federal funding, treatment facilities in the United States are required to use government-defined "best practices," such as cognitive-behavior therapy (CBT). Social workers and therapists have taken over the previous roles of alcohol and drug counselors. One expert, who recently retired after 35 years as an alcohol and drug counselor in both private and prison settings, explains the changes like this:

> There are a couple schools of thought on treatment – the holdouts, who are very 12-Step oriented, and the devotees of the money. The money comes from the Feds for treatment. The national model shifted from 12-Step into cognitive-behavioral therapy (CBT). The conundrum is, no one in either camp knew shit about each other, so that was a battle from the git-go, where 12-Step people didn't trust the

mental health world, and vice versa. There aren't a lot of professional counselors who really understand the depth of meaning of what the 12-step program is all about. The money came down to cognitive behavioral therapy, which basically says you can't just change behavior like, to stop drinking, you have to change the thinking too. So, they were actually espousing a lot of what the 12-Step people say. All the treatment programs in the U.S. that were getting federal monies had to follow the mandates to do the treatment the way they told them to, which was not a 12-Step program because they thought the 12 steps were a religious program. Even the Feds mandated that criminals could not be "forced" to attend 12-Step programs. Now today, bigger programs that have a lot of money can do more than cognitive-behavioral therapy (CBT). For example, experiential. But treatment today is about social workers, not drug and alcohol counselors. Most social workers know shit about addiction and recovery.[65]

Yet many of the theories and practices the Walker Center instituted in what was considered 'out there' at the time are now integrated into most modern treatment plans, including treatment for depression and anxiety, and addressing underlying childhood trauma. A more holistic approach is common, introducing patients to integrated healing with yoga, meditation, music and massage therapy. The majority of treatment facilities still emphasize attending 12-Step meetings but it's not a requirement.

Medication and therapy are still the first lines of treatment for depression. Dialectical behavior therapy (DBT), a type of cognitive-behavior therapy (CBT), is currently the preferred method.   There has been one exciting possibility: In 2019, the Food and Drug Administration (FDA) authorized a new pharmacological intervention for treatment-resistant depression, a drug called esketamine. This drug is available as a nasal spray. The medication is derived from the anesthetic ketamine, a drug with hallucinogenic and dissociative effects, used as an anesthetic.

According to Johns Hopkins, esketamine like ketamine, can cause audio and visual distortions during the first two hours of treatment, which is why it has to be administered in a clinical setting. It's also prescribed in conjunction with conventional antidepressants. Esketamine increases the levels of our brain's most abundant chemical messenger, glutamate. This is interesting, given recent evidence has implicated glutamate receptor-associated complexes in several neurological and psychiatric disorders including Alzheimer's disease, schizophrenia, autism, and mental retardation as well as in chronic pain and drug addiction.[66]

I wondered if the drug would have been an effective intervention for me during my most severe bouts of depression. It's possible, but with my other symptoms at the time, taking something that would increase my dissociation and distort my perception of reality would have been counterproductive. In fact, potential side effects of the drug sold as Spravato include "may cause sleepiness (sedation), fainting, dizziness, spinning sensation, anxiety, or feeling disconnected from yourself, your thoughts, feelings, space and time (dissociation)."[67]

LSD and other once-illegal drugs are showing promising results when administered in a clinical setting, in helping a patient's depression and symptoms of trauma. For me, any hallucinogenic drug scares me, probably because of the terrifying experience that happened to me in California when I was unknowingly given one.

Ask almost any addiction counselor if they believe childhood mistreatment played a part in their client's disease. I've heard percentages between 85 and 100 percent. Ask an educator or school counselor if they believe adverse childhood experiences (ACEs) – defined by the Centers for Disease Control as "potentially traumatic events that occur in childhood" – contribute to a student's learning, behavioral and emotional issues and their answer is nearly always yes. Then, there's this shocking fact: About 61% of adults surveyed across 25 states reported that they had experienced at least one type of ACE, and nearly 1-in-5 reported they had experienced three or more types of ACEs.[68]

To recap, nearly *two-thirds of adults* surveyed reported potentially traumatic events in their childhood. And if two-thirds of adults in the U.S. were traumatized through abuse or other means as kids, then it makes sense to believe that two-thirds (nearly 48 million) of our current child population of 73 million are being or have been traumatized. For me, abuse/trauma was so prevalent and sustained I thought it was normal. By the sheer numbers, it's still covertly accepted.

Here's another unfortunate reality: vast numbers of children are publicly abused but the witnesses don't report it. Many times, witnesses hesitate because they think the maltreatment is not serious enough.[69]

When I was growing up it was common to see a child being slapped or spanked in public. It was even common to see a father punch his teenage son for mouthing off. "I'm making a man out of him!" Relatives and neighbors don't want to cause trouble for themselves despite anonymous reporting mechanisms in every state. Too often the spouse of the perpetrator looks the other way and either pretends that nothing is wrong, excuses the abuse, or is too afraid to speak up.

We know what happens to the two-thirds of us who experienced abuse, trauma, and/or neglect. Many grow up to become addicts and perpetrators. Others like me, suffer mild to profound dissonance in their self-esteem and relationships. Some suffer long-term mental illnesses as I did. Many figured out how to blend in and even stand out as caretakers and leaders, trying twice as hard to succeed. That doesn't mean those people are unnaturally resilient. I used to believe that meant they had learned how to fit the currently accepted norms in their behaviors and stated belief systems.

But more recently I learned there are indeed some people with a biologic ability to deal better with stress and trauma than others. Dr. Stephen Porges proved that a high heart rate variability is better at coping than a low heart rate variability. He used the analogy of the old toy called a Slinky, that expanded and contracted like a wire spring. Most encouraging, because heart rate variability can be strengthened with lifestyle changes, it's possible to increase resiliency and social engagement in children and adults.

John Bradshaw wrote that toxic shame is at the core of codependency, addiction, compulsions, and the drive to super achieve. But as I read today's research into child abuse, I see trauma at the root. As mentioned previously in this book, exposure to trauma in childhood is a risk factor for many forms of psychopathology, including post-traumatic stress disorder (PTSD), anxiety, depression, disruptive behaviors, and substance abuse. [70]

Amazing discoveries are happening right now in the field of trauma research. Dr. Esther Sabban, from the New York Medical Center, is researching a powerful signaling protein called, neuropeptide Y (NPY), that is delivered to the brain via a nasal spray. Tests showed the spray prevented PTSD from occurring in traumatized rats. Human trials are still sparse. Dr. Sabban's work could revolutionize treatment for PTSD.[71] "Current pharmacological treatment for stress-related neuropsychiatric disorders includes selective serotonin reuptake inhibitors (SSRIs), which take weeks to elicit an effect, and reduce symptom severity rather than leading to remission of the disorders," said Dr. Sabban.

EMDR is now at the forefront of effective treatment for trauma, including PTSD. As I wrote in chapter 2, the common symptoms and behaviors point to trauma response, regardless of the diagnostic lens.

The question I used to ask myself, "What's wrong with me?" has disappeared and been replaced by a gentle, "Hey, what's really going on? Why am I feeling this way?" A similar question I tend to ask now is, "What happened to you?" when talking with someone who carries the pain of trauma.

When I started my healing journey there was no ACES test or information, no substantial research into what Dr. Janet Woititz called, 'adult children' of alcoholics, drug addicts, overeaters, workaholics, abusers, etc. There wasn't an understanding of how our brains develop or how trauma affects us, particularly as a child.

When I was desperately seeking answers, the few options available maintained a rigid distance from each other. Psychiatry had no use for 12-Step group treatment, and 12-Step groups disdained treatment paths that didn't include them. The idea that there might be an underlying core common to psychiatric disorders like depression and anxiety and the 'isms' of addiction, and the many learning and behavioral issues of certain students in school, was only beginning to emerge.

More recently, Dr. Bruce Perry introduced the neurosequential approach to healing trauma. Since our brains develop from the bottom up, starting with our most primal needs, it makes sense that treating the deepest wounds of an injury first would be more effective.

For example, if that model was initially used in my therapeutic journey, the clinician's first approach would have been to help me feel safe and supported, something I didn't learn as a baby. More trauma responders and even doctors are taking a cue from psychologist Stephen Porges' Polyvagal Theory and applying his insight that helping trauma victims feel safe allows them to heal psychological and physical wounds more quickly.

Art therapy has come into its own as one of the many holistic tools toward healing. One path is to let your non-dominant hand hold the pen, crayon, paintbrush, etc. My first attempts with crayons were self-conscious and crude drawings. I felt like I was holding a squirmy, unruly, unlikeable child on my lap who kept trying to grab my crayon. Disgust and shame battled inside for a minute until I decided that was that. I was not going to do that again. Years later, I tried again, this time sitting still and opening my heart and feelings to my inner child ... but with reservations. I felt anxious and uneasy, wanting but not really wanting her to have any voice. I was still punishing myself for the child I was, still unwilling to acknowledge I had been a victim, a helpless child. But as my healing continued, I began to feel compassion towards myself. Most recently, I've given myself permission to paint without agenda or purpose. I love watercolors because they blend and flow together so gently.

Today's teenagers are finally getting the truth in libraries across the nation. Where I struggled to find even on book about sexual health on my school's library shelf – or public library, for that matter — the local library's shelves feature titles about dealing with eating issues, abuse at home and school, sexual abuse, trauma, body image, relationships, etc.   Most of the books I've seen are supportive and informative and empowering. Of course, nothing reaches our youth better than social media platforms.   There is some good information out there, but too often not. Peers are a powerful link in spreading misinformation, for both teens and adults.

My story certainly isn't unusual. But it should be, because doctors now know any form of abuse can be traumatic, and trauma damages a child's developing brain in ways that can lead to post-traumatic stress disorder (PTSD), and in some cases permanent problems. I truly believe the mindset that parents 'own' their children is key to any real hope and change.

21

true.

You're not a victim for sharing your story. You are a survivor setting the world on fire with your truth. And you never know who needs your light, your warmth and raging courage. ~Alex Elle

The onion analogy is often used to describe the journey of self-discovery. I used to think it looked like that, peeling back layer after layer of protective defenses built up over a lifetime of response to trauma.

Now I see my path shaped like a spiral, chambered nautilus. At the beginning was the pure light and promise of my birth. The boxes I created to store memories were buried deep under my internal ocean, inside a cavern, inside the first spiraled chamber.

I also used to believe I suffered from a myriad of disparate problems and spent much of my life addressing them one at a time. Hallucinations. Paranoia. Depression. Anxiety. Codependency. Eating Issues. Workaholism. Relationship Addiction. The aftereffects of sexual abuse, like self-mutilation and fear of intimacy, and avoiding gender labels. Hating my body. Fear of intimacy.

Like John Bradshaw's conclusions, I believed the core of my struggle was a toxic shame. The same core of shame others exposed in thousands of 12-Step meetings, in group therapy sessions, and in private sharing. It seemed as if shame was the initiating factor of all addictions.

Today I know that shame can be a toxic byproduct of trauma.

My recovery is slow and imperfect with many pauses. Each chamber in that nautilus analogy was painstakingly cleared and cleaned, then a deeper chamber was revealed, and a new cycle of struggle, pain, and healing took over. Growth continues, and I hope I will always be open to it.

Most recently, I learned something new about myself. I offered to help with our town's big annual event, and the committee was so delighted they appointed me the event coordinator. I love organizing details. Then I bumped into an old barrier: working well with the team. I've always told myself I'm a good team player, and a servant-leader when I need to be. But as I felt the old struggle of frustration, irritation, confusion, and lack of boundaries, I did something different: I didn't blame the other team members for my feelings.   Instead, I started reflecting on the type of jobs I've held, the barriers I've encountered, and how I dealt with them.

Here's what I realized: Almost every job I've had, I worked alone and was accountable to (usually) only the boss. My absolute favorite jobs were when I worked alone: radio broadcaster/DJ, project manager and writer. The jobs I struggled the most in were secretarial, line work, and team coordinator.   Then the truth hit me, so obvious I laughed it took me over 60 years to see it: I am not a good team player.

I thought of a general contractor: he/she is hired to take the plans and ideas and turn them into a house. A general contractor oversees every tiny detail, listens to input then makes the decisions, tracks the budgets, and approves everything.   So, when the homeowner wants to change plans mid-stream, or nitpick small details, the general contractor gets cranky.

Yep. I'm a general contractor.   With wonderous gratitude for my healing, I have no desire to beat myself up for my limitations with team projects.   Instead, I feel a sense of empathy toward myself, and the frustration I felt toward my teammates is gone - poof. Now that I know what I am, I am aware, and will work harder to be understanding with others. I feel empowered.

Would my journey have been different if I knew then what I know now – if I knew that shame is perhaps the first protective shield we use to cover or hide trauma? Because trauma is at the core of every single problem I have or had. Would it have made a difference if I'd tackled the root first, and not spent so many decades on the individual trauma responses I developed? I don't know, but I'm guessing not. I had to spiral through each chamber to reach that underwater cavern, to open and reclaim those locked boxes. It takes what it takes.

Every relationship in my life to that point was impacted by my illness. My one true regret is that my daughter grew up feeling the weight of my trauma. But despite all odds, Andie grew into a truly extraordinary, talented, smart and loving being, who gives to others with a true and open heart. I jokingly say, "God and the village did an incredible job raising her!" and that's not far from the truth. I was never burdened by the idea that she was 'mine,' and I welcomed and encouraged her relationships with other stable adults in her life.

Andie and me were talking recently about this book, and I asked what her feelings were, after she read a draft. She honored me by speaking her truth, "I grew up with no emotional boundaries. In so many ways, I felt like I had to be the parent. There were times I felt so alone, like you had abandoned me."

Every person, who's loved one deals with the aftermath of trauma, should relate to her words. Abandonment takes place when someone is unable to be fully present to themselves. The ensuing responses to major trauma include denial, fear of intimacy, addiction, depression, anxiety, and the other go-tos our psyche uses to cope.

Many of my actual childhood memories are still dark. I've recovered so much, and with the help of research and therapy I stand firm in my true self. I don't expect any more surprises. That is, until something jars another realization.

I recently got an email from my second cousin. She is older than me, and we've had rare contact through the years. As a child, I was given many of her hand-me-down clothes, but I have no memories of her. There is a hazy glimpse of being at her parent's house one Thanksgiving. I am crouching on a stair landing leading to their second floor. I think she and her two brothers are nearby.

It had been years since I had any contact with her. The email was a surprise. No note, just a photo attached. It was a black and white photo with the scalloped edges but no date on it. I am a child, sitting in a metal patio chair with my legs drawn up to my chest. In my hands is some kind of long bar with attachments on the ends. I am smiling the extra wide smile that kids do when they are told to smile for the camera. Looking at the photo, the sense of unease I felt grew. I was holding my breath, my body tense, my stomach hollow with anxiety.

Then I saw it: two markings on the little girl's legs. My legs. One was on the side of my right calf, a scraped looking injury that I immediately decided was the kind kids get when they slide in the grass or roughhouse. But on my right ankle, right over where the anklebone protrudes, was a dark circle. In the old photograph it's impossible to zoom into a clear close-up, but there is no mistaking the unnaturally round shape of the injury. Fear flooded through me as I looked at it, and even without direct memory I recognized it as a cigarette burn. It wasn't just a single round burn from the tip of a cigarette; the circular injury was larger, the result of more than one application.

It makes even more sense now why I wanted to destroy photographs of myself as a child.

Over the next few days, I try to process my feelings. I am looking for other reasons why a round, dark burn-looking sore would be on my ankle. Maybe my shoes didn't fit right? I google images of foot sores from shoes and can't find anything that looks remotely like the wound in the photo. Maybe I stood too close to something round and hot and touched my ankle bone against it? Maybe I had a small sore on my ankle from something, and I picked at it and made it bigger and shaped it into a circle?

I realize I'm in denial. I don't want to accept that the photo shows an injury that was deliberately caused. The photograph is evidence I can't deny. I feel exposed and hurt. Did anyone ask my parents what happened to my ankle? What would my parents have said? "Oh, she was being clumsy." I can almost hear it in my head. What did my mom say when she first saw it?

Then I felt a welling up inside of compassion and love for the child sitting in that chair. I look at the photo now and see myself as the child I was — strong and resilient, who found ways to survive – and thrive – in a world of fear and abuse. I retold my story to myself in different ways, in ways that made sense to me as a child, in ways that felt safe. I wasn't abandoned every summer; I had grand adventures travelling with my parents up and down the West coast. I spent days on the giant Ferris Wheel, looking up at the rolling sky. I was a princess waving from atop a beautiful float in the Portland Rose Parade. When Mom returned from the Puyallup Fair after my birthday each year, she threw me magnificent parties and invited all the kids in school. Each child went home with bags full of leftover carnival prizes. And most important, I was never abused. Ever.

The child I was became the person I am today. I am highly intuitive, curious and bold. I am kind to myself and others and will always root for the underdog. I am learning to love myself.

Over the years, I've gradually incorporated holistic elements into my daily routines, like aromatherapy, deep breathing, musical healing and meditation. I get enough sleep. I emphasize anti-inflammatory foods, because like many survivors, my body still reacts more intensely to stress. I'm conscious of healthy eating, with occasional splurges. I'm still learning to experience the joy of body movement.

My life today is whole and true. I wake up nearly every morning and give thanks for my life and family. I love my community. I look for the best in others, but I also accept people for who they are in this moment. Sometimes I feel the old pull to get sucked into the darkness of this world – there are loud voices from every direction shouting doom, gloom, conspiracy, fear and anger. I can choose to listen and dive down into the cesspool with them. But I don't. I listen to my internal compass that points me forward one step at a time, and that keeps me focused on my own behavior and attitudes. I know my life today would not be possible without everything I did to heal from my past, and I am grateful.

We humans are so much the product of our upbringing – not only our parent's political, moral, community, and national beliefs, but where we live, the diversity of life and cultures we're exposed to, our spiritual teachings, our wider family of relatives, and so on. Yet there's truth that we're the same. Same core. Same yearnings. What I learned in thousands of 12-Step encounters and stories and in countless group therapy sessions is when you strip away last names, what someone does for a living, what church they attend, what political beliefs they espouse, where they live, who their family is, what movies they like, how much (if any) education they had, etc. --- at the core we are the same.

This truth was borne out in my job for Dr. Abdullah's projects in Oregon, when we held focus groups among various stakeholders and asked the same questions about what they wanted for their children and for their community. We received the same answers from everyone: to make a good living, to keep family close and safe, to raise children to be their best, and to share in community life. Overwhelmingly, despite feeling unsure about the people they perceived as different, there was a common desire to feel safe, to be accepted and to be loved.

I believe life is about relationships. There is my relationship to the universal divine, which I call God. The strength of my relationship is directly in sync with my relationship with myself. If I'm hiding, lying, fantasizing, in denial, and reacting from my wounds, then my relationship with myself is not true. Nor can my relationship with the Divine be true. My relationship with myself informs my relationship with other people. If I'm not true, then my relationship with them isn't either.

Recently, I was diagnosed with emphysema. I felt immediate calm and acceptance, thinking "Ah. So that's how I will probably go."

Now I work harder to build my health. I want to maintain the best quality of life possible until I die. And who knows when that will be?

Deep in my bones, I'm ready whenever it's time. In the Christian faith I was raised in, I see death as a homecoming. I believe I will be with Linus after our deaths, and I know I will see those I've loved and those I've learned from. In the Tibetan Book of Living and Dying, Sogyal Rinpoche wrote, "Perhaps the deepest reason why we are afraid of death is because we do not know who we are." I don't fear death. I know who I am. One of my favorite writers wrote of death, "And what is it to cease breathing, but to free the breath from its restless tides, that it may rise and seek God unencumbered?" [72]

I am keenly aware that I'm very privileged to have an income that affords me a life beyond day-to-day survival. Still, echoes of my earlier life whisper when I'm riding in the car with my husband. I automatically scan the landscape for obscure spots to sleep or hide a shopping bag if I were homeless. I scope out how accessible a public restroom is to people who are homeless. Linus mentioned the public library often has displaced people who seek warmth in the winter, cool air in the summers, and access to the free computers, books, and magazines, and my first thought was, I should have thought of that!

I still go on alert when I see someone walking along the road where I'm driving. I briefly worry they might jump in front of my car to commit suicide. The response is still woven into my brain cells, even though the thoughts have changed to potential suicide avenues for other people, and never myself.

Today I live my life in truth. One time I was asked to be a keynote speaker at a recovery retreat, and after sharing my story there were people who approached me asking about specific therapies and tools I've used. I'm happy to share my own experience, strength and hope, but I like to remind people to trust their own journey. For me, it took leaping off cliffs of fear and self-doubt at times, other times gradually opening one of the steam valves to slowly let the pressure escape. I reached a point where I realized I was worth it, and the next time I sought a therapist, I arrived with a full and honest mental health history, notes about what I was there to work on, and most importantly, a willingness to trust the process.

In my experience, every time I open myself up to the truths I don't want to see or admit, I make progress. And that is *true*.

Epilogue

To my fellow survivors

You are not alone. What happened to you was not your fault. Your body and mind and soul responded in many ways to what happened in order to protect you. Some of those ways served you well as you moved forward in your life. Many of them now work against you and hold you back from becoming your true self.

Hurtful relationships. Lack of confidence, low self-esteem, shame, overwhelming anger, impression management, debilitating fear, focusing on trying to control others (including your children), numbing out with food, sex, drugs or alcohol, carrying old baggage of anger and blame, feeling disconnected, depressed, hurting others or allowing others to hurt you ... all of these and more are often byproducts of what happened to you.

Change is possible. You can uncover and reclaim your true self.

It's not easy and I believe it's not possible to do it alone. Walking with others who are on the same road, working with professional guides, and perhaps needing temporary or permanent medication are key.

Striving toward healing and wholeness in every aspect of your life is worth it. You are worth it.

In the following pages you will find some resources that may help you continue your path forward.

I wish you light and strength on the journey.

Catherine Ada Campbell
www.truecampbell.com

Acknowledgments

Immense gratitude for the mental health professionals who helped me along the way: JC Smith, CADC, CCS, Catherine Pasley MA, LMHC, Counselors Elberta Askew, Gail Ater, and Howard Carroll LCPC, Dr. Evelyn Reilly PsyD, Dr. Charles Kaufman PhD, the Walker Center in Gooding, Idaho, and others whom I can only recall their first names: Sasha, Karen, Diane, George, and Bob, and to the counselors and doctors who staffed the Lily Drug Company pharmaceutical trial I took part in.

Love and gratitude for these inspirational influencers: my mentor Anne Adams, Dr. Sharif Abdullah, Beverlee Koutny, Dr. Jeff Fox, and my brothers at the Monastery of the Ascension in Jerome, Idaho.

Thank you Rosita N'Dikwe, Rosela Moseng, Kris Wallace, Linda Hall, my Al-Anon sponsors and sponsees, dear friend (and unpaid editorial assistant) Max Hartman, sisters of my heart Karen Woods, Cheri Garey, Dagmar Smith and Barbara Bacon, and bonus relatives Jamie Chupa, Caelan Coppinger, and Matt and Heidi. There are thousands of people I've been privileged to witness and share with in 12-Step meetings, recovery conferences, group therapy, experiential therapy and/or in-patient treatment. Each of them shared their truths and helped guide my way.

I'm very grateful for input and encouragement from my friends Karin Manns, PhD. and Vicki Miller and the other early readers whose comments and critiques made this book much better. Thank you to Dr. R.Y. Langham, who helped edit and review the clinical content.

Resources

Where to begin? Begin where you are at. There is no one way, no one-size-fits-all, and no one has the right to judge how you travel your journey. I encourage seeking professional input. Mental health professionals are specifically trained to help you onto the best path.

Note: Check your local public library first for book titles, research and more. Most libraries offer books, computers, movies, and magazines.

General
National Alliance on Mental Illness, www.nami.org
The Walker Center for Addiction Treatment and Mental Health Services, Gooding, Idaho
The Artist's Way by Julia Cameron, Tarcher Perigee, 2016

Addiction
Look online or in your local phone directory for contact

numbers to the following 12-Step groups:

- Al-Anon

- Alcoholics Anonymous

- Narcotics Anonymous

- Overeaters Anonymous

- Sex Addicts Anonymous

In the Realm of Hungry Ghosts by Gabor Maté, M.D. North Atlantic Books, 2020

Is it Love or is it Addiction? Falling into Healthy Love by Brenda Schaeffer, Hazelden Books, 1987

It Will Never Happen to Me by Claudia Black, Ballantine Books, 1987

Many Roads, One Journey: Moving Beyond the 12 Steps by Charlotte Davis Kasl, Ph.D. Harper Collins Publishers, 1992

Out of the Shadows: Understanding Sexual Addiction by Patrick Carnes, Ph.D. Hazelden Books, Third Edition, 2001

Stage II Recovery: Life Beyond Addiction by Earnie Larsen, Harper One, 1984

Stage II Relationships: Love Beyond Addiction by Earnie Larsen Harper One Publishing, 1987

Substance Abuse and Mental Health Services Administration, www.samhsa.gov

Anger

The Dance of Anger, by Harriet Lerner, PhD., originally published in 1985, recent edition by William Morrow, 2005

Anxiety

first, we make the beast beautiful: a new journey through anxiety by Sarah Wilson, Dey St Publishing, 2018

The Dance of Fear: Rising Above Anxiety, Fear, and Shame to Be Your Best and Bravest Self, by Harriet Lerner, PhD., Perennial Currents, 2005

Body and Brain

A Molecule Away from Madness: Tales of the Hijacked Brain by Sara Manning Peskin, Lakeside Book Company, 2022

www.Human-Memory.net

When the Body Says No: Exploring the Stress-Disease Connection by Gabor Maté, M.D. John Wiley & Sons, Inc., 2003

Codependency

Adult Children of Alcoholics by Janet Geringer Woititz, Ed.D. Health Communications, Inc. 1983

Beyond Codependency by Melody Beattie, Harper/Hazelden Publishing, 1989

Codependence Misunderstood-Mistreated by Anne Wilson Schaff, Harper and Row Publishers, 1986

Codependent No More by Melody Beattie, Harper/Hazelden, 1987

Who's Driving Your Bus?: Codependent Business Behaviors of Workaholics, Perfectionists, Martyrs, Tap Dancers, Caretakers, &

People-Pleasers, by Earnie Larsen and Jeanette Goodstein, Wiley 1993

Daily Meditation
The Language of Letting Go by Melody Beattie, Hazelden Publishing, 1990

One Day at a Time, Al-Anon Family Headquarters, Inc. 1984 (updated regularly)

Depression
National Suicide Hotline: 800-273-8255 (or, pressing 988 which may be available in your area)

Reinventing Depression: A History of the Treatment of Depression in Primary Care 1940 – 2004 by Christopher M. Callahan and German E. Berrios

The Noonday Demon: An Atlas of Depression, by Andrew Solomon

The Upward Spiral: Using Neuroscience to Reverse the Course of Depression One Small Change at a Time by Alex Korb, PhD

Domestic Violence
National Domestic Violence Hotline www.thehotline.org, 800-799-7233

Also, many states have a 24/7 phone number 2-1-1, with referrals to local domestic violence shelters and other resources.

Eating Disorders
goodbye ed, hello me: Recover from Your Eating Disorder and Fall in Love with Life, by Jenni Schaefer, McGraw Hill Education,

2009

When Food is Love by Geneen Roth, Penguin Publishing, 1992

Family

Bradshaw on: The Family – A New Way of Creating Self-Esteem by John Bradshaw, Health Communications, Inc. 1990

Healing the Shame That Binds You by John Bradshaw, Health Communications, Inc. 1988

Recovery of Your Inner Child by Lucia Capacchione, PhD, Simon & Schuster Fireside, 1991

Relationships

Addicted to Love by Stephen Arterburn, Servant Publications, 1992

Getting the Love You Want – A Guide for Couples by Harville Hendrix, PhD, Henry Holt & Co., 1988

Keeping the Love You Find – A Personal Guide by Harville Hendrix, PhD, Atria Books, 1992

Love Is Letting Go of Fear by Gerald G. Jampolsky, M.D. Celestial Arts Books, 1979

Whole Again: Healing Your Heart and Rediscovering Your True Self After Toxic Relationships and Emotional Abuse by Jackson MacKenzie, TarcherPerigee, 2019

Sexual Abuse

National Sexual Assault Hotline, 800-656-HOPE (4673)

Sexual Violence Resource Center, www.nsvrc.org/survivors

Rape, Abuse, and Incest National Network, www.rainn.org – RAINN operates the national Sexual Assault Hotline at

800-656-HOPE (4673)

Survivors of Incest Anonymous, www.siawso.org

Survivor Space, www.survivorspace.org

Child Molestation Research & Prevention Institute, www.childmolestationprevention.org

Trauma – PTSD, EMDR, etc.

The Body Keeps the Score by Dr. Bessel van der Kolk, Penguin Books, 2014

What Happened to You? Conversations on Trauma, Resilience, and Healing by Bruce D. Perry, M.D. PhD., Oprah Winfrey, Flatiron Books, 2021

Trauma Through a Child's Eyes by Peter A. Levine and Maggie Kline, North Atlantic Books, 2007

homecoming: Healing Trauma to Reclaim Your Authentic Self by Thema Bryant, PhD., Tarcher Perigee, 2022

Healing Trauma by Peter A. Levine, PhD, Sounds True, 2005

Our Polyvagal World: How Safety and Trauma Change Us, by Stephen W. Porges, Seth Porges, W.W. Norton, 2023

Memoirs I've read that inspired me and gave me hope:

Educated, by Tara Westover

first, we make the beast beautiful: a new journey through anxiety by Sarah Wilson

Half Broke by Ginger Gaffney

Happiness is Running Through the Streets to Find You: Translating Trauma's Harsh Legacy into Healing by Holly Elissa Bruno

Hell If We Don't Change Our Ways by Brittany Means

Mommie Dearest by Christine Crawford

Never Tell, A True Story of Overcoming a Terrifying Childhood
by Catherine McCall

What My Bones Know, by Stephanie Foo

About the Author

From early childhood, Catherine Ada Campbell struggled with trauma, homelessness, abandonment and mental illness, not knowing the childhood she remembered was false. A single mom by the time she was 20, she sought wholeness through 45+ years of traditional and experiential therapies, medication, research, education, and self-help groups.

Professionally, she was a popular radio morning show host, and worked in the non-profit sector as a coordinator and service provider. She lives in a small town in the Pacific Northwest with her husband and a multitude of visiting wildlife.

Readers are invited to contact her through her website at https://www.truecampbell.com

Endnotes

1. *The Prophet* by Kahlil Gibran, Alfred A. Knopf, Inc 1975, pg 17

2. Ibid pgs 30-31

3. *Our Polyvagal World, How Safety and Trauma Change Us*, Stephen W. Porges and Seth Porges, W.W. Norton and Company, 2023, pg 19

4. *Farnham's Freehold* by Robert A. Heinlein, published G.P. Putnam 1964

5. Silverman, Phyllis and Worden, William, *Harvard Child Bereavement Study*, in article written by Ira Nerken, published The Washington Post 1990.

6. United States Department of Health and Human Services, Trauma and Adverse Childhood Experiences, Early Childhood Learning and Knowledge Center. https://eclkc.ohs.acf.hhs.gov

7. *The Secret and Life-Changing Impact of Early Childhood Abuse*, Milissa Kaufman, MD, PhD. January 13, 2021, www.mccleanhospital.org

8. Dan Siegel, M.D., *The Neurobiology of Trauma*, National Institute for the Clinical Application of Behavioral Medicine

9. Silverman, A. B., Reinherz, H. Z., & Giaconia, R. M. (1996). *The long-term sequelae of child and adolescent abuse: A longitudinal community study.* Child Abuse and Neglect, 20(8), 709-723.

10. Teicher, M. D. (2000). *Wounds that time won't heal: The neurobiology of child abuse.* Cerebrum: The Dana Forum on brain science, 2(4), 50-67. De Bellis, M., & Thomas, L. (2003). *Biologic findings of post-traumatic stress disorder and child maltreatment.* Current Psychiatry Repots, 5, 108-117. Springer, K. W., Sheridan, J., Kuo, D., & Carnes, M. (2007). *Long-term physical and mental health consequences of childhood physical abuse: Results from a large population-based sample of men and women.* Child Abuse & Neglect, 31, 517-530.

11. *The Grieving Brain* by Mary-Frances O'Connor, Harper One, 2023

12. *homecoming* by Thema Bryant, PhD, Tarcher Perigee, 2022, pg 40

13. *Codependent No More* by Melody Beattie, published 1987 Harper and Collins, pg. 6

14. Ibid pg. 28

15. Ibid pg. 33

16. *It Will Never Happen to Me*, Claudia Black, Ph.D., M.S.W., Ballantine Books, 1981, pg. 16

17. Ibid pg. 18

18. Ibid, pg 18

19. *Adult Children of Alcoholics* by Janet Geringer Woititz, Ed.D, published by Health Communications, 1983. Pg 38

20. Ibid pgs. 119-120

21. https://psychcentral.com

22. Diagnostic and Statistical Manual III by the American Psychiatric Association, published 1980 pg. 330

23. *first, we make the beast beautiful*, Sarah Wilson, Dey Publishing 2018

24. *The Impact of Early Life Trauma on Health and Disease: The Hidden Epidemic*, ed. Ruth A. Lanius, Eric Vermetten, Clare Pain, Cambridge University Press, 2020

25. United States Conference of Catholic Bishops, Liturgy of the Hours

26. Office of the Sacred Congregation for Divine Worship

27. *Living With Contradiction: Reflections on the Rule of St. Benedict*, Harper and Row, 1989, pg 139

28. Wolf M. Mehl K. *Experiential learning in psychotherapy: ropes course exposures as an adjunct to inpatient treatment.* Clin Psychol Psychother. 2011 Jan-FebQ18(1):60-74. Doi: 10.1002/cpp.692. PMID: 21110401

29. Symptoms and Causes of Major Depressive Disorder, Mayo Clinic, www.MayoClinic.org

30. *History of Depression*, Allan; Horwitz, Jerome C. Wakefield, and Lorenzo Lorenzo-Laces, The Oxford Handbook of Mood Disorders, edited by Robert J. Derbies and Daniel R. Strunk, Oxford University Press, 2015

31. Burton, R. *The anatomy of melancholy*, New York, NY: New York Review Books

32. Shorter, E. (2013) *How everyone became depressed: The rise and fall of the nervous breakdown.* New York, NY: Oxford University Press

33. Nancy Schimelpfening, *The History of Depression: Account, Treatments, and Beliefs through the Ages.* http://www.verywellmind.com

34. *History of Depression*, Allan; Horwitz, Jerome C. Wakefield, and Lorenzo Lorenzo-Laces, The Oxford Handbook of Mood Disorders, edited by Robert J. Derbies and Daniel R. Strunk, Oxford University Press, 2015

35. Ibid.

36. Ibid. Horwitz, A. et al, 2015

37. Ibid. Blazer, 2005; Francis, 2014; Horwitz and Wakefield, 2007; Shorter, 2013

38. *Anxiety Disorders in Children and Adolescents*, ed. Tracy L Morris, John S. March, second edition, The Guilford Press, 2004, pg 333

39. *Post-Prozac Nation*, Siddhartha Mukherjee, Sunday Magazine, April 22, 2012 pg 48

40. *What has serotonin to do with depression?*, Philip J. Cowen, Michael Browning, University Department of Psychiatry, Warneford Hospital, Oxford, UK. World Psychiatry 14:2, June 2015.

41. *Post-Prozac Nation*, Siddhartha Mukherjee, Sunday Magazine, April 22, 2012 pg 48

42. *Large-scale evidence for an association between low-grade peripheral inflammation and brain structural alterations in major depression in the BiDirect study*. Opel, Nils MD, Cearns, Micah, BPsy, et al. Journal of Psychiatry Neuroscience, July 15, 2019

43. Bradshaw, John. Healing the Shame That Binds You, pg 41. Health Communications Inc., 1988

44. Castellani Rudy, DeJong Joyce, Schmidt Carl. *Homicidal Abuse of Young Children, A Historical Perspective. Journal of Forensic Science and Medicine* (Vol. 3, Issue 2), Medknow Publications and Pedia Pvt. Ltd. 2017. 2. Myers, John E.B., *A Short History of Child Protection in America*, Family Law Quarterly Vol. 42 No. 3, 2008. 3. Centennial Series: Child Abuse Prevention and Treatment Act. Children Welfare Information Gateway, Children's Bureau Express 2012. 4. *The History of Private Life*, Vol. 1. Philippe Aries and Georges Duby, General Editors. Harvard College, 1987. Pgs 9-14. 5. *Infanticide*, Dianne R. Moran. 6. Brewis A.A., (1992) *Anthropological Perspectives on Infanticide*, Arizona Anthropologist 8.

45. Pinker, Steven, *The Better Angels of Our Nature: Why Violence Has Declined*, Viking Press, 2011, pg 419

46. Ibid.

47. Steven Mintz, *Placing Childhood Sexual Abuse in Historical Perspective*, The Immanent Frame, July 13, 2012. Social Science Research Council, ssrc.org

48. Ibid.

49. The American Era of Child Labor, VCU Libraries Social Welfare History Project, socialwelfare.library.vcu.edu

50. 2020 Findings on the Worst Forms of Child Labor, Bureau of International Labor Affairs, U.S. Department of Labor, dol.gov

51. Ashley Pettus, *Repressed Memory*, Harvard Magazine Jan-Feb 2008

52. https://human-memory.net/the-study-of-human-memory/

53. *The Body Keeps the Score*, van der Kolk, Bessell M.D. Penguin Books, 2014 pg 182

54. *The Impact of Early Life Trauma on Health and Disease*, ed. Ruth A. Lanius, Eric Vermetten, Clare Pain, Cambridge 2016

55. *Lost and Found, Unexpected Revelations About Food and Money*. Geneen Roth, Wheeler Publishing, 2011. Pg 95

56. https://www.emdr.com/theory/#theory

57. *The Body Keeps the Score*, van der Kolk, Bessell M.D. Penguin Books, 2014 pg 256

58. Ibid. pg 80

59. *Our Polyvagal World, How Safety and Trauma Change Us* by Stephen Porges and Seth Porges, W.W. Norton and Company, 2023, pg 78

60. Ibid. pg 156

61. https://www.somaticexperiencing.com/home

62. Dr. Stephen Greb, Kentucky Geo Survey, https://www.uky.edu/KGS/education/clockstime.htm

63. Beer is believed to have been invented around 4,000 BCE by the Sumerians.

64. Pinker, Steven. *The Better Angels of Our Nature: Why Violence Has Declined*. Viking Press, October, 2011

65. Interview with John C. Smith, Certified Alcohol and Drug Counselor, Certified Clinical Supervisor, October, 2021

66. Dr. Richard Huganir, Johns Hopkins University School of Medicine

67. www.spravato.com

68. United States Center for Disease Control, Violence Prevention http://www.CDC.gov

69. *Child Abuse and Neglect* Volume: 19 Issue: 9 dated: September 1995, Pages: 1083-1093, Author E Gracia, 1995

70. McLaughlin KA, Green JG, Gruber MJ, Sampson NA, Zaslavsky A, Kessler RC. *Childhood adversities and first onset of psychiatric disorders in a national sample of adolescents.* Archives of General Psychiatry, 2012:69:1151.1160.

71. Esther Sabban, Ph.D., *Works to Reduce Prevalence and Provide New Treatments for Stress-Triggered Neuropsychiatric Disorders*, New York Medical College, Dec. 2021

72. The Prophet, Kahlil Gibran, pg 81. Alfred A Knopf, 197

Printed in the USA
CPSIA information can be obtained
at www.ICGtesting.com
LVHW041113260724
786405LV00006B/15/J